D1478247

CONFESSIONS
OF A
FISH DOCTOR

CONFESSIONS OF A FISH DOCTOR

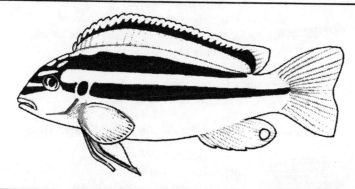

BY SCOTT BODIE

WITH CORINNE BROWNE

ILLUSTRATIONS BY THE AUTHOR

WORKMAN PUBLISHING COMPANY
NEW YORK

For my mother.

Library of Congress Cataloging in Publication Data

Bodie, Scott.
Confessions of a fish doctor.

Includes index.
1. Aquarium fishes—Diseases. 2. Aquarium fishes.
I. Browne, Corinne, joint author. II. Title.
SF458.5.B6   639'.34   76-25474
ISBN 0-911104-83-6

Workman Publishing Company
231 East 51 Street
New York, New York 10022

Manufactured in the United States of America

First printing May 1977
10 9 8 7 6 5 4 3 2 1

CONTENTS

FOREWORD

Every week, I find New York City homes for fifty young Sumatran refugees. They have been plucked from their jungle wetlands, packed like sardines, shipped on jets, and whisked through U.S. Customs. When they come to me in their plastic bags, they are shy and confused; they have been neglected. I pop open their polyethylene bags and watch the excitement as they investigate their new surroundings, bumping into residents that hail from Taiwan, Tanganyika, the Amazon, and North Dakota. Within moments, the newcomers have disappeared among the rocks and under the gravel.

People stop to peer through the window, waiting for me to unlock the shop door. They stroll in before I can get the lights on. They ask questions before I can get my coat off. Some drop in every day, looking for new arrivals, fish food treats, or just conversation.

One morning, a young woman parked her bicycle outside the shop, came in, and asked a common question: "Which fish would make an ideal addition to my community tank and also function as a vacuum cleaner?"

"I have some kuhli loaches that may be just what you're looking for. Come and see them." I guided her to the tank where my new refugees were hiding.

Silently, we watched. Brazen angelfish were the first to acknowledge our presence, hoping that a between-meals snack was on its way. A school of zebra fish paraded back and forth with military precision, not seeming to notice us at all. We waited. My client seemed to be losing patience, so I rolled up my sleeve, plunged my arm into the tank, and shifted a rock shelf. Chaos! Kuhli loaches dashed out in all directions.

An elderly woman who had joined our vigil nearly knocked me over as she turned away in disgust. "Worms!" she cried. "I wouldn't have them in my home!"

But the young woman pressed closer to the tank. "Can I pick my own?" she said softly.

"Sure, you'll fall in love with them. The kuhli loach is gentle and a great housekeeper, but most of all, it has a real *personality*."

She looked at me in disbelief. I went about my business and let her watch them for a while.

The young kuhli loach is an agile little devil, squeezing into minute crevices in rock formations in search of scraps of leftover food. It is fast, elusive, and impetuous. It sports brown and gold tiger stripes. At first, it is nocturnal, just as it is in nature, but after a few weeks in a home aquarium, it reorganizes its life and becomes extroverted and inquisitive. With a few months of good treatment, the kuhli loach grows chubby and lethargic, spending most of its time on the aquarium floor. It comes to resemble a pudgy little dachshund as it plays hide-and-seek and snuggles up with its friends in little love knots.

I rejoined the young woman. "So, do you agree that they have a personality?"

She nodded, and one more refugee had a home.

Months later, the same young woman, whose name was Judy, called me. She was frantic with worry about the kuhli loach, which her children had named Pluto. Usually, I can diagnose and solve problems over the telephone, but in this case, I felt a house call was in order. I got my bag, headed for the subway station, and hopped onto the Broadway local.

People were pushing and shoving mindlessly, and I couldn't help wondering how they would react if they knew that my bag contained tetracycline, chlorophenicol, and kosher salt—all for the purpose of treating a sick fish. Sometimes, at parties, when I tell people I'm a fish doctor, they look at me as if I'm crazy. They can't believe there really is such a thing. But that is my trade, and there I was, on the subway with my little black bag.

Judy and her children met me at the door and hurried me to the tank. It seemed unsettled, and the fish were very nervous. Pluto had tripled in size, and I could tell by his plump shape and rich brown color that he had found a good home. However, a deep gash ran from his pectoral fin all the way to his tail. I knew what had happened, but I listened as Judy explained how the kids had bumped the tank, causing a large, jagged rock to tumble down onto poor Pluto, who had become too lazy and fat to scurry out of harm's way.

"Will he be all right?"

"Can you fix him up?"

I unpacked some kosher (i.e., uniodized) rock salt and sent the oldest child to get a cup of warm water. Fortunately, there was an empty 1-gallon mayonnaise jar in the kitchen, and I filled it with water from the aquarium. Even though Pluto was wounded, netting him was no easy task. Once he was safely in the jar, I took a closer look at his side. I added 3 drops of methylene blue dye to the water, then dissolved 1½ teaspoons of the kosher rock salt in 1 cup of warm water and put 1 tablespoon of salt water into the makeshift infirmary. I explained that since a wounded fish is prone to infection within hours, the dye and salt were added to the water to prevent bacteria and fungus from attacking the wound. After instructing the family to add 1 tablespoon of the salt water at hourly intervals until it was used up, I admonished them to watch Pluto carefully and to call me in three days to let me know how he was doing.

Back on the subway, I felt happy that I had made the trip. And after only two days, Judy called to say that Pluto was healing nicely, so I recommended that he be restored to his home the following day.

Of course, I was pleased to have helped Pluto, but this was just one day in his life. His well-being depended upon other factors. First of all, Judy had made a good choice. She had selected a fish that she and her family found appealing, and he had thrived in direct relation to the attention they had given him. No factor is more important to a pet's well-being than love. You can spend a week's paycheck on aquarium paraphernalia, but if you don't care *about* (as well as *for*) your fish, they will be just another possession, rather than an experience.

Aquarists come to know their fish intimately. They learn, through daily observation, that fish have both intelligence and distinct personality traits. Consequently, choosing a fish whose personality suits your own is the key to creating a successful aquarium.

In my Manhattan apartment, I maintain twelve aquariums. Each tank has its own metabolism and unique appearance. All are balanced, and I can leave them unattended for periods of up to two weeks. Still, inevitably, I miss them terribly and wind up returning home ahead of time. Visitors often glance casually at my aquatic menagerie, paying little attention at first. But it seldom takes them long to settle down in front of one tank and begin to watch. They've discovered an environment that strikes their fancy. A small lecture almost always elicits comments such as "I had no idea fish were like that!" Meantime, I discover delightful qualities about my guests.

There is a wealth of information and fascination to be derived from a fish tank. The only qualifications required are vulnerability and curiosity. Five minutes of daily observation is all it takes to keep an aquarium healthy. First, of course, you must learn what specific things to look for, but that is true of any special interest. Once your perceptions develop, subtle changes and nuances will become apparent to you, as if your vision had suddenly cleared.

Prepare for an underwater journey. You need no scuba gear, and the water is as warm as a stone hearth fire. I will guide you through a living world that is yours to own, enjoy, and admire. Here are observations, tips, and enthusiasm to help you develop a growing, changing, thriving aquarium that will be a never-ending source of joy, amusement, peace, and learning.

TO BEGIN WITH FISH

I slid across the lobby's marble floor, reached for the double doors, which reflected the crystal prisms of the chandeliers, and strode out onto Park Avenue and into a rainstorm. I stopped long enough to look back at the doormen who framed the building's palatial portico. One of them grinned and gave a proper little wave.

They had stared in disbelief when I identified myself as a fish doctor on a house call. The taller man, who spoke with a French accent, had said, "You know, in Montmartre, thirty years ago, my little brother kept fishes, and he spoke to them! In front of the tank he sat, day after day. He thought that his puffy old goldfish could recognize him, and, you know, I believed him." He had chuckled and beamed at the memory, and I had nodded and said I would have believed him, too.

Now I jumped into a cab, waved good-bye to them, and sat back. As I stared out at the checkerboard of apartment windows that lined the avenue, I thought about the boy in Montmartre. What did he have in common with me and with many of my clients? The word *receptivity* stuck in my brain. We can't enjoy the marvels of the natural world around us any more than we can sense what is happening inside our own bodies unless we are receptive. And to be that way, we have to be willing to take risks; we have to be open and vulnerable.

Just then, a stream of water ran out of a crease in my raincoat and dripped down my back. I didn't need any philosophy to understand that I was cold and tired. My workday begins at noon, so I knew it had to be past midnight. The day had been a busy one: three epidemics of ich at three points of a triangle in Manhattan. I wondered how many other aquariums were bounded within that triangle, how many of their owners would be telephoning me for help.

In some cases, I give clients my home phone number. I have mastered the technique of leaping out of a sound sleep, hurtling the bedpost, and grabbing the telephone in two seconds flat. As soon as I have rubbed the sleep from my eyes, I can offer calm advice to a distraught aquarist calling to report an unnerving development in the overdue labor of a prize pregnant platy. I don't mind being awakened; I'm always pleased by the sincere regard that many people have for their fish, the sense of wonder mixed with respect for nature that turns them back into inquisitive children.

With 22 million enthusiasts, fish keeping rivals photography as the second most popular hobby in the United States. (Only stamp collecting can claim more devotees.) Worldwide, there are at least 70 million of us, and our numbers are constantly increasing. Consequently, I am kept very busy. Aquarists tend to form thriving friendships. Special fish societies and clubs exist all over the world. I have met some aquarists who seem shy and slightly embarrassed about their preoccupation with fish and some who devote all their spare time to hunting down rare species and exotic hybrids. But we all love to share our experiences and discoveries, and we all have a compulsion to communicate with and care for our own private communities of living creatures.

The taxi pulled up in front of my apartment building. I dripped my way to the elevator, clutching my doctor's bag and a bucket filled with odds and ends. In the quiet of my apartment, the sound of the rain merged with that of the bubbles echoing among my aquarium-lined walls. My fish were resting in slings and hammocks formed by the coral and quartz furnishings of their homes, but they were not asleep. Fish do not have the luxury of sleep because they have no eyelids. Although less active at night, fish must maintain a constant flow of water past their gills.

They all rushed to the front of their tanks as I drew near. I knew they were hungry, so I went to the freezer, where I keep a supply of brine shrimp—their favorite frozen dinner. I placed a hunk of the frozen shrimp in a fine-mesh net, ran cold tap water over it to thaw and clean the shrimp, and swirled the netful of tidbits to an eager bunch of eaters. Even before it touched the water, the fish leaped to bite the net that fed them.

My fish are accustomed to eating promptly when I return in the evening. They become alert and excited when I approach their tanks, often churning the water surface and splashing me to get my attention. One of my African cichlids has actually become so frenzied at the sight of his approaching dinner that three times he has jumped clear out of the tank—but only when I have been right there to rescue him.

I brewed a cup of coffee and sat down in my captain's chair, which is the only piece of furniture in my African cichlid room. Well, actually, it's a hallway that I painted chestnut brown. When the doors are closed and the sunlight is locked out, the aquarium illuminates the shades of Prussian blue and tangerine on the bodies of my fish. I leaned back and shut my eyes, lulled by the sound of the bubbles. But I began to see more fish—fish swimming around the corner of my bedroom closet, swimming in midair—

The phone jarred me from what could easily have become a nightmare.

"Did you get home all right, Scott? It's Mrs. Gould. I've forgotten whether you told me to leave my tank lights on all the time or off all the time."

I knew I should have written it down for her! "Ich is a parasite that needs light to reproduce," I said, "so turn out all your lights and go to sleep. I'll see you the day after tomorrow. Don't worry. Your gouramis will be fine."

"Thanks. You're a darling. Good night."

I turned out all the lights in my twelve tanks and got into bed. The moon was out now and cast a wide beam through the aquarium nearest the bed. From the corner of the tank, a red eye was watching me. I grabbed a sock from the floor, threw it at the tank, and distracted the nosy angelfish. That peeping tom is always behaving as if *I'm* invading the privacy of *his* room. I could feel him watching me again. How could I sleep?

As insomnia set in, I thought about my fish collection and the course of events that led me to the unlikely role of fish doctor.

My first experience with tropical fish was in Kathy Brown's basement. She had invited me to play at her house after school. I was reluctant to give up my afternoon of back-yard adventures, but as soon as I saw that basement, I was glad I had come. Kathy's father was a retired police detective whose hobby was tropical fish; the basement was his breeding room. He came down (while I was there) and explained that the hundreds of fish in his aquariums had come from three original pairs. I was so fascinated that I didn't even hear Kathy's mother call us to come up for ice cream.

From that day on, no one could keep me out of the Browns' basement. Kathy's father spent many hours with me, talking to me and answering my questions. He pointed out that fish come in a great variety of shapes and sizes and that the shape of their tail and fins determines how they move. I wanted to know what it was like to be a fish, what kinds of feelings they had. He explained that fish are very aware of temperature. Each kind of fish is comfortable within a particular range of water temperatures. Most fish are friskier and more romantically inclined when the water is at the warmer end of that range because heat quickens a fish's metabolism.

Basic Anatomy of a Fish

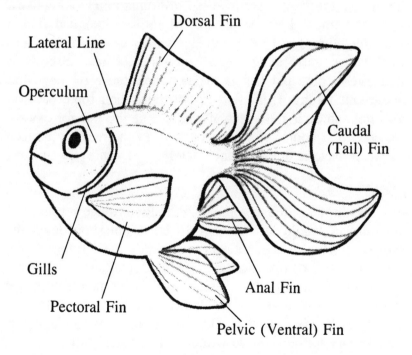

Dorsal Fin

Lateral Line

Operculum

Caudal (Tail) Fin

Gills

Pectoral Fin

Anal Fin

Pelvic (Ventral) Fin

I also learned that fish have a keen sense of smell—probably because of water's effective chemical transmission of odor—which human beings are incapable of detecting. Kathy's father told me about the salmon battling upstream, guided at every turn by its sense of smell, which leads it back to the very same stream bed where its life began.

On my tenth birthday, Kathy arrived at school with a small casserole, which she carefully placed on my desk. It was full of water and contained two baby guppies that her father had picked out for me. I watched them all day, and when I got them home, I put them in a place of honor on the dining room table. I was crazy with the anticipation of raising thousands of fish. Every day, I raced home from school to see them. But one afternoon, I arrived to see my casserole aquarium looking like a bowl of oatmeal. I was devastated. My little brother had tried to feed my guppies and had emptied a whole can of fish food into their water, suffocating them. Since then, I have discovered that overfeeding pet fish is the common cause of most first aquariums failing. If the fish do not finish their food, bacteria will flourish on it and eventually challenge the fish for oxygen or attack the bodies of weakened fish. In the race for oxygen between bacteria and fish, the bacteria will win every time.

My brother used to go to the orthodontist once a week, and my mother would let me visit an aquarium shop down the street. For forty-five minutes every week, I was left to my own devices in that damp, cavernous place. It smelled of cedar, and it was filled with wonderful creatures. The woman who owned the shop always sat behind the counter with a cup of coffee and a copy of *Reader's Digest*. She wore long skirts and kept herself wrapped up in a shawl winter and summer. At first, it was hard for me to talk to her, but after a while, she sensed my enthusiasm and encouraged me to ask questions.

After I had been visiting the shop for a few months, she told me to call her Aunt Etta. By then, I had saved my quarters and bought a chrome-plated 5-gallon tank from Kathy's father. But I couldn't afford a pump and filter, which were necessary equipment if I was to have a thriving aquarium—or so I thought. I decided to consult Aunt Etta.

"You can learn to keep a fish tank healthy and well balanced without using any equipment," she said. "If you can master the most important rules for aquarium maintenance, you won't have to depend on little motors that can break at any time.

"Now, first of all, in nature, there are laws and principles that enable fish to live surrounded by water. To care for your fish tank properly, you must abide by these rules. Then your fish will be as healthy and happy as they can be."

Aunt Etta reached behind the counter for a scrap of cardboard and began to write something on it.

"Do you know the story about the boy who cried 'wolf'?" she asked.

"He kept sounding the false alarm," I answered.

"Well, when you say 'wolf,' you will be reminding yourself of the ways to avoid future problems with your aquarium. Each letter stands for one of the four factors that make a successful fish tank. Here, this will help you to remember."

On the cardboard, she had written:

W = water quality and temperature
O = oxygen dissolved in the water
L = lighting (sunlight and artificial)
F = feeding (how much food and what kind)

Water quality is vitally important. Fish will not stay healthy if you let their water become stagnant. Like all living creatures, fish consume food and excrete waste materials.

These wastes may accumulate in the tank and pollute aquarium water. Frequent changes of water prevent these toxic chemicals from reaching dangerous concentrations. Removing one-third of the water and replacing it with tap water removes these toxins.

Water temperature must be kept constant. Check the thermometer daily and avoid any sudden temperature changes. Fish can adapt to a wide range of temperatures, but you *must* keep that temperature constant. A 10-degree drop within a few hours or two could lead to serious problems and leave your fish susceptible to disease.

Fish draw breath from oxygen, which enters the water at its surface. Unfortunately, the oxygen in H_2O is not usable because of its strong molecular bond to the two hydrogen atoms. But fortunately for fish, oxygen dissolves readily in water at mere contact. This is why the total water surface of an aquarium is so important: not only because fish need a ready source of oxygen, but also because they must expel carbon dioxide. If aquarium water is stagnant, chances are it is already saturated with CO_2, making proper respiration impossible. Artificial aeration by means of an air pump will increase the absorption of oxygen and release of CO_2 by constantly moving the oxygen-rich surface layer of water. But your first aquarium doesn't need an air pump *if* you remember to circulate the water daily by hand. Just take a cup—make sure it is very clean and free of detergent—and scoop up some water from the tank. Hold the cup about 2 feet above the surface and pour the water back into the tank. Repeat this three or four times a day.

Ideal tank lighting includes 2 hours of filtered sunlight daily and from 10 to 16 hours of indirect or artificial light, which is especially important for plant growth. Although plants do best when exposed to a combination of incandescent and fluorescent light, fish seem to prefer the soft and flattering purple hues of fluorescent plant bulbs. Incandescent bulbs cast a yellow hue over the aquarium and often generate too much heat for the tank's well-being. The key principle to remember when it comes to light is the same as that for temperature: Keep it at a constant level. Aquarium lights should be turned on and off at about the same time every day. This will give your fish a sense of normalcy. Leave the room lights on for at least 10 minutes when you turn the tank lights on or off. You don't want to startle your fish by throwing them into pitch-darkness or blinding light.

Proper food that is high in protein is another important factor in keeping healthy fish. If your fish like what you feed them and you don't give them more than they can finish in five minutes, there will be less left over to decay and attract bacteria. A varied diet of high-protein food will ensure your fish of proper digestion, and they will excrete less waste materials.

Don't expect any fish, especially the larger cichlids, to be healthy and prolific on a diet of nothing but dry food. All fish, whether or not they are natural vegetarians, enjoy live brine shrimp in the aquarium. Brine shrimp are readily available at most pet shops, but they can also be cultivated at home (see page 235).

Aunt Etta told me I was ready to start my aquarium, and she sold me my first pair of flamingo guppies *(Lebistes reticulatus)*. I can still remember exactly what they looked like. The male's pointed tail shimmered neon green; the female was fat and golden. There was a magical quality to the way their jeweled scales sparkled red and gold when they caught the light. I chose them for their unique individual personalities. They were intelligent, frisky, and far from timid, especially when I fed them. And I was sure that they recognized me. Also, they were fast breeders, which appealed to me because I wanted lots of fish. Happily, the female was already pregnant. I decided to leave her with Aunt Etta until she had given birth since I knew nothing about birthing babies. I thought I had never seen anything more beautiful than that pregnant guppy. She seemed to glow like an unfurling rose.

I was full of questions about guppies, so Aunt Etta sat me down with some reference books. I learned that, like mollies, platies, and swordtails, guppies actually give birth to live babies. Because of their relative hardiness and prolific nature, live-bearers are popular with novice aquarists. They have a tendency to produce mutations and dissimilar offspring, and all live-bearers have been hybridized and produce beautiful new man-made varieties of fish.

Reverend John Lechmere Guppy sent the first specimens of the little fish that bears his name to the British Museum in 1866. German aquarists were quick to propagate them. Today, guppies are found in freshwater streams throughout tropical America, but no one knows whether the fish are native or were introduced to these waters. These wild specimens bear little resemblance to the fancy veiltail varieties seen in aquariums. The males were the first to begin differentiating multicolored patterns and concentric circles. The females were devoid of color, but through selective breeding, they have developed multihued tails. A tankful of guppies can outshine a rainbow.

But guppies have more than appearance to recommend them. They are easily fed and cared for when kept with compatible tankmates. Ideally, they should be kept alone or with a few *Corydoras* catfish to help with tank maintenance. They are not at all timid and can be handled and moved from tank to tank with little worry of trauma or pH shock.

To better the original strain, immature male guppies must be isolated and their long filmy tails protected from wear and tear. If male guppies are allowed to breed before they are full grown, they will remain stunted for life. When properly cared for, guppies will begin to reproduce at 3 months of age and

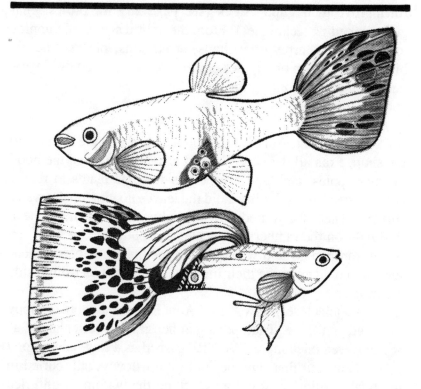

Guppies *(Lebistes reticulatus)*

will continue to give birth to an increasing number of fry every 28 days. A single male may fertilize a harem, which makes selective breeding remarkably practical.

The optimum temperature for breeding guppies is 78 degrees, and fry grow faster at 82 degrees. Mature guppies live longer at 72 degrees because that temperature retards their metabolic rate.

No other fish offers as many possibilities for improvement and variation as the guppy. Devoted breeders work relentlessly to improve their guppy stock (see page 239 for professional guppy breeding techniques). From the hybrid swordtail guppies to the fabulous array of veiltails, snakeskins, blacks, and albinos, a collection of guppies presents a breathtaking display of nature and man working together.

One evening, Aunt Etta telephoned and told me to hurry to the shop. I ran all the way. When I arrived, she lifted the hood of my guppies' tank and brushed aside some plants to reveal half a dozen babies darting amid the leaves floating on the water surface. Then she turned out the lights and had me shine a flashlight on the mother. Her scales and body had become virtually transparent, and we could see the unborn babies twitching. We could even see their little eyes staring at us from inside the mother.

"Watch closely now," said Aunt Etta as the mother guppy quivered and froze. The opening at her gravid spot enlarged as she quivered once more. We both gasped as a tiny baby guppy popped out, tail first, and began to drop slowly, still curled in the fetal position. Just before reaching the bottom, it unfurled and shot back up to the surface, where it hid among the floating leaves. "Baby guppies are born perfectly formed, like tiny adults. They are fully equipped to fend for themselves even one minute after birth."

Before long, I counted a dozen babies already born. Aunt Etta told me that we could expect between 50 and 100 more by morning. She said that the record for baby guppies is 212.

"How can we keep them alive?" I asked.

"We need enough plants to hide the babies, because sometimes the parents decide to gobble them up," she said. "We'll have to make sure to feed them twice a day. We'll also give them lots of live baby brine shrimp. And, of course, they must have clean water. We'll turn off the outside filter so that it won't suck in the babies. Instead we'll use an air stone—a porous chunk of compressed sand—attached to the air pump to make plenty of bubbles. Newborn fish are quite sensitive to water quality, especially when there are so many of them. If you put them in a bowl with no aeration, they would surely die. With a little patience, you'll raise guppies whose beauty will surpass that of their lovely parents."

She patted my head and sent me home. I felt that I had witnessed a miracle.

After three days, we took the babies out of the tank so that they wouldn't be bothered by their parents. Aunt Etta showed me how to scoop them up using a siphon tube as a slurp gun, and we put them into their new home, a 10-gallon tank without gravel and a box filter.

"It was a good idea, Scott," she said, "to choose live-bearers for your first fish. They are easy to raise, and they don't need any care from their parents. In fact, they're better off when they're raised away from their parents, for then it is possible for an entire brood to grow to maturity. Of course, some people prefer to breed egg-laying fish because they can produce thousands of tiny eggs, but those eggs must be tended by their parents."

She explained that female live-bearers can retain enough sperm from a single contact with a male for four or five batches of babies. They are even susceptible to free-swimming sperm in aquarium water, not requiring the actual touch of the male gonopodium (sex fin). Experts are not sure whether the male actually enters the female's vent or whether a fraction of the sperm released nearby find their way up the female's reproductive tubes to fertilize existing eggs. Either way, this makes co-ed tanks taboo for selective breeding. Virgin females must be separated from immature males to ensure fertilization by a chosen mate. Brothers, sisters, mothers, and fathers can all interbreed with no apparent weakening of the strain.

I wanted to leave my baby fish with Aunt Etta a little while longer until I learned how to care for them. Even though she reassured me that it wasn't difficult, I was afraid that if I didn't learn exactly what to do, my guppies would share the fate of the fish in my casserole aquarium. I was determined to raise a healthy family.

Aunt Etta explained that the water temperature for live-bearers may range between 65 and 85 degrees and that 78 degrees is ideal for guppies, platies, mollies, and swordtails. They require no specific water conditions but are most comfortable with a neutral to slightly alkaline pH and a mild concentration of rock salt. "Because they are omnivorous, they should have a variety of foods. Give them weekly treats of live brine shrimp and tubifex worms, and supplement these with aquatic plants and algae," she said.

Aunt Etta advised using water sprite, a floating fern that has since become my favorite for live-bearers' tanks. Sprite and live-bearers flourish under the same conditions, so sprite may be used as a barometer of proper water conditions. Old leaves float to the surface and sprout a blanket of lovely new round-leafed plants, all dangling their gossamer roots and providing shelter for newborn babies. Sprite also creates areas of filtered light that live-bearers enjoy; it gives them a sense of security.

"Now that you've seen the babies born," said Aunt Etta, "you realize that these are living creatures and that they must be treated with respect. If you give them a clean environment—and remember, above all else, that water changes keep the environment clean—then these fish will give you all the babies you have room to raise."

One day, Aunt Etta showed me the other live-bearers in the shop. She spoke of them with such affection and enthusiasm that I have always remembered the sound of her voice. We stood in front of a tank of swordtails *(Xiphophorus helleri)* which were pale green with a red stripe from mouth to tail. She told me that wild swordtails hail from central Mexico.

"All the fancy varieties you can buy today are descended from these green fish, and they have lost none of their fiery Latin temperament along the way. They move quickly and gracefully. Just look at them. The males are like brightly costumed matadors. They joust for supremacy whether or not a lady fish is watching them. Only the male has the elongated swordtail, and he uses it the way a matador uses his cape, distracting his opponents and courting his mate with it. They are bold and fierce, but they fight to show off, not to kill. They are constant jumpers, so a tank that contains swordtails should always be covered."

Aunt Etta told me that there are many color varieties among swordtails. Bloodred swords are the ones that most appeal to me today. Velvety smooth and aristocratic, they are always active and spellbinding, filling the tank with excitement and an intense flash of red. Green swords glimmer with a faint, pearly sheen. They are less flamboyant and slightly timid, but they grow quite large and often give birth to over 200 babies.

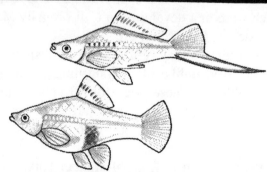

Swordtails *(Xiphophorus helleri)*

Tuxedo swords have a bold streak of black and blue sequins along their sides. Wagtails have a jet black tail and matching dorsal fin. Berlin swords are speckled with irregular black patches.

Aunt Etta's tank also contained golden swordtails, gentle fish that glitter softly and offer a lovely contrast to the red varieties. Then there were the golden albinos—even lighter, with transparent bodies and eyes like tiny pink mirrors. And she had black swordtails, shining with the reflected blues and greens of a peacock's tail. Their individual scales sparkled like opals, and I was fascinated with their expressive silver-rimmed eyes. Aunt Etta told me that they are extremely responsive to their owners, and she showed me how they accepted bits of her chicken sandwich right from her fingers! She turned to me and said, "Hand-feeding is an easy way to win your fishes' confidence. Larger fish love bits of raw meat, and any nonspiced cooked meat, such as ham or chicken, is fine, too. As you can see, my black swords are very partial to chicken. Most fish will eventually come right to your hand for a nibble of food. They will let you stroke them and even lift them right out of the water. Just be calm and patient, and they will soon learn to trust you."

Then she pointed out the high-finned and lyretailed hybrids, which were first developed in California by Mrs. Thelma Simpson, a devoted swordtail breeder.

"The swordtail's long, graceful fin extensions are striking and dramatic. And unlike other long-finned fish, swords are quite comfortable with these extensions. But you should always remember to keep them away from sharp coral and rocks. And don't put swords in the same tank with aggressive fin nippers like barbs."

When we stopped in front of another tank, I said, "That one looks like a swordtail without its sword. Its body is more compact, too."

Platies *(Xiphophorus maculatus)*

Aunt Etta explained that this was a platy *(Xiphophorus maculatus)*. Both platies and swordtails are bred in a variety of colors and patterns, and some have elongated dorsal fins and black tails. They are as easy to breed as guppies, and they are less likely to eat their own young. The varieties (or subspecies) will interbreed and produce new hybrids.

"Platies aren't aggressive, but they aren't shy, either. Their active nature, as well as their variety of colors, has made them a favorite since they were first imported from Mexico.

They are inexpensive, too. And they don't require much space. A small tank—five to ten gallons—will house up to thirty platies happily."

Then we went to look at the mollies *(Mollienesia sphenops)*. They are similar to platies in shape, but they are a bit more delicate. Mollies are inquisitive and more intelligent than their colorful counterparts. Once, they were green, black, or marbled black and white. But now, specimens with brilliant orange and blue speckles are being bred throughout the world for their jewellike ornamentation, lyre tails, and jet black, sparkling gold, or green body color. Males are bred with outrageously oversized veillike dorsal fins.

"Mollies inhabit brackish waters along the Gulf coast of Texas and down to Venezuela. Because they are accustomed to a combination of fresh and salt water, mollies should have an average of one level tablespoon of rock salt per gallon of aquarium water. They are natural vegetarians and should have plant material in their diet, but they will accept most fish foods with little coaxing. Add some dolomite to a tank housing mollies; this keeps the pH level high in alkalinity. Mollies range in size from one inch to four inches when mature. They are very prolific and rarely eat their own young. It's true that they need some pampering, but their playful personalities justify the trouble. They are delightful cartoon characters."

Over the years, I've remembered Aunt Etta's words. Mollies are indeed funny fish. Don't feel slighted or inadequate if you have absolutely no success with them. Either they thrive and flourish in the home aquarium, or they waste away before your eyes. There is no middle ground with mollies.

But back to the story of my guppies. I grew impatient to bring my new family home. Finally, confident and eager, I cleaned my 5-gallon tank twice, once with salt water and once with fresh. I washed a pot of gravel under warm tap water until it ran clear and then spread it along the tank bottom. I positioned the tank near my bedside window. Just for luck, I taped the card on which Aunt Etta had carefully printed her formula:

W = water quality and temperature
O = oxygen dissolved in the water
L = lighting (sunlight and artificial)
F = feeding (how much food and what kind)

I remembered all she had said about each requirement. How could I lose with such guidance?

I let the water stand for a day. Then, at last, I was ready to bring home my fish. I pleaded with my school bus driver until he agreed to take a detour and drop me off at Aunt Etta's aquarium. Aunt Etta had my little guppies in a plastic bag, all ready for their trip home.

"Here's a little present." She grinned and scooped up a *Corydoras* catfish. "He'll help to keep your tank clean and keep an eye on the baby guppies since I won't be around."

I left the shop repeating Aunt Etta's advice: "Above all, keep the tank clean to prevent disease. Remember, it is easier to keep fish healthy than it is to cure them if they get sick. If you will spend at least five minutes with them every day, your reward will be a healthy, happy aquarium. Enjoy them."

I walked home slowly, trying not to shake up the fish. I knew I had discovered something very special, more than a unique hobby or plaything. My fish tank was to be a microcosm of nature to study and enjoy; it would grow as my understanding grew. From that day until this very moment, I have never been without an aquarium.

FISH ARE LIKE PEOPLE

When I was in my early teens, I began assisting Aunt Etta at her shop on Saturdays, feeding the fish, changing tank water, helping customers. Aunt Etta had grown accustomed to my questions, and she seemed to take pleasure in teaching me more and more about our aquatic charges. In exchange for my help, she presented me with a 10-gallon tank and a starter kit of basic equipment (pump, filter, and heater) and let me bring home new fish from time to time.

I had added swordtails to my guppy tank, and I was eager to try out new inhabitants. At first, I chose fish only because I liked their appearance. I wanted a pair of young albino convicts (*Cichlasoma nigrofasciatum*). They were handsome and completely unlike the fish I had in both shape and temperament. They were about the size of a quarter and seemed quite active. I could tell the male by his long, pointed dorsal fin and the female by her rosy-gold blush. And unlike most albino species, their eyes were black and alert.

"It is important to know what to look for when choosing a fish," said Aunt Etta. "The wrong choice can completely upset the balance of a thriving aquarium. First of all, you must know what you are looking for. You should decide which family of fish is suited to your needs and appeals to your personality, and then you must learn to pick the healthiest, most desirable specimens.''

As I stared at the tank that contained the convicts, I noticed Aunt Etta looking at me somewhat doubtfully. Still, I was sure that they were what I wanted.

"Which one would you choose?" she asked.

I pointed to a small one that was swimming to and fro in a rather frantic manner.

Aunt Etta shook her head. "Never choose the smallest fish in the batch. In most large broods of fry, there are a few runts who will never attain full size or coloring. Now take another look. Examine the dorsal and anal fins to see if they maintain tension and are extended fully at least from time to time.''

I nodded, studied the fish, and chose another—a larger one with extended fins.

"Watch the tank for fish that pay attention to you, for any fish that will come to the glass and peer at you. An attentive fish is easily fed. He will not be afraid of you, and there is every chance that he will become your friend.''

The idea of a fish being my friend seemed strangely wonderful, but I didn't interrupt.

"To select a fish in prime condition, look for a plump body, unbroken fins, clear eyes and color, and a smooth scale surface.''

I chose a pair of convicts that fit Aunt Etta's criteria and took them home with me.

I kept wondering what she had meant by fish becoming friends. The idea fascinated me. So the next Saturday I asked her about it.

"Fish are like people. They may lack concepts of time, death, and deity, but they do have definite personalities. As species and as individuals, they are more or less intelligent, sweet or cranky, hardworking or lazy, vain or shy, sinister or gay, serene or rambunctious. Choosing a fish for an aquarium, therefore, is as delicate an affair as choosing a friend.

"But, first, before choosing a single fish, you should acquaint yourself with the different ways in which an aquarium can enhance your life. If, for example, you want fish that will recognize you, distinguish between you and other people, and acknowledge you as their master, then you must choose clever fish. If you find it rewarding to feed fish by hand, you must choose bold fish. And if you want to share your secrets with a friend who will only listen, then you must choose a fish who seems to care.

"Now, Scott"—she looked at me with her funny little frown—"how are those convicts doing?"

"Fine," I said. "It's my other fish I'm worried about." Lately, I'd noticed that the other fish in the tank were vanishing, gone without a trace. The albino convicts, on the other hand, were growing so fast, they were like a circus attraction. Finally, I caught the male chomping away on the remains of a tuxedo swordtail, and I realized what had been happening.

I had mixed emotions about keeping the convicts.

Their rate of growth fascinated me, and they were alert and responsive. At first, they had rushed over to the glass whenever I came into the room, and they quickly learned to eat raw hamburger from my fingers. But then they began courting. They no longer greeted me at mealtimes. In fact, they hid whenever they saw me coming. (When I described this behavior to Aunt Etta, she explained that convicts are such intensely territorial fish that they will not tolerate the presence of any other living creature near them when they are spawning.) I began to resent being made to feel like an intruder in my own room. True, their courtship ritual was intriguing, especially the way they locked their jaws together. But in the process of preparing their nest, they destroyed the landscape of the tank, moving pebbles around with their mouths and digging a hollow in the gravel in a far corner.

At last, in order to restore peace and harmony to my room, I decided to get rid of them, realizing that they weren't at all suited to my temperament and that I had grown to hate them.

Somewhat sheepishly, I took them back to the shop and asked Aunt Etta if I could trade them in.

"Well," she said, "they're more than twice the size they were when you took them home three months ago, and that means their value has more than tripled."

Wholesale distributors generally have a good supply of baby fish, but mature breeding pairs are always in demand and usually bring a good trade.

"Now, your convicts are members of the family Cichlidae, or cichlids. Cichlids and similar fish are relatively long-lived, and their market price is based on their size and rarity. That makes them a good investment for pet dealers, who are usually eager to trade lots of little fish for one large specimen in prime condition. So if you enjoy raising these fish to maturity and don't mind the time it takes, this is a thrifty way to populate your aquarium."

As I watched Aunt Etta dealing with customers, I realized that she always made a special effort to find out why they were fish hobbyists, what basic human needs they wanted their aquariums to fill. From then on, I listened very carefully and learned everything I could about what makes a successful match between fish and aquarist.

I didn't bring home any new fish to replace my two convicts for quite a while. I had learned a vital lesson, and I wanted to give myself plenty of time to think about what I wanted from my aquarium and which fish would suit my personality. I knew that that was the only way to be sure my fish and I would be happy together.

There was plenty of time to read on those Saturday afternoons. Aunt Etta brewed her coffee and occasionally clipped something out of *Reader's Digest,* and I devoured the natural science books she kept behind the burlap curtain in the back room.

I learned that two-thirds of the globe is covered with water and that life beneath the oceans and seas outnumbers life on land by 100 to 1. Small crustaceans, the insects of the sea, outnumber all combined insects, birds, mammals, reptiles, and amphibians on land. Life originated in the water, and many living fossils, such as trilobites and lungfish, still dwell there, untouched by millions of years of evolution. The 40,000 living species of fish are unrivaled among the vertebrates for adapting to unpromising living conditions, surviving at varying depths and pressures—even beneath the polar caps and in steaming volcanic pools.

It seems that for thousands of years men have been fascinated by fish, to whom we still have a kinship in the form of the gill markings that appear during our embryonic development. The Sumerians kept live fish for food in 2500 B.C., and the Chinese domesticated the carp more than 2,000 years ago. And there are occasional mentions of fish in literature. Guillaume Rondet, a Renaissance student who died in 1566, claimed that his wife kept a fish alive in a glass of water for three years.[1] In his diary entry for May 28, 1665, Samuel Pepys wrote: ". . . then home to see my Lady Pen, where my wife and I were shown a fine rarity: of fishes kept in a glass of water that will live so for ever; and finely marked they are, being foreign."[2]

In 1853, there was a public exhibition of aquariums in Regents Park, London, and this stimulated great interest in the

[1]Herbert Axelrod, *Tropical Fish as a Hobby* (New York: McGraw-Hill Book Company, revised edition, 1969).
[2]*Ibid.*

hobby. Until that time, it had not been possible to produce the large sheets of clear glass necessary to construct an aquarium. In fact, the word *aquarium* was not used to indicate a container of water housing aquatic animals until 1852. Other major European cities soon acquired their own public aquariums, and in 1872 the Brighton Aquarium was built—the biggest in the world, with a tank that held 110,000 gallons!

E. G. Boulenger, author of *The Aquarium Book,* relates a number of anecdotes about visitors to the London Zoo aquarium. A World War I general wanted to know which fish were edible. And a group of lamas from Tibet were amazed to discover that the fish did not become seasick.

The Germans became interested in tropical fish as early as 1900, but in the United States, it was not until the time of World War I that aquarists showed much enthusiasm for tropical fish. P. T. Barnum, who had an instinct for anticipating what the public would like, was the first to display live fish in America; he even managed to keep a whale in captivity—a rare feat even today.

Prior to World War II, Hamburg was the center of tropical fish activity, but today, New York is the tropical fish capital of the world. And because it is now possible to ship fish by air to almost anyplace on the globe, fish are big business indeed.

I daydreamed about going to the Amazon River basin to collect my own fish. I knew how it was done. Native fishermen cast a long, narrow net, called a seine, that has weights attached to its bottom edge and corks attached to its top edge. In the misty shallows of such exotic places as Ceylon, they draw nets through the water slowly and carefully. The specimens they catch are sorted into collecting buckets and then immediately sealed in plastic bags and packed in insulated freight cartons.

Very often, native collectors have a family member or friend who functions as a middleman, receiving the shipment at his fish farm, unpacking and placing the specimens into huge holding tanks and vats until it is time to repack them, and sending them off to wholesale distributors, or jobbers. Owners of aquarium shops often visit jobbers in order to handpick the best stock. When such a visit is impractical, a telephone call usually brings an immediate delivery. This urgent race to move tropical fish from their native waters to the pet shop and finally to the hobbyist must be accomplished with a great deal of care. The markup on fish at the retail level is surprisingly high; a fish purchased for $.15 may easily sell for $1.00. But these prices reflect the high risks involved in the business.

I was suddenly aware that every fish in Aunt Etta's little shop had gone through a long and dangerous journey—final destination still unknown.

One day, a woman came into the shop while Aunt Etta was in the back room. She dropped her shopping bags and a knapsack on the counter and asked if I could give her some advice.

She explained that her son's birthday was the next day. His name was Alex, and he visited the shop almost every day on his way home from school. "I can't spend much money," she said, "but I'd like to give him a fish that won't die right away like goldfish. He keeps talking about the 'boxing fish.' What are they?"

"I think Alex solved your problem for you." I said shyly. "I can give you a Siamese fighting fish, a bowl, some gravel, a banana lily plant, and two and a half years' worth of food for less than five dollars."

Still a bit surprised at the authority of my sales pitch, I escorted Alex's mother to the betta tank.

"Here they are. The *Betta splendens,* or Siamese fighting fish, belongs to the family Antibidae, which also includes the gourami and the paradise fish. These fish are hardy and easy to maintain, and, in fact, they were one of the first to be kept

Siamese Fighting Fish *(Betta splendens)*

successfully in aquariums. In their native habitat, they're found in shallow, stagnant rain pools and rice flats. It is nearly impossible for them to derive oxygen from these muddy waters; consequently, they've evolved a sort of lung called a labyrinth that enables them to breathe directly from the atmosphere. They're often seen gulping down air at the water surface.

"Originally, bettas were plain gray, but because of their sport value, they have been bred selectively over the decades to produce many different hybrid varieties in breathtakingly flamboyant shades of Prussian blue, cobalt blue, turquoise, lavender, magenta, and crimson. Breeders take great pains to isolate young bettas, keeping them in individual bowls, in which they spend most of their lives. The betta's territorial instinct has been developed to such an extent that two mature males in the same tank inevitably go to war.

"The Siamese fighting fish has muscular little jaws that serve the same purpose as a porpoise's spout: to breathe air. But the betta's mouth is also its greatest weapon. By the way, a fish's mouth is a pivotal characteristic. It is possible to identify closely related species by the shape and character of the mouth and teeth, which are adapted to its predominant source of food. The size of a fish's mouth can tell you something about temperament, too. Fish are aggressive in direct proportion to the relative size of their mouth.

"When a betta prepares for battle, his sequined gill plates flare out, making his head seem three times larger than it really is. He flays his fins, which makes them look like hair standing up on a cat's arched back. He hangs suspended in the water, quivering, trying to psych out his opponent. For a few moments, the foes flash their brilliant colors at each other. Then one of them starts to snake in and suddenly darts at the other, trying to rip his fins from his body.

"In between bouts, they go to the bottom and retreat to their own corners, like boxers. Then they rise, slowly, to the spot where they began their encounter. They continue in this way until one fish is so torn and battered that he slumps away in embarrassed retreat. In nature, the victorious betta always finds a lovely lady rooting from the sidelines, fully aware that she is the prize.

"The male betta also engages in some very interesting breeding behavior. He rises to just under the surface of the water, takes in a little air with a sucking motion, and begins to construct a bubble nest, which he holds together with his sticky saliva. He blows hundreds of bubbles, continually driving the female away, until the nest is completed. It may be as large as three to five inches across and one inch high. Then, with flamboyant fin spreading and frantic advances, he entices the female beneath his nest, and they curl up in the nuptial embrace. With each embrace, six to ten fertilized eggs drift slowly toward the bottom. The male catches them in his mouth and spits them back into the nest, which will become a nursery in less than forty-eight hours. After spawning has occurred, the female leaves the nest and should be removed from the breeding tank for her own protection. The male will incubate the eggs and tend the babies, keeping them safely afloat."

Alex's mother seemed fascinated with the fighting fish. She chose a brilliant blue male and asked me to wrap up everything so that it would be a surprise.

I rang up my first sale with considerable aplomb. As soon as she had left, I sat down on Aunt Etta's stool and leaned on the counter. Aunt Etta came out from behind the curtain and gave me a big smile. I was so proud of myself, I had to look away.

"Soon you can run the place without me," she said, patting my shoulder.

I took a big breath, and we were both quiet, listening to the peaceful bubbling of the tanks in her old cedar-smelling store.

When I was older and had gone to work in an aquarium shop in New York City, I often thought of my friend Aunt Etta sitting behind her counter, calmly watching the world go by. If she could have known where her inspiration had led me, if she could have watched me during a typical afternoon in those early New York days, she probably would have apologized for selling me my first guppy.

My most difficult task was to open the shop (which is located on the West Side of Manhattan) promptly at noon every day. One morning, I jumped up from a deep sleep. The alarm hadn't gone off, and it was 11:55. I rushed out, haggard and unshaven, grabbing a breakfast donut on the way.

Anxious people were waiting for me at the shop door. Two boys peered through the picture window. They seemed convinced that someone was hiding in there and was purposely keeping them out. A huge delivery truck sat at the curb, its motor running. I stopped at the corner, out of their line of vision, and pulled myself together. I had overslept because it had taken me all night long to hang a new glass-windowed front door for the shop—perfectly understandable, but no one would want to hear any of my excuses. I knew it was going to be one of those days.

I tried to keep them all at bay as I switched on the lights. I showed the deliveryman where to stack the boxes full of merchandise and equipment, but the old shop door, weighing 800 pounds, was balanced against the display racks, blocking his way. He was swearing and sweating. The kids were running circles around me, asking questions.

I gagged. A strange, horrible smell filled the store. I looked around, then remembered. I had unplugged the brine shrimp freezer while using the electric drill and had forgotten to plug it in again. Sixty pounds of brine shrimp had melted and oozed between the cracks of the freezer.

"I'm afraid you'll all have to wait," I said. I ran around, twisting fluorescent bulbs and plugging in banks of lights, telling myself not to stick one hand into a tank while the other one was on an outlet.

The boys closed in on me. I followed them just to get them to quiet down. Then I saw what they were excited about.

"Who left the cover off the elephant-noses?" I shouted. "I check every night to make sure they can't jump out." They're a special favorite of mine. Their comical profile and clownlike antics make them a delight. But if they are given the slightest opening, they will jump out of the tank to explore during the black of night. There was only one left in a tank that had housed two dozen fish the night before. We picked up twenty-three flat little bodies from the floor. I was almost in tears.

Meanwhile, the shop was filling up with cardboard boxes. "Here's the invoice," grunted the deliveryman. "Wanna check it out?" Simultaneously, another voice growled, "I have a live fish delivery here. Where were you at noon?" And his partner began piling air freight cartons from Guyana on top of the equipment cartons.

The shop was also filling up with customers; it positively bulged. I sloshed through the brine shrimp mess, leaving a trail behind me, scooping up neons and goldfish by the bagful to fill dozens of orders. The ring of the register blended with that of the telephone until, finally, I had to dig through bottles of fish medicine to find my bottle of aspirin.

Just then, a harassed grade school teacher pushed her way to the counter. "They're driving me crazy with their fish," she moaned. "I don't know if I'm supposed to have an appointment or something, but I can't get anything done in class till this aquarium problem gets solved. Can I let the children in?"

Without waiting for a reply, thirty kids wearing name tags streamed into the store.

"Show him!" yelled Tommy. "Show him the bag!"

"He's a cannibal!" cried Rosemary. "He ate up all the babies."

"I wanted to flush him down the toilet!"

"We came to give you back your gourami."

Only a month before, I had set up a 10-gallon community tank of gouramis and swordtails for this class. All the children knew me, but still it wasn't very easy for me to quiet them down and get their attention.

"Now, I want you to tell me what happened. Begin at the beginning."

I looked into the plastic bag, and the giant blue gourami *(Trichogaster trichopterus)* peered back at me. Judging from the children's story, their tank had been peaceful until hundreds of baby swordtails were born, whereupon the blue gourami promptly went on an eating spree, sending the tank and the class into pandemonium. So they had come to return a fish that was no longer compatible with its tankmates or its owners.

I tried to explain the chain of life to them. "If every baby born to every mother fish survived, the seas would be so crowded that the fish would bump into each other. Nature controls her populations by the survival of the fittest. Only the strongest animals survive to have babies, and they pass along all their best qualities to their offspring through genetics so that their children may lead a happier, healthier life."

None of this consoled them for the loss of their baby fish, and the only bargain we could strike was to trade the blue gourami for a pregnant swordtail with a promise of many generations of little swordtails.

This incident left me more convinced than ever that, aside from choosing a healthy specimen, the most important factor in picking a fish is being aware of its personality. The children had been right to trade in their fish, just as I had been right to trade in my convicts so long ago, because it no longer made them happy.

The day had piled up on me, but now there was a lull and I set about making order out of the deliveries. The old metal-frame door was obstructing the entrance to the tank room, so I hoisted it on my back and propped it against the picture window. I was momentarily distracted by a group of children standing outside with their noses pressed up against the window glass, and in that instant the door came crashing down on the huge display tank, smashing the custom-designed hood into three pieces and tipping the tank. The children were hysterical. Two prize discus leaped through the air and plummeted to the floor amid gallons of water. I steadied the tank, replaced the discus, and prepared to drown myself in a puddle. Just then, a beautiful woman appeared in the doorway.

"Scott, I've had nothing but problems today and to top it off I ran out of fish food, and, oh, how are you?" she said hurriedly.

I handed her a bag of thawed brine shrimp and pushed her out the door. "Pepper, I need some cheering up."

I locked the shop and took a big breath, relieved to remember that there was a life outside. Pepper and I got some coffee and sat on a bench under a tree in Riverside Park. The sight of her long, shining hair and the warmth of the sun on my skin began to put me back at ease.

After I had enumerated to her all the incidents in my day, she asked, "Do you ever think of quitting?"

"Sure, but I'm hooked on fish, forgive the pun. I guess people are in this business for all sorts of reasons: for money, for aesthetics, for drama, for experimentation, for entertainment. I'm in it for all that plus love."

She nodded. "Have people always had aquariums? Who were the first to make them?"

"It goes way back. The earliest record of putting fish into glass containers dates from first-century Rome. In true Roman style, they found it entertaining to watch the fish change color as they died.[3]

"Long before the second half of the first century A.D., Sperlonga cave was used as a seaside villa. It was decorated by Faustinus, who incorporated fish motifs in the mosaics and frescoes of its baths and temples. The base of a huge group of

[3]Herbert Axelrod, *op. cit.*

sculpture is still standing in the middle of the circular pool that occupied most of the floor space. The pool was fed by fresh-water springs and was part of a series of ponds for the fish that the Romans admired 'almost to the point of mania.'[4] They were specially constructed for breeding, and seats were added so that guests could sit and watch the goings-on. A special system was designed to give the fish fresh seawater with every tide. They were given shelter from the summer sun and winter cold. It must have been very beautiful at Sperlonga, with all those rainbow-colored fish swimming back and forth in the crystal-clear water that mirrored the polychrome sculpture and the cliffs overhead.

"In his *De Re Rustica,* Varro wrote about the extravagan-cies of his contemporaries. He said that the fishponds of ordi-nary men were sweet, meaning that they contained fresh water and that they produced fish for the table. But the ponds of the nobles were bitter because they contained salt water with fish no cook cared to touch because they were so expensive.

"Apparently, Lucullus, a Roman general, consul, and pa-tron of the arts who lived around 110 B.C. nearly went bankrupt because of the elaborate fishponds he had built for himself at Baia. He even had channels tunneled through the rocks to make a mixture of seawater and fresh water for his fish.

"Often, in the great Roman houses, the fishponds were connected to the kitchen and the banquet hall by canals. During banquets, the live fish would be exhibited in the ponds while other fish were being served for dinner.[5]

"So you see? We're not the first!"

Pepper laughed and suggested that we go feed her guppies.

At her apartment, she dropped her bag on a table, told me to make myself at home, and disappeared.

---

[4]Georgina Masson, *Italian Gardens* (London: Thames A. Hudson, 1961).
[5]*Ibid.*

When I make house calls, people welcome me in many different ways. One woman has vodka and tonic brought on a silver tray. A West Side couple always serves me dinner and Irish coffee. Another couple on the lower West Side lives in a one-room apartment. The most expensive thing they own is their aquarium. The last time I went there to cure their *Geophagus* cichlid of tail rot, they sent me home with an aloe plant, after showing me how to break off a leaf and rub it on my skin in case I ever got a burn.

Pepper returned with a lavish antipasto. *"Mangia,"* she said with a grin.

Pepper leads an interesting life as a model, and she loves pretty, shimmering things around her. I was not surprised when she chose veiltail guppies for the aquarium I had helped her set up. She had hesitated for a long time before buying an aquarium because she didn't want to bring fish into her house if they might die easily. And, with her busy schedule, she had been worried about having enough time to give an aquarium the proper attention. But guppies are easy to keep, and veiltails are as shimmery and as delicately beautiful as Pepper herself, so her choice had been a good one on all counts.

At last, Pepper sat down to relax in the love seat beside me. "I went for an interview today," she began, "and I caught my stockings on a chair in the waiting room just before going in. My watch is broken, so I've been late all day. I'm frazzled, but just look at Heathcliff." She was pointing at her aquarium. "Best-looking male guppy on the West Side and his tail is in shreds. He's dying, isn't he? Scott, I love that little rogue, but you can tell me the truth."

"I smiled. "It's not unusual for male guppies to joust for the attention of a female. Their long, frail fins often tear, but fish have the remarkable ability to regenerate lost tissue quickly. In fact, you'll be fascinated watching his tail mend in a matter of days."

"I wish my stockings could do that." She giggled.

I added 3 tablespoons of kosher salt for each 10 gallons of water. "This will discourage bacterial infection while Heathcliff is recuperating."

We fed the hungry guppies a pinch of brine shrimp, watched and marveled as their appearance changed. Within five minutes after they had eaten, they looked as though they'd returned from a health cure. Their stomachs bulged, they were friskier, and their colors intensified. Before, they had carried their tails as though the weight was too much for them, but now they seemed lighter than water as they paraded back and forth, showing off their brilliant colors, like courting peacocks.

Pepper pointed out her favorite, a gorgeous male with a red splotch, like rouge, under his eye. "You're right. He looks more like himself already."

Pepper had another appointment, so I reluctantly said good-bye to her and went back to the shop.

When I told my boss about everything that had happened, he said to take the rest of the afternoon off, to go home and relax. I jumped at the chance and ran out into the sunshine before he could change his mind. The tree in front of the five-and-ten had begun to bloom and the sidewalk passersby seemed suddenly cheerful.

I ran into several customers on their way to the shop for advice. One man described his swordtail's symptoms, which sounded to me like dropsy: swollen body, protruding scales, and lethargic behavior. Unfortunately, there is no sure cure for dropsy. Successive strong salt baths (1 tablespoon of uniodized salt per gallon for 10 minutes) are the only treatment I've had success with, and I suggested that he try it. The added salt raises the water density and causes the fish to secrete more protective body slime, which is a fish's best pick-me-up.

"Excuse me now," I said to him, "while I run home for a salt bath myself."

As I learned more about the personalities of fish, I also learned a good deal about people because I found that many people think of their fish as extensions of themselves. Some fish are difficult; some people are even more difficult.

My boss asked me to make a house call in Greenwich Village early one Saturday morning. August sunshine warmed the busy streets, which were crowded with jewelry sellers and artists, and people were in fine tempers because it was the first time in a week that the air pollution dropped below the hazardous level. But as I climbed the stairs to the apartment, the air turned dank and foul.

Horace met me at the door, a can of beer in his hand, his huge belly hanging out of a Hell's Angels T-shirt that had shrunk beyond the point of decency. The apartment smelled like a stable.

"Like some breakfast?" Horace gestured with the can.

"I don't have much time," I blurted out. "I see the tank in the living room."

"Yeah, there it is. Careful where ya walk."

The room was brown—walls, ceiling, and thick pile rug. The only furnishings were two tremendous leather couches, a stereo, and two octagonal fish tanks, one free-standing and one modified as a coffee table. A circular oil painting of a squinty-eyed bulldog named Butch hung over the mantel, surrounded by monochromatic pornographic paintings that suggested sex after death. I took off my glasses and tried not to look at anything. The free-standing tank was green and slimy, its windmills and sunken ships creating a pitiful scene.

"Are there any fish in there?"

"Sure. Can't you see Moe, my catfish? Take a closer look."

I did, just to get farther away from Horace. My stomach turned as he plunged his arm into the green water, snatched up the foot-long pink catfish, and flung it to the floor. "He's a walking catfish from Florida. He and Butch—where is Butch? Butch. Butch?—he and Butch are chums.''

How appropriate for Horace to have chosen a walking catfish. The albino clarias *(Clarias batrachus)* comes right up onto land during floods. In Florida, they've been known to attack dogs and children; in fact, their importation has been outlawed in many states. They just eat and grow, consuming everything in the tank except rocks and gravel and getting more obnoxious and ornery all the time.

I looked at Butch's portrait, then at Horace, then at Moe, who was making a beeline for the front door. I tried to smile, but I was close to choking. "Do you live here alone?" I asked, trying to make conversation.

"Just Moe, Butch, and me! Listen, can you clean the whole thing out today?"

"Clean it? Why should I clean it? The algae gives it character and a lovely shade of green, and there's enough garbage in there to satisfy Moe for a long time. Keep up the good work. I'll let myself out."

"Stay for lunch!" he shouted, but I was already halfway to the subway stop, on my way home to burn my clothes.

When I got to work that day, my boss handed me the keys to the rickety Dodge van, gave me an address to hunt down in the uncharted wilds of the Bronx, and told me to get back fast with a package he needed. In my haste, I left behind my wallet, which contained my license and I.D. As I tooled along Riverside Drive, I was completely unaware of the adventure that lay ahead.

I was soon aware, however, that I was stuck on the approach ramp to the George Washington Bridge heading for New Jersey—the opposite direction from the Bronx. I breezed past the tollgate and pulled into a gas station six miles up the road, not realizing that I couldn't get back to Manhattan without paying a toll. I didn't have a cent in my pocket. A kindly mechanic listened to my story, and as soon as I uttered the words "fish doctor," he knew my tale was too farfetched to be anything but the truth. He crossed my palm with two bucks and wrote out directions to get me to Baychester Avenue in the Bronx. And I was off again in a cloud of exhaust.

An hour later, I pulled into a parking lot and entered an unmarked storefront where I was supposed to find a livestock wholesaler. A short man who resembled Sydney Greenstreet took my half of the invoice, the only official document I was carrying, and handed me a heavy styrofoam box. It was marked DANGER. I put the box into the back of the van, lifted the lid, and immediately recognized the intense muscular jowls of two mature red-bellied piranhas *(Serrasalmo mattereri)*. I didn't need a second look. I needed a cold shower.

For lack of anything better, I stopped off at a burger joint and used the remains of the $2 for a Coke. My mind raced. Piranhas are illegal in New York State, aren't they? Didn't they devour an overgrown musk ox in a Humphrey Bogart flick? Aren't there dozens in the New York City sewer system, along with scores of alligators flushed to freedom by mothers everywhere?

Two killer piranhas confined in that little box of water. They must be pretty angry. They were full grown (about 1 foot long), with teeth sharp enough to bite the foot off a hippo with surgical accuracy. What could they do to a styrofoam box? This is the most dangerous and feared animal in South America, perhaps the most dangerous fish in the world. They will attack fearlessly if there is any commotion in the water, and the taste of blood will send them into a frenzy and draw schools of 1,000 fish or even more to the attack. Yet no legislation prevents their importation because they have never bred in captivity. I hallucinated two piranhas with feet running around the truck.

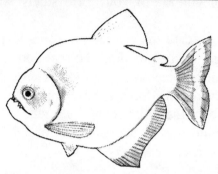

Piranha *(Serrasalmo mattereri)*

I was talking to myself as I started to pull out into traffic again. Suddenly, I felt a definite resistance at the van's left rear bumper. I seemed to have attached myself to an innocent Dodge Charger. As I maneuvered to free the locked bumpers, a madman came screaming out of the burger joint. I had done no damage except to the emotional state of the car's owner, but that appeared to be irreparable. It was difficult to decipher exactly what he was screaming, but I did hear the words "I'm gonna kill you!"

There I was—no license or registration or money, a madman threatening my life, and a pair of bootleg piranhas in the trunk. I thought about turning myself in to the nearest policeman, but I decided that my best option was simply to run away. I figured that if this lunatic followed me back to Manhattan, he would be forced to deal with my employer, who was capable of talking a walrus into buying ice. So I floored the gas pedal and broke the speedometer as well as the speed limit.

I was halfway home and drunk with a false sense of security when the same Dodge Charger appeared alongside me like a storm cloud. I could see its driver still mouthing that same phrase: "I'm gonna kill you." He surely was a determined individual.

He managed to run me onto the shoulder of the road and pin me up against the guardrail. His car door flew open and out popped a stocky man with the face of an overfed Doberman pinscher. I locked the doors as he charged at me wielding a gaff hook the size of the Grim Reaper's scythe.

How could this be happening to me? I loved my parents and kept my room clean. Why was I destined to die like a clumsy tuna fish?

The man was climbing all over the windshield, making certain I understood every profanity. He pounded on the door, putting three holes in the sheet metal and threatening to smash the window and drag me up and down the service road. I began talking to myself, naming all the people I'd rather be.

Where are the police when you really need them? Surprise! A highway patrolman had stopped on the overpass a quarter-mile away and was waving encouragement. At least I *assumed* he was encouraging me. Moments later, my assailant and I were being questioned separately. "He's the town hothead," explained the patrolman. "You're lucky he didn't draw blood."

I thought that if this had happened to someone else, I would really have felt sorry for him. I headed toward midtown, but I was so distracted, I had almost forgotten how to drive. Just as my pulse rate began to calm down and I pulled into 125th Street in Harlem, I heard the piranhas jumping around in their carton. It took me a moment to realize that they could only be making so much noise in a dry box. I glanced back. The carton was punctured, and the van was flooded.

I swerved into a service station, jumped from the driver's seat, and explained to the attendant exactly why I was hysteri-cal. He gaped as I rushed the box to a tap. I was shaking again, and I let the water run too fast. As the two very dry, very angry piranhas felt the surge of water, they made an immediate dash in my direction, upsetting my balance and causing the entire contents of the box—piranhas and all—to fall into my lap. For a second, I was paralyzed. Then I found the strength to overcome fear itself. With lightning reflexes, I grabbed the piranhas with my bare hands and tossed them back into the box.

The man at the gas pump had watched this whole experience motionless. I took a few deep breaths, refilled the box carefully, and drained out the back of the van.

Back on the road, I could only wait for the car doors to fall off or the tires to explode.

Suddenly, I was back at home base. The van started lurching—a belated nervous seizure—as I guided it alongside the piles of garbage that lined the shop's sidewalk. Knees knocking, I transferred the piranhas to a very private holding tank, dried myself with a paper towel, and lit a bent cigarette.

What type of ghoul would want to own a pair of these beasts, anyway? They're as ugly as they are dangerous. Who could love a creature that might bite off the hand that feeds it?

In strolled my boss.

"I had some trouble—"

"So have I," he snarled. "I've had a terrible morning. Don't bother me. In fact, why don't you take the rest of the day off?"

I looked at my watch. It was full of water and had stopped.

"But first, would you deliver those piranhas?"

"I thought I just did."

"Run them down to the Village, and the van is yours for the night."

"Where in the Village?"

"They're for Horace."

I took the keys to the van and shot them at him. "You take them. I'm going to join the merchant marine."

I ran out into the twilight of car horns and headlights,

heading for my apartment, hoping for something to cheer me up. Once at home, I settled down amid the serenity of the blooming hibiscus on my terrace, where the air smells as sweet as dusting powder. The fragrance emanates from the tropical water lily in the corner of my rooftop garden. I can understand why ancient cultures worshiped the lotus. Its blossoms are shades of blue, lavender, and magenta, and as one closes at dusk, a tight new bud rises to replace it and bloom the following morning. The lily flowers with amazing precision, day after day, all summer long.

My lily pond is a round fiber-glass pan measuring 30 inches deep and 4 feet across. I rooted the lily in soil in a big plastic pail, covered the soil with sand, submerged the pail about 18 inches below the surface of the water, and anticipated the prolific growth of lily pods and blossoms. Before the first frost, the planting pail must be wintered indoors. No special care is required, other than occasional watering.

A variety of fish will thrive and breed outdoors. Goldfish, of course, and koi are ideally suited for this, but the larger gouramis also adjust nicely.

Koi *(Carassius hybrid),* or Japanese carp, often grow to over 1 foot in length and are considered to be outdoor pool fish. They are extremely hardy and breed readily, scattering thousands of tiny eggs into the roots of floating plants. Selective breeding has provided striking calico patterns of vibrant reds, orange, metallics, yellow, and black, with prize hybrids valued to $10,000. Yet serious Japanese breeders do not part with reliable breeding stock, believing mated pairs fall in love.

Perhaps the most beautiful outdoor fish is the paradise fish *(Macropodus opercularis).* They are remarkably tolerant of adverse conditions, such as minimum aeration and extreme temperatures, whether they are kept in an aquarium or in an outdoor pool.

Paradise Fish *(Macropodus opercularis)*

The paradise fish is gaily painted with pearly bands of crimson and blue that blend into its gossamer, threadlike fins and tail. It weaves slowly and self-confidently through the water with balletic poise and grace. Its personality reminds me of a cat's: alert and aloof. It is a simple, easygoing fish that appeals to the same kind of person.

Paradise fish were among the first dozen species to be kept alive in home aquariums back in the 1800s, when they first arrived in Europe. Like their cousins the bettas, they are quite

vain and will display a bit of a mean streak if placed with any
other fish that dare to rival their beauty.

If well fed, paradise fish will breed like rabbits, demanding very little in the way of special conditions. When I was
fourteen, I had a lovely blue breeding pair. I needed a separate
tank for them, but by then I already had three tanks of guppies
and swordtails, and my parents absolutely refused to allow me
to have another tank in my bedroom. Undeterred, I filled a new
10-gallon tank with water, put in the two fish, and hid them in
my shower. Within a week, before my parents could even discover my new aquarium, it was full of babies.

And now my lily pond was full of baby paradise fish. Just
like bettas, the parents built a bubble nest beneath a lily pad and
protected the fry until they were self-sufficient. By winter,
when I brought them indoors, they looked like their handsome parents, with long, flowing fins and lacy lyre-shaped tails
with the blue and red iridescence of fine opals. It is a pleasure to
watch them break the surface tension of the water as they rise to
gulp in air, creating rippling rings as they do.

I've noticed that most of my clients at the shop arrive in
pairs. Funny how fish people always like to get their friends
involved with their enthusiasm.

Two dancers from American Ballet Theatre were passing
by the shop on their way home from rehearsal and decided to
take a look at the fish. They went from tank to tank, comparing
the different fish to their fellow dancers.

"That fantail clumps around like your partner. Look how
its fins drag along the gravel."

"Those catfish dash around like us doing that new Balan-
chine piece."

"The gold angelfish looks like Elizabeth doing the dying
swan."

"That kissing gourami looks like you!"

One of them decided to buy a complete setup (a 10-gallon tank, pump, heater, filter, and accessories) for about $20. I sent him home with the aquarium and a fish manual.

The following morning, his friend was back. He bought exactly what his buddy had chosen the previous day, babbling about how he just had to own a pair of kissing gouramis because he could really identify with their amorous nature.

Kissing gouramis *(Helostoma rudolfi)* are a most popular aquarium fish because they kiss and also because they are a lovely shade of rose pink and have a handsome oval shape and a charmingly casual personality. They are about the largest domesticated gourami, growing to almost 1 foot long if kept in a large aquarium. Other gourami species, including dwarves, thick lips, honeys, opalines, and pearls, all make excellent community tank citizens.

"Why do they kiss so much?" he asked.

"No one really knows for sure, but they kiss only if both fish are about the same size. It's almost impossible for anyone—except, of course, another kissing gourami—to determine their sex. At any rate, they kiss so often and breed so

Kissing Gouramis *(Helostoma rudolfi)*

seldom that I doubt it has any sexual meaning. And they kiss most energetically right after eating, so I would guess that they are helping each other to digest their food.''

''That's harder to relate to, but I still adore them,'' he squealed. ''Don't sell them to my friend. I want them all to myself.''

And so a competition developed between the two dancers. If one came to buy a fish on Tuesday, the other would arrive on Thursday, duplicating his friend's purchase and then going him one better, as if they were playing poker.

People who share an apartment often find themselves sharing an aquarium as well. Two elderly sisters visit once a week, examining every tank in the shop for an addition to their 5-gallon community of platies.

In this case, platies seem a particularly appropriate choice: gentle little live-bearers, perky, sensible, wholesome, and plain—a good fish for the modest aquarist. Their reasonable price (usually about $.50) means that almost anyone can afford to put as many varieties into a tank as space will allow (about 1½ platies per gallon).

Invariably, the only fish the sisters ever agree on is a platy. It appears to be the only kind that fills their major requirement: that the fish must love both sisters equally.

Vernon and his wife Daffy are an eccentric couple who write comic books. They have read a few fish books and like to come to me with solutions instead of problems. Together, they are striving to develop a new strain of guppy, which they intend to call ''Broadway Blues.''

Little John and Rocco have appeared in several rock musicals. Their brightly colored, wildly combined clothes make them look like guppies. In addition to their clothes, they share a two-room apartment and a 30-gallon community tank. They are

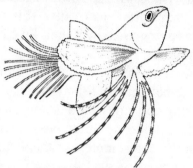

Butterfly Fish *(Pantodon buchholzi)*

always on the lookout for bizarre creatures for their aquarium. Butterfly fish *(Pantodon buchholzi)*, with delicate, winglike fins and lacy markings, glide on top of the water like trapeze artists. Elephant-noses and rope fish *(calamoichthys)* bump around on the tank floor like clowns, and Ginger, a dancing stingray *(Potamotrygon laticeps)*, is the main attraction. In short, their aquarium has the same circus quality that they create every time they visit the shop.

Sharing an aquarium can be just as practical as Dutch treat dating. In fact, sometimes that's just where it leads. One afternoon, my boss asked me to make a house call in Turtle Bay. Mr. Hanson was concerned about some white spots that had begun to infect his son's favorite silver dollar; the boy was away at summer camp, and I had promised to keep an eye on the aquarium while he was gone. I rang the doorbell. No one answered, but the door was unlocked, so I went on in—and received a little surprise. Mr. Hanson was entertaining Mrs. Solomon in a very romantic fashion in the tank room. Mrs. Solomon's jaw dropped as I blushed my way into the room.

You see, I had visited Mr. and Mrs. Solomon only two days before to treat their ailing swordtails. This was quite a coincidence, and I was dying to know if their love for tropical fish had brought them together.

Later, I remembered a passage in Jung that has always struck me as fascinating: "In fish symbolism every conceivable form of devouring concupiscentia is attributed to fishes, which are said to be 'ambitious, libidinous, voracious, avaricious, lascivious'—in short, an emblem of the vanity of the world and of earthly pleasures."

The second-best erotic fish story I've heard was told to me by Susan, a beautiful photographer with a somewhat active night life.

"I met this man in a singles bar. He talked a lot about his fish tank, so we had a mutual interest. When I went home with him, I was mesmerized by his aquarium. It curved around the wall behind his water bed—a fabulous headboard. When the room lights went out, the tank was lit with red and blue spotlights that cast rippling shadows across the bed, like waves lapping against the shoreline. You know, I can remember that water bed aquarium clear as a bell, but I can't for the life of me remember what that guy looked like!"

SCHOOL FISH

During my apprenticeship at the shop, I came to understand that in order to help a person start an aquarium, I first needed to figure out what kind of aquarium would fit in with his or her life-style, as well as what fish would suit that individual's personality. This is very important if the aquarium is to be a pleasing diversion rather than a chore. I discovered that many people want a fish tank that will help them to relax and forget their daily cares.

A tall blond man came into the shop one day. He was balancing a small goldfish bowl on his Columbia University notebook. He approached the counter and said, "This goldfish looks so lonely and unhappy that he keeps me worried all night long. I want a fish tank that will help me get to sleep."

"Doctor's prescription?" I grinned, but he was clearly not amused. "That's not so crazy," I said reassuringly. "Many communities of fish have a calming, soothing, and relaxing effect on their observers. Their whirling activities are hypnotic. I know a psychiatrist who is an aquarium enthusiast himself. The tank in his apartment sits on top of his stereo speaker, and the fish dodge and weave in time to the music—so he says. It is true, of course, that fish hear or feel vibrations by means of a network of exposed nerve endings visible along the fish's body from gill plate to tail and known as the lateral line. It is, therefore, unwise to tap on a tank full of fish because sudden vibrations cause fish to experience a loss of equilibrium, which can lead to a state of shock and symptoms of distress. He prescribes fish tanks as a soothing pastime for his patients, and he has given almost two hundred full aquarium setups to patients as gifts and as therapy.''

By the time I had finished my speech, the young man, whose name was Josh, was noticeably excited. It was closing time, and I asked Josh if he would like to see a good example of what I had been describing. I had to make my weekly house call to check up on the fish of a doctor who doesn't make house calls, and I was sure that his peaceful aquarium would appeal to Josh.

The patients in the doctor's waiting room regarded me with suspicion as I lifted the huge top off the aquarium and leaned over to sniff its contents.

"What are you doing?"

"Why are you sniffing in there like that?"

"What are you looking for?"

"Do you have permission?"

"Yes, I'm the doctor's fish doctor. Maybe I should have worn my white coat.''

I explained to Josh that in a well-kept aquarium the water should be colorless and should have a pleasant, earthy smell. There should be no pungent or foul odor. The fish should be alert but not frightened. Debris should be netted from the gravel as it accumulates and algae buildup scraped from the glass. This tank water was very old, and when I peered into the tank from the side, it looked brownish; a water change was needed. I removed one-third of the brown water and replaced it with tap water of equal temperature to that in the aquarium. Then I put the top back on and sat down next to Josh to watch the tank. The patients, quiet now, were watching, too. The room was silent except for the gurgling of the tank water. The 55-gallon aquarium resembled a primeval kingdom, with its shining shoals of copper-colored harlequin rasboras, crimson-hued serpae tetras, and brilliant blue and red neon tetras weaving through the undulating banana lily streamers and wide blades of Amazon swordplants. The fish paid no attention to us; they were in their own world.

I spoke to Josh in a low voice. "These fish can provide the same type of relaxation that many people derive from meditation. They are school fish. There are no stars, no major performers in a school tank, although there is usually a leader, who tends to be the fastest member of the school. As individuals, school fish are no great thrill. They are aloof, and they won't recognize you. But when their shapes, their colors, and the geometric patterns of their markings interact, they create a moving picture that is fascinating at first and then soothing. The bubbling of the tank is relaxing. At night, if the tank is lit, it creates a vibrant focal point in a darkened room."

"It's really magical," Josh whispered. "And I think from now on, I'm coming to this doctor. But I could never get such a huge tank of my own. I don't have room, and even if I did, I couldn't afford a tank like this."

"But you can have one, only on a small scale. These fish are not expensive. And they can be maintained in a ten-gallon aquarium, which is also quite thrifty."

We went back to the shop long enough to grab my fish encyclopedia and then went out for coffee. I guided Josh through the book, pointing out the school fish in particular.

"Although many fish will coexist in a community of mixed tankmates," I explained, "few ornamental or tropical fish live in similar communities in nature. Many fish may have a dinner party and congregate when lots of food is on hand, but there are species that identify primarily with their own fraternity members. These are school fish. They are mostly smaller fish, such as barbs, tetras, and danios. School fish are considerate. They help each other cope. Schooling is an orderly, evenly spaced swim formation wherein all the schoolmates submit their individual senses to a group identity. Their practice of schooling is usually a defense adaptation. If a hungry fish threatens them, they instinctively scramble in every direction, confusing the attacker until it is safe for them to reunite. That's why bunker fish jump when striped bass are running. In many species, the sentinel fish, who is a kind of troubleshooter, alerts his friends to an approaching threat by releasing a so-called fright substance into the water, a chemical message to its friends to take it on the lam."

As we read and talked, it occurred to me that I could use some peace of mind, too. I needed a community tank in my apartment. I knew that Josh wasn't ready to spend money, and I wanted to be able to give him the best possible advice, so I decided to set up a tank for myself first and then, after a while, set one up for Josh. He liked the idea and said he would come back in a month to see the results.

At home, I studied the notes that I had been compiling on school fish. They were a mixture of historical facts and practical observations.

Most school fish are characins (members of the family Characidae), which is the most familiar and diversified group of fish to be kept by aquarists. They are native to still waters throughout South America and Africa. Characins have adapted to a great variety of conditions, and they range in temperament from the timid tetra to the voracious piranha. A characin may be identified by the small, round adipose fin on its back right beside the base of its tail. Many species are carnivorous and require periodic feedings of live goldfish and guppies. They can also be given tubifex worms or brine shrimp a few times a month. They can attain surprising size for their individual species when well fed and cared for. A tank of little white cloud mountain fish will multiply without much attention if their diet is high in protein.

The largest and most popular group of characins is made up of the tetras. Tiny luminescent neon tetras *(Hyphessobrycon innesi)* were first netted in secluded ponds and streams in the Amazon River basin by a French butterfly collector. Impressed by their clear, vivid blue and red stripes, he brought some back to France. German aquarists were eager to propagate and enjoy these beautiful fish and sent the first neons to the United States by way of the *Hindenburg* a few weeks before its tragic explosion. To this day, fish collectors trudge through muddy Amazon jungles in search of new species of tetras that might forever bear their names.

Neons and their cousins the cardinal tetras *(Cheirodon axelrodi)* are not often bred in the aquarium, and they are not

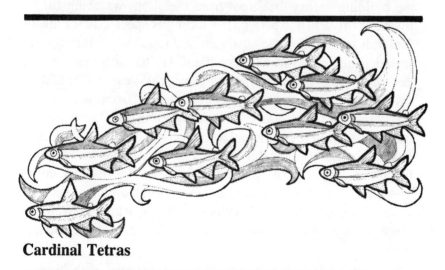

Cardinal Tetras

the easiest fish to keep happy. Because they like aged water and need special attention to their individual pH requirements, a tank of tetras should be carefully supervised to maintain a soft, slightly acid water quality through the use of plants, peat moss, or black water tonic—a commercial liquid preparation. Cardinals are easily identified by the solid red line that extends from gills to tail below the lateral line. Neons have less red; it starts in the middle of the body and extends to the tail. These fish are considered delicacies by most fish large enough to swallow them.

Thanks to economic transportation, there is always an abundant supply of these fish. This is fortunate because tetras are like potato chips—you can't get enough of them. The demand is so great that we often need to order a couple of boxes—that's 2,000 fish—directly from Guyana. Strays and babies of many varieties are often accidentally included in the shipments, and sharp eyes can spot varieties not commonly available. This makes collecting tetras a pastime in itself.

I'm convinced that a nervous client of ours must hide in the building across the street from the shop, watching for deliveries of live fish to arrive. His timing is spectacular; I always find him scrutinizing the newly arrived tetras while they are still sealed in their plastic delivery bags. He has a 60-gallon tank devoted exclusively to tetras and close relatives, and he adds an average of ten neons to it every few weeks. Because he knows that tetras prefer a relatively dark environment, the bottom of the tank is covered with volcanic pebbles that are dark. This makes his fish comfortable indeed, for they shine with celestial brilliance, and the tank pulsates with over 200 fish. He comes home from work in the early evening, turns on his stereo, and finds nirvana within the confines of his apartment. Watching large schools of neons and cardinals induces a natural intoxication.

This is precisely the kind of school fish tank I wanted for myself. I began by preparing my planting trays. I chose two squat glass bowls and added ½ inch of drainage pebbles, 2 inches of African violet potting soil and peat moss, and 1 inch of gravel. I rooted some cryptocorynes, swordplants, and hygrophila and covered the soil with an inch of coarse pebbles. I let the containers soak for 10 minutes in the sink, until the soil was drenched and none escaped from under the gravel mulch, before placing them in the tank full of day-old water.

After the plants took root and began to grow, I added two varieties of school fish. Twelve rasboras *(Rasbora heteromorpha)*, copper-plated and tastefully decorated with a handsome black triangle from midbody to tail, were first in the tank. These active, hardy fish rarely grow to more than 1 inch in length, and schools have been known to thrive in aquariums for years without a single death. Always popular for its unique geometric markings, rasboras were one of the first tropical fish to be profitably imported.

Six rummy-nose tetras *(Hemigrammus rhodostomus)* were obviously delighted with their well-planted new home, for their

Rasboras

Rummy-nose Tetras

noses grew bright red within minutes after I let them loose, which indicates that they are happy. They raced excitedly through the plants like little stock cars, an image enhanced by the vivid black and white racing stripes along their tails, especially when they grow large. In the store, these fish had been crowded in a bare tank and had seemed quite plain, but how marvelously different they looked now as they came to life in my school tank.

To complement these two schools of fish, I added eight zebra danios *(Brachydanio rerio)* a week later. They are a metallic white gold with seven to nine cadet blue stripes running horizontally along their bulletlike body, fins, and tail. The females are easy to recognize because they bulge with eggs, and given proper conditions they are very easy to spawn. Danios are native to the swift-moving streams of India, Burma, and Sumatra. They are active, darting about nervously in schools of six or more. They may reach a grand 2 inches in captivity, and as they grow, tusklike barbels appear at the sides of their mouth.

I sat back and enjoyed the optical illusions produced as these three schools of geometrically contrasting fish intersected.

Zebra Danios

It was a bit like having my own combination op art exhibit and light show.

A month later, Josh reappeared at the store, and I took him to see my school tank. This convinced him that he was ready to try an aquarium of his own. He was anxious to buy fish right away, but I cautioned him against it. "Don't think about buying fish until your aquarium has been filtering for twenty-four hours so that the gases in the pressurized tap water have had time to dissipate. Then plants must be added, and they will need an additional forty-eight hours to adjust before the fish are added because some fish will try to uproot plants."

To help ease Josh's impatience, I went on to explain that the right choice of plants is very important to the well-being of the fish community. Fish consume solid food and manufacture solid feces (mulm). They also use and convert oxygen to carbon dioxide. If there is proper aeration, a tankful of fish is never dependent on the plants for oxygen, but a well-planted aquarium will stay sweet-smelling for years. Green plants feed on mulm that has been broken down by bacteria and fungi into usable nitrogen fertilizer.

As Josh and I walked through the shop, I pointed out

different plants. "There are three kinds of aquatic plants," I told him. "The floating plants are on your right; the rooted plants are in the bottom tanks. Throughout the store is algae, which is no bargain at any price."

Creating the proper environment for a tank of school fish is a good deal of fun. They need no special nests or caves, and they will be happy in any tank that supports healthy plant growth. Even the most delicate black phantom tetras (*Megalamphodus megalopterus*) or Von Rio tetras (*H. flammeus*) adjust and thrive in such an aquarium. The shelter provided by corkscrew valisinaria or feathery tufts of cabomba is reassuring for these timid fish. But more important, aquatic plants both require and help to maintain the soft, sweet, slightly acid water quality these fish need. Plastic plants don't help to cleanse the tank water of gases, but it's not a bad idea to keep one or two bushy ones handy for the times when your plants are dormant or sparse.

Many fish take on more vibrant colors when they are surrounded by rich green foliage. A tank of cardinal tetras well stocked with tangles of deep green anacharis or wisteria vibrates with an unforgettable display of red and blue sparkles.

We chose lots of leafy hygrophila and corkscrew to create a moody grass thicket in Josh's new 20-gallon tank. I recommended a small motorized outside filter strong enough to filter and circulate that amount of water and sent him home with a heater and a fluorescent hood light.

When the tank was ready for fish, I warned Josh against starting with too many. "Listen," I said, "people call the shop three times a day with the same problem: 'My tank was doing fine for two weeks, and suddenly, yesterday, I lost half my fish.' I ask how large a tank, and they say, 'Ten gallons.' 'How many fish?' 'Twenty-five.' I say that I'm surprised they lasted as long as they did. Dumping twenty-five fish into ten gallons of water is like trying to carry six bags of groceries home in one trip. It's just not done that way. A balanced community of fish must be built gradually, with a pair or two introduced every week. A ten-gallon tank can easily support twenty-five small fish, but only if they have all been allowed a period of adjustment and are introduced into a balanced environment, that is, one with plenty of oxygen, an adequate culture of purifying bacteria, and comfortable tankmates."

Josh agreed to begin with one kind of fish. We walked through the shop and stopped in front of a tank of danios and barbs. "These fish establish an order of rank within their community and pick on each other like little boys during recess," I explained. "They rely on the brilliance of their coloring to determine superiority, and they have a repertoire of signals and protocols to communicate that status. It's a bit like the army. A zebra danio will assume a slumped-over, submissive attitude to indicate respect for a fish of greater stature."

I told Josh that these fish often breed in large groups, and so the *machismo* courtship and wooing tactics apparent in Siamese fighting fish have no parallel among school fish. All school fish are egg scatterers or adhesive-egg layers; they assume no parental responsibilities. And even though school fish are rarely bred by the hobbyist, it's important to know their breeding habits in order to provide a proper environment. They are most likely to spawn when the males outnumber the females 2 to 1. They dash through fine-leaved vegetation and chase each other for long distances, allowing the fertilized eggs to disappear in the gravel.

"Because they relate so politely to one another and relate to you only when you feed them, you don't have to dote on them if you want them to thrive. You have fewer responsibilities with this type of microcosm, so you can watch your fish in a detached manner, observing their peaceful world without having to disturb it or participate in it in order to enjoy it.

"School fish are visually oriented. Their behavior is dictated by colors, patterns, and movement. We fellow 'eye creatures' are well equipped to understand their world. That's why it is important to choose your fish according to your taste and sense of color," I said. "You may enjoy a tank with one or two large schools more than a tank with a pair or two of many different species."

The long 20-gallon aquarium, densely planted at one end, created an ideal home for the five black tetras *(Gymnocorymbus ternetzi)* that Josh chose as his first fish. They are flat and shaped like a silver dollar, with severe black coloring throughout the fanlike dorsal and anal fins. They are large for tetras, reaching a diameter of 2 inches for males and 3 inches for females. They remain peaceful and are not difficult to breed. They are very hardy fish, ideally suited for the beginning aquarist because they are always the last to die. Schools dart

Black Tetras

about with distinctive swoops rather like a fleet of flying saucers.

Two days later, he was back for four serpae tetras *(Hyphessobrycon serpae)*, which are half the size of black tetras and have similar lateral black stripes. Their translucent crimson hue is accented by a dash of white and black in dorsal and anal fins. The serpae's swimming pattern is less frantic than those of most tetras, and although they are timid, one or two pairs will thrive as successfully as a few dozen.

Josh was fascinated by the bleeding heart tetras *(Hyphessobrycon rubrostigma)*. They are named for the bloodred spot in the center of their round silver bodies. I recommended only one pair for his mixed community because they would make a very dramatic accent. Males develop an imposing arched dorsal fin trimmed in black and white. Young bleeding hearts are often confused with their dainty cousin the ornatus, but they reach a maximum size of 3 inches, whereas an adult ornatus is not even half that size.

A week later, we added six tiger barbs *(Capoeta tetrazona)*. Barbs have large metallic scales that reflect sparkles of light; they remind me of the mirror ball in a dance hall. They

Tiger Barbs

are hardy, easy to feed, and very playful, even impish in their tendency to nip at the fins of slow-moving tankmates. But if they are added to an aquarium when they are young and in groups of six or more, tiger barbs are usually too preoccupied with each other to bother with other fish. Tiger barbs are as popular as neon tetras and zebra danios. Their striking golden sides are braced with four distinct vertical black bands located at the tail base, dorsal fin, gills, and eyes, and their fins are blood red. Males are distinguished by their rosy-red nose.

Josh bought eight silver hatchetfish. Because of their bizarre shape, characterized by an enormous drooping stomach, they look like the blade of a hatchet—a hatchet with wings, for that is what their long, feathery pectoral fins resemble. With their flat silver bodies, they made a fine contrast to the black tetras and tiger barbs. Hatchetfish like to cluster at the water's surface and are capable of gliding through the air at high speeds, much like flying fish. They have been known to sail for distances as great as 15 feet, so Josh added a glass canopy to his list of accessories. Hatchetfish are shy, frail, comical creatures. They resemble nothing so much as a fleet of awkward flamingos.

Hatchetfish

A week later Josh took home a dozen cardinal tetras and a single brass tetra for color contrast. These tetras have a lovely metallic shine. They are wonderfully sociable and will eagerly join a school of different fish. A brass tetra will stand out among the schools of other fish like the star atop a Christmas tree or a shooting star in the night sky.

Josh has been extremely successful with his school tank. He comes back to the shop at least once a month to give me reports on his fish. His school fish tank brings him pleasure, peace, and relaxation. And he has never slept better in his life.

GOLDFISH

I'll never forget one particular day when my boss was out of the shop. The store was filled with customers, and I was rushing around, filling orders and answering the telephone. A man stood near the counter; he was holding a plastic bag and thumbing nervously through the latest issue of *Tropical Fish Hobbyist*.

"Sorry you had to wait," I muttered, drying my hands on my shirt.

"My goldfish is choking," he whispered.

"I beg your pardon?"

"My goldfish is choking! He swallowed a piece of glass gravel this morning. It's still in his throat. So I took the day off to bring him here."

This man wasn't kidding. I folded a length of paper toweling, soaked it with water, and cleared a space amid the paper bags and rubber bands that cluttered the counter. I grabbed a flashlight. "Put him on the operating table, and I'll see if I can help," I said, trying to deepen my voice.

He produced a beautiful lionhead oranda, its telescope mouth extended. It looked up at me mournfully as I stroked its head for reassurance—mine as well as the oranda's. I placed a length of air-line hosing in its mouth and tried to suck the glass chip free. The fish twitched uncomfortably, so I gave that up. Next, I broke apart a wooden matchstick and carefully prodded the glass, readjusting my angle and taking great care to prevent the glass splinter from tearing the fish's delicate mouth. And all the while, I had to remember to keep the fish damp.

At least fifteen minutes passed, and I was beginning to despair. But suddenly, the goldfish popped the glass chunk from its mouth and began flapping its tail gleefully. I put it into a container of aquarium water with a pinch of salt for the ride home.

"Any special instructions, Doc?" asked the man.

"Don't let it play the trumpet for three days," I said, and packed the oranda in a plastic bag. I felt exhausted but pleased.

I had been so absorbed in my "surgery" that I hadn't noticed my boss's return. He was standing a slight distance away from the counter, smiling proudly at me. Now he turned to the owner of the goldfish and explained that what I had just done was an extremely delicate operation and that an amateur should not attempt to do such a thing at home.

"How can I thank you?" the man asked.

"Throw out the glass gravel," I said. "It's dangerous, especially for goldfish because they love to poke around for bits of uneaten food and because they—or any other fish—can easily cut their bodies on the sharp edges. Furthermore, these food pockets harbor fungus and bacteria."

"Here's my card," he said. "If you ever need any help, professionally speaking, give me a call." He waved and left the shop, smiling at his goldfish.

I glanced down at his card: "Dr. Bernard Blustein, Psychiatrist."

My boss and I laughed. The telephone rang, and he answered it. I heard him say, "A fish doctor? Just a moment, please." He handed me the telephone. "Scott, it's for you. I think you've earned the title."

On their way from their native waters to the hobbyist's aquarium, fish undergo a difficult, even traumatic journey. They arrive at the aquarium shop frazzled and frightened, and if they do not receive proper attention, they may die. Someone has to care for them. That is why you will find a fish doctor in the vicinity of every aquarium shop. He may not use that title, but he is respected by fellow hobbyists and is invariably eager to help his friends with the problems and diseases that afflict their tropical fish.

I have a responsibility both to the fish I handle and to the people I sell them to. It is my job to guard the fishes' health, to help people make good choices in stocking or adding to an aquarium, and to make sure that aquarium conditions match the fishes' needs. I do everything I can to see to it that fish and owners are compatible.

One day, I received a call from the director of the New York Center for Scientific Realism. When I arrived at the center, I discovered that it occupied two floors of offices in a huge West End Avenue high rise. Houseplants climbed along the window frames, and lighted terrariums brought a touch of nature to dark corners of the rooms. I don't remember ever seeing so many smiling faces. At the hub of all the activity is an earth mother figure who sits behind an antique breakfront desk, solving problems and guiding people through their lives. She is a busy woman, concerned with financial as well as socio-psychological matters. She is surrounded by people who are looking for reassurance and peace of mind. Where does this woman go to find her own sanctuary?

Two years ago, when the original members of the center moved into their present headquarters, Marian's staff gave her a 20-gallon aquarium, fully prepared and ready to welcome its first residents. Marian bought two angelfish. Because of her interest and daily care, they grew quickly, came to recognize her, and habitually congregated at the end of the tank nearest her desk, hoping for attention. They behaved in this way even before she entered the room, which indicates that they could recognize the sound of her approaching footsteps.

By the time of my visit, class enrollment had more than doubled, which meant that twice as many students visited Marian's office and shared her aquarium. And although the center had accumulated a number of other pets, including cats, dogs, and parakeets, the fish were everyone's favorites. So Marian decided that her office aquarium should be large enough for each person in the office to have his or her own favorite fish. After spending two years in close proximity to an aquarium, there was not a single member of the staff who did not take an active interest in fish.

She wanted me to install a massive tank that would fill an entire corner of the office and provide proper conditions for as many fish as possible. The 20-gallon tank of angels was moved into Marian's apartment, and the office was in happy turmoil over selection of the proper fish to replace them.

Installing an aquarium in an office is a delicate matter because an office is unoccupied for considerable periods of time. An office aquarium should be planned with a minimum of maintenance requirements. Catfish and algae eaters are good janitors in a small aquarium, but a whole community of scavengers would be needed to keep an office tank clean. That is why I recommend goldfish or African cichlids for office tanks. They have very agile mouths adapted for retrieving food that other fish miss. An African has gritty little teeth that enable it to chew the algae off rocks, and a goldfish has a mouth like a plunger. I have found that either of these fish will be able to keep its own tank clean if ample filtration is also provided.

Both of these fish come in a wide diversity of shapes, sizes, colors, and personalities. Africans are alert, active, and aggressive; goldfish are slow, clumsy, and playful. Either fish would have been suitable for Marian's situation, and the decision was not easy for her. While she was making up her mind, I went through the equivalent of a six-week course in life awareness by chatting with her. In appreciation, I invited her to my apartment for brunch one Sunday. By then, I had accumulated six tanks, the largest of which was a 29-gallon tank devoted to fancy Japanese goldfish, and I wanted Marian to have a chance to see them.

My boss and I had gone on a buying trip to a jobber in New Jersey who had just received an overwhelming variety of hybrid goldfish from Singapore. I had raced from tank to tank, excited by the thousands of colorful, pudgy creatures, each with a face and personality all its own. When my boss disappeared into the office to negotiate, I grabbed a bucket and a net and snatched my favorites with lightning speed and accuracy. When my boss came back out, I stood there grinning sheepishly, holding a plastic bag full of goldfish.

"What's in the bag?" he inquired.

"Nothing much at all," I said. "Just a few goldfish I can't live without."

"We'll pick some up next time. I've already written the check."

"Take them," echoed a raspy voice from inside the office. The jobber emerged, a bald, rosy-cheeked little man who was perpetually chewing on an inch-long cigar. "Take them as a bonus. You're good customers. Besides, I've got so many, I don't know what to do with 'em."

"They are my pride and joy, Marian. Ten fish handpicked from thousands."

She smiled, eager now to see them. "I've always thought goldfish were too commonplace to be terribly interesting. You see them everywhere, even in the lake in Central Park."

I couldn't argue with her. Children come into the shop all the time with goldfish they have caught in the park, asking if they can trade them. "I understand what you're saying," I replied. "But take a look at my tank before you make your final decision."

We sat down on the couch in front of the tank, and in less than sixty seconds, Marian leaped to her feet, laughing out loud.

"Look at those black ones. They're so funny. One looks happy, and the other one looks grumpy."

I nodded. "They're my favorites. I call them Jekyll and Hyde. They're black moors."

"Tell me more. They enchant me."

I explained that the first fancy goldfish were actually freaks of nature. Every hybrid strain of goldfish available today is a direct descendant of the common species *Carassius auratus auratus*. After centuries of crossbreeding mutants with double tails or bulging eyes, Oriental fish breeders are still developing bizarre varieties. The secret of these deviations lies, somehow, in the alteration of a single chromosome. After continued breeding of selected freaks, the characteristics are adopted as dominant genetic traits and are passed on to future generations. Although the only true pigments possessed by goldfish are orange, yellow, and black, some varieties display vibrant reds, blues, and browns derived from combinations of these three original colors.

"How far back in history do goldfish go?" Marian wanted to know. She was moving her pinkie along the glass as she followed the progress of a calico fantail.

"During the Sung dynasty, which was A.D. 960 to 1126, hybrid goldfish were kept as pets. After several centuries of

Goldfish *(Carassius auratus auratus)*

selective breeding, goldfish became a fascination throughout the Orient not only as a hobby or curiosity but also as an art form. Prized for their grace of line and fantastical appearance, they were popular subjects of lovely scrolls and paintings. The Chinese were fascinated by gargoyles, dragons, and monsters, and they adopted the goldfish as part of their pictorial tradition, treating these hybrids with respect and aesthetic delight. A Chinese myth explains the appearance of the first goldfish. In the Chou dynasty, seven centuries before Christ, the world was without rain for one hundred days. Sacrifices made to the gods brought forth a bubbling spring. A goldfish leaped from that sparkling spring, and the rain began to fall."

"What a lovely story!" Marian's eyes were shining. "But how were goldfish introduced into other parts of the world?"

"It seems that in the first half of the eighteenth century, goldfish were brought to England. At first, they were kept in wealthy people's ponds, just as they had been in China. Sir John Hawkins, editor of Izaak Walton, wrote in 1760, 'These fish are usually kept in ponds, basins and small reservoirs of water . . . and I have known a few of them kept for years in a large glass vessel like a punch bowl.' The goldfish gained in popularity and in numbers very quickly. In 1784, only twenty-four years after he first wrote about them, Hawkins changed a footnote in *The Compleat Angler* to 'it is a now very common practice to keep them inside.' So, you see, between 1775 and 1784, the goldfish bowl came into existence—and with it the myth of the balanced aquarium."[1]

"Why is that a myth? I'm not sure I know what you mean," said Marian, who by now was examining the tank from the side.

"Well, there was a chemist named Robert Warington who set up a tank with goldfish and tape grass *(Vallisneria).* In 1850, he read a paper before the Chemical Society of London, stating that the fish consume the oxygen and furnish carbonic acid, feed on insects and young snails, and excrete material for food for the plants. He believed that the plants consume the carbonic acid, appropriate the carbon, and liberate the oxygen, at the same time feeding on the excreted matter. This concept was not refuted until 1931, when Charles Breder, Jr., who was a research assistant at the old New York Aquarium in Battery Park, proved that the oxygen from photosynthesis contributed

[1] Herbert Axelrod, *Tropical Fish as a Hobby* (New York: McGraw-Hill Book Company, revised edition, 1969).

little because there was plenty of other oxygen—an 'over or under saturation returns with extreme rapidity to equilibria' with the air above the water. In other words, you can't keep oxygen out."[2]

"How did goldfish get to be so popular here?"

"You mean in this apartment?" I teased her.

She shook her head, smiling a bit sheepishly.

"At the same time that they were becoming popular in England, Louis XV was taking advantage of newly established trading arrangements with the East. And among the imported gifts he lavished on Madame de Pompadour were live goldfish. The famous mistress—who was born, incidentally, with the name Poisson—adored the fish and kept them with the rest of her prize possessions at Versailles. In Russia, not to be outdone, Prince Potemkin had his banquet hall decorated with goldfish bowls.

"By 1878, goldfish were being sold in New York. A certain Admiral Daniel Ammen imported them for the U.S. Fish Commission, and when they were displayed in Washington, D.C., they created a sensation. In fact, until World War I, the principal interest of American aquarists was the development of elaborate and fantastic strains of goldfish.

"It's true that today goldfish are available literally everywhere. In Japan, it's common to see an old street vendor with two buckets of goldfish hanging from a pole slung over his shoulders. But, nevertheless, some varieties are so rare that a single specimen can command as much as a thousand dollars. I know that sounds outrageous, but it can be considered an investment. After all, a pair of goldfish can spawn dozens of times before they reach their declining years, and a single spawn may contain five thousand eggs. But I must tell you that goldfish propagation requires a great deal of care, space, and

[2]*Ibid.*

food. Even though one spawn can produce many eggs, only a fraction will reach maturity.''

Marian had become so engrossed in watching the goldfish that she scarcely seemed to notice I had stopped talking.

"What are all their names?" she chuckled.

"They don't all have names."

"Well, tell me about the ones that do. What about Mr. Jekyll and Mr. Hyde?"

"That's *Dr.* Jekyll."

"Oh, then he's a fish doctor, too!"

"Yeah, but he charges scale." I laughed, she groaned, and I continued. "As I told you, they are Black Moors, friendly, playful, and altogether delightful. Their velvety, copper-hued black fins are like a butterfly's wings. Their billiard ball eyes, located at the sides of the head, give them a baffled expression, as if they had just lost something. They are hardy in the aquarium, but breeding them is a challenge. The best stock have one black and one red parent. Watch how they come to kiss my finger." I dangled my finger in the tank in front of Jekyll, and Hyde charged forward, blowing bubbles and finally giving me a little kiss.

Black Moors—"Jekyll and Hyde"

"How delightful," she sighed.

"Now, this celestial has a less fortunate face. Celestials' eyeballs point straight up, which is an unsettling sight at first. They look as if they are peering toward heaven, hence the name. They were first bred in Korea by Buddhist monks, who kept them as sacred pets in the pools outside their temples. I call her Celeste.

"That bright red chubby one with the puffy face and full fantail is Kathleen, a lionhead oranda, named for a friend of mine who is a real Leo."

"What sign are you, Scott?"

"I'm Cancer, the Crab."

"Well, that certainly makes sense," she said laughingly.

"The two elegantly sequined beauties with the long, flowing, silky fins are named Jackie and Dame Margot. They are calico fantails, and they rarely leave each other's side. That sublime creature swimming in circles at the back of the tank is a silver veiltail. She often sits alone beneath the Amazon swordplant or in semiseclusion under a rock. I named her Miss Garbo."

"They really are beautiful," said Marian. "I think that they will be perfect for the office. How soon can we set up a tank?"

"We can begin tomorrow," I said.

The next day, Marian came to the shop, and we looked at all the goldfish. She took a great interest in learning everything that she could about them.

As we walked round the store, I rambled on. "Goldfish hatch from microscopic eggs within five days and must have a constant supply of protozoans and algae to eat. It takes six to ten weeks of continual eating for them to grow to one inch, and few survive the first few weeks of life. It is impossible to guarantee how many offspring will look exactly like their parents, that is, 'breed true.' However, each spawn presents the chance for new hybrids.''

''You know,'' she said, ''I'm involved with helping people to change their lives, to change and free themselves, rather like butterflies. I think I'm going to enjoy having fish that offer such a magnificent example of transformation. Even the way they move is so different.''

''That's true. Goldfish scurry and dance around. Their silhouette is always changing. It all depends on what angle you look at them from. They're like a 3-D cartoon.

''But goldfish are also very stable creatures. Their size and life expectancy depend upon living conditions, but a friend of mine has kept two goldfish healthy in a ten-gallon tank with daily attention for over sixteen years. Even though they are comets—the species closest to the common goldfish—they have developed long, graceful tails and fins. The record for goldfish age is ninety-nine years, so your goldfish may well outlive you.''

''I like all the different colors.''

''No two goldfish have exactly the same coloring. They are born silver, but after three to six months, they begin to show irregular black and white spotting mixed with gold flecks. A few weeks later, the black and white disappear, and the fish begins to assume its bright gold scales and true coloring.''

Marian gasped, ''Oh, I must have this one. Its body is like mother-of-pearl.''

I scooped it into a container of aquarium water. ''That's a pearl-scale goldfish. It's called a scaleless goldfish because its clear scales look like skin.''

''And two black moors—and what is that one, the one with the sleek white body and carrot top head?''

''A red cap oranda. The fleshy crimson growth on the top of its head indicates that it is related to the lionhead oranda.

This growth is more extensive and grotesque in appearance in the lionhead, but unlike his cousin the oranda, a lionhead has no dorsal fin, and with its clumsy, humpbacked body, this sad fish is unable to navigate, often swimming upside down or bumping into the sides of the tank. The fleshy growth eventually covers the head, often interfering with the gills and blinding the fish. Lionheads resemble human infants, and they need almost as much pampering. They require cool temperatures to keep their metabolic rate low, and even in a well-aerated tank, some specimens die of suffocation.''

"Oh, I don't want a lionhead," said Marian.

"Good. I haven't got any in stock," I answered.

We selected twelve goldfish and placed them in a holding tank marked "Sold."

At the center, I readied the tank, an 80-gallon octagon, perfect for the office corner. I decorated it simply, with dark gravel and massive chunks of rose quartz.

The members of the staff gathered around as we put the fish into the tank. They were all excited and eager to help. And they all had questions about care and feeding. Everyone wanted to be part of this adventure.

"First of all," I said, "goldfish will eat just about any-thing, so feed them only their own goldfish food. With their retractable telescopic mouths, they can pick up gravel in search of buried food, so they are good housekeepers. But be careful to feed them only as much food as they can finish in five minutes. When goldfish die, they've usually been killed by kindness, not by neglect. They are one of the few kinds of fish capable of eating themselves to death. In nature, fish search for food ac-tively all day. But in the aquarium, the reverse is true. Abun-dant food and little room for exercise produce fat goldfish. That's why I stress *sparse* feeding for goldfish, every other day. Your fish will love raw seafood—clams, shrimp, oysters, and other such things—as occasional treats. These should be chopped up and rinsed in a net under cold tap water to prevent the tank water from clouding. And regardless of treats, they should get their flake food every second day.

"Keep an eye on the water temperature. Goldfish like it cool, between sixty-five and seventy degrees. That is one reason why they should not be kept in the same tank with tropical fish that prefer very warm water."

I reached into the tank and gently petted one of the big old orandas. Then I placed a piece of chicken between my fingers. The fish circled once and finally nibbled the meat. It glanced along my wrist, its back smooth and solid, and then it swam on to join a fantail near the back of the tank.

Marian's friends watched quietly, and I knew that each one was thinking, I can't wait to try that.

Marian walked with me to the front door and thanked me once again.

"I'll be back in a week to check to make sure everything is going all right," I said. "If there are any problems, give me a call. But I'm sure there won't be any. I can see that these goldfish have found just the right home."

FISH
AS PETS

Some fish are so intelligent and have such interesting personalities that their owners think of them primarily as pets. Such a fish can be ideal for a nature lover who cannot keep a dog or cat but who would like some living creature to share the space he or she lives in. Some fish really do become family members. But, like children and domestic animals, the amount of affection that they give will be in proportion to the care and attention that they receive.

One of my pets is a mudskipper *(Periophthalmus barbarus)* named Clarias. He is a delightful comedian, with a frog face and popeyes on top of his head. His body is pale gray, and he has flecks of startlingly iridescent blue on his jagged top fin. He is a lovable misfit, caught somewhere in evolution between fish and amphibian.

In nature, mudskippers inhabit long stretches of mud flats along the African coast and around the shores of the Indian Ocean as far as Australia. Their versatile pectoral fins can be used as legs and are strong enough to enable them to jump twenty feet or climb up tangles of mangrove roots to survey their territory. They can see things both in the water and in pure air. Their eyes are close together and individually suspended and can be raised and lowered at will. Mudskippers are thus ideally suited to a shallow aquaterrarium that includes a cork or rock island to climb onto when they want to be out of the water. And they are happiest if given a sunny but cool exposure.

Mudskippers have tremendous mouths and will eat live worms and small fish, such as baby guppies. They may also be taught to eat fresh meat or cold cuts such as liverwurst, diced cooked chicken, or ground chuck, which they may nibble gingerly from your hand.

Home for Clarias is an old 10-gallon leaker tank divided into two sections: the watertight side for water and the leaking corner for earth. He shares this vivarium with a hellbender salamander named Sammy, a spotted salamander, two green frogs, and two Japanese newts. Their antics are wonderful to observe, and Clarias is the runaway favorite with visitors.

Their aquaterrarium was really quite easy to set up. I cemented a strip of rigid plastic to the aquarium sides with silicon glue and waited 24 hours for the glue to cure and dry. Then I covered both sections with 1 inch of pebbles (no. 5 gravel). I went on to put together the terrestrial section, which is really just like any terrarium. I mixed together equal amounts of potting soil, humus, and perlite and patted the mixture down gently. Next, I added water to the aquarium section and provided it with a small inside box filter. Then I covered the plastic divider with a long piece of cork. Finally, I added a deep rock cave and a couple of spider plants to make a perfect haven for the salamanders.

Clarias took an immediate liking to the cork strip. He often crawls completely out of the water and rests on it, enjoying the morning sunlight that streams through my bedroom window.

Not long ago, I received a call from a client named William. He sounded melancholy, and after a few minutes, he blurted out, "Valentino, my arowana, died last night."

It is always difficult to cope with the death of a fish, especially an expensive one, but it is worse if the fish has been a pet. I was tempted to tell William to come into the shop and to look for a new fish, but I knew that even if he did, he would still be sad. He would have to get over his loss in his own way.

"I had him for five years," he said. "He grew from six inches to two and a half feet long. He recognized me. He could even tell when I was coming; he knew the sound of my footsteps. He outgrew tank after tank, and he ate like a pig, but he really was my friend."

I offered condolences. I knew just how he felt. There was no point in saying, "You'll feel better tomorrow," or "You'll forget about it soon." I knew that Valentino had become a part of William's life.

William told me that he wanted an autopsy performed. He had been sure that Valentino was in perfect health, and so it was very important to him to find out what had gone wrong.

I hate doing autopsies because there is no guarantee of discovering the cause of death. I have sent fish to the microbiology lab for tests, which can cost from $15 to $25. But in this case, I felt an obligation to perform the autopsy myself.

I slit Valentino open, squeamishly realizing that there was enough arowana to make a dinner for two. There were no external signs of disease. I probed the vital organs but found nothing blatantly unusual. However, closer inspection revealed tiny pinhole lesions of the left eye. When discus succumb to brain worms or hole-in-the-head disease, the cause is an evil little fungus called *ichthyophonus* (not to be confused with the parasite *Ichthyophthirius*, which causes ich, or white spot). It can attach itself to just about any internal or external organ and thus turns out to be the cause of most undiagnosed aquarium deaths. I took smears from various locations and viewed them under the microscope. My diagnosis was correct. The liver, kidneys, and gills all revealed a high concentration of spherical brown fungus. The only consolation I could offer William was to tell him that treatment for this particular fungus is seldom successful.

The Amazon River basin is the home of the arowana *(Osteoglossum bicirrhosum)*. Young specimens are often collected in an unfortunate manner. The mouth-brooding female is killed, and the babies are taken from her mouth while they are still being nourished by the yolk sac. If the yellow sac is still attached to their bellies, the babies were robbed from their mother prematurely and are not likely to survive.

The arowana's graceful silver body is shaped somewhat like the blade of a knife. It swims like no other fish, gliding through the water like a Japanese kite in the wind or a panther pacing in its cage. Because it has an erratic temperament, is easily frightened, and is likely to jump out of the aquarium, it needs the protection of a padded cell, that is, an aquarium with

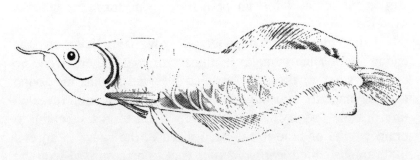

Arowana *(Osteoglossum bicirrhosum)*

no sharp edges. However, the arowana has an extremely sturdy constitution and is seldom sick. A pet arowana can live happily for ten to twenty years in a 55-gallon aquarium. There are just a few points you need to remember if you want to have success with this fish: Keep the water clean and at a temperature of 78 degrees, and move the arowana as little as possible.

One thing about the arowana: It is *constantly* hungry. Consequently, it never seems to stop growing. Live goldfish are the preferred food, but I have taught arowanas to eat a variety of chopped meats (raw beef and chicken hearts, beef liver, lean beef, chicken, lamb, ham, shrimp, and clams) from my fingers. I've also learned that it's a good idea to have lots of scavengers in the tank with arowanas; they are sloppy eaters and need someone to clean up after them.

An arowana is best kept by itself with one or two tankmates who are its natural close neighbors in the Amazon, particularly the less aggressive South American cichlids, such as members of the species *Festivum, Geophagus,* and *Severum,* and even their enigmatic cousin the oscar.

The oscar *(Astronotus ocellaturs)* comes from Paraguay, Guyana, and the Amazon and is undoubtedly the most popular of all the South American cichlids. Like the arowana, it prefers a diet of live fish, but it will (in most cases) settle for red meat, which is a relief to owners who are queasy about feeding it live baby goldfish. And like the arowana, the oscar will respond extremely intelligently to its keeper. It soon learns to recognize its owner and to differentiate him or her from anyone else who stops to visit its tank. An oscar will eat its dinner right from the palm of your hand and even splash water on you as you pass by to let you know it's hungry. My friend Wallie, who lives in a ground-floor apartment in a brownstone across the street, displays his tank of oscars in his picture window. Passersby get a free aqua show when he has his oscars swim through hoops to earn their dinner.

The oscar is a most engaging creature. It always seems to be smiling. The larger it grows, the more its owner feels responsible for its growth. If you have an oscar, you just can't help taking pride in it. I have talked to dozens of aquarists who say, "The oscar is my friend." When asked why, they usually say, "It's his personality."

When I visited a large fish farm in Miami, the proprietor, Mr. Brown, led me to a huge concrete pond and waved his hand above the water. Instantly, the surface began to move. I peered into the water and was met by the inquisitive eyes of at least thirty foot-long oscars.

"Stick your hand in," Brown said. "They're wonderfully gentle." I did so and experienced a wild sensation. Several of the oscars approached my hand and then glided against my skin while others came and bumped my fingers, looking for food.

The perimeter of the tank was divided into dozens of foot-long cubbyholes separated by slate partitions. "These oscars would never let you approach them like that if they were breeding," Brown explained. "Each separate cubby is a breeding chamber, supplied with a removable slate sheet. When the oscars pair up, each pair chooses its own chamber. Slates bearing hundreds of fertilized eggs are removed daily, and the young are hatched and reared separately in a big nursery tank.

"Oscars have become so popular that they have been introduced into the freshwater channels and canals surrounding Miami. I foresee them becoming a game fish before too long. They'll certainly give freshwater anglers an excellent fight on a fly rod."

There is no disputing that a fish which will rub itself against your arm in order to display affection can truly be a pet. However, these fish require a particular kind of care. Oscars may demand greater (even constant) attention and more time than you are willing or able to give them. For instance, oscars are best not left alone for much longer than a weekend. If you

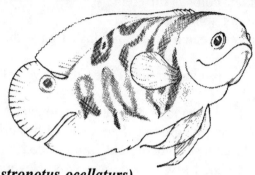

Oscar *(Astronotus ocellaturs)*

are away any longer, you will risk alienating them. And it is actually dangerous to leave them alone. They are capable of knocking off the aquarium hood and leaping from the tank in a desperate attempt to find you when you don't show up for their accustomed feeding.

Mrs. Newman has been a client of mine for a long time. She inherited her oscars from her son, who had to leave them behind when he went to college. He had started with two baby red oscars, only 1 inch long, in a 20-gallon tank, and he quickly fell in love with their gregarious nature. Since he left, the oscars have grown spectacularly. They are now well over 1 foot long, and they swim around happily in an 85-gallon tank right next to the television in Mrs. Newman's living room. She explained to me that at first they offered a distraction from commercials, but more and more, they command as much interest as prime-time programs and soap operas. Guests aren't in the house for more than five minutes before they're plunked down in front of the tank to say hello to Mrs. Newman's babies.

Mrs. Newman calls me constantly about her oscars.

"Scott, their color is different."

"They're not sporting their fins."

"They haven't eaten all the goldfish I gave them yester-day."

"The water is evaporating faster than ever. I'm afraid there's a leak."

One day, her husband called, but I could hear Mrs. Newman's voice in the background. She sounded hysterical. "I'll pay your cab fare. Just come quick!" he pleaded.

When I arrived, I saw at once why Mrs. Newman was so alarmed. The beautiful velvety red markings on her prize oscars were mottled and clouded by an advanced bacterial infection; a grainy white film covered their bodies and eyes. Bits of food clung to the gravel and plastic plants. The excess food had supported a bacterial bloom, which, in turn, was trying to consume all organic matter in the tank, *including* the fish.

The oscars, Fred and Ethel, were definitely in a state of melancholy. I had seen this condition and treated it on many occasions, and I told Mrs. Newman so in my suavest tankside manner while she practically stood on my shoes, repeating anxiously, "What's wrong? What's wrong?"

"You can relax, Mrs. Newman. This won't take long."

I disconnected the power filter and drained off one-third of the water, replacing it with fresh tap water. I then added 17 tetracycline capsules (250 milligrams each) to the tank water and carefully sprinkled 25 tablespoons of kosher salt over the bodies of the fish.

The amount of medication given in any case is related to the size of the tank. In a well-stocked 10-gallon tank, there may be only 7½ gallons of water. That's why I believe in being cautious when dosing an infected tank. (Symptoms and treatments, based on my conservative philosophy, are included on pages 246–247.)

"There, they should feel a lot better now," I said, turning to Mrs. Newman.

"Scott, how could you tell what was wrong and what to do for them?"

"Well, you yourself realized that something was wrong. It's easy to tell when your fish are sick because, after all, you know them so intimately that you are quick to notice even a subtle change in their appearance or behavior. A fish is a beautifully symmetrical organism, and proper preventative measures will protect it most of the time. But when a fish is in ill health, that symmetry is visibly distorted. If there are white bumps, red splotches, lumps, or fuzz on any of a fish's extremities, that's a sure sign that something is wrong.

"You were right to heed that warning and call me at once. It's actually not difficult to diagnose most aquarium diseases. The real trick lies in knowing what medication to prescribe for what symptoms and in what dosages. It's best not to experiment with treatment on your own because a novice eager to help an ailing fish is likely to overlook one very important fact: A sick fish is a weak fish. And a weak fish can just as easily be poisoned by a medication as cured by it. That's why my first and foremost prescription is a salt bath. Fish absorb and excrete minerals through their skin, as well as their gills. A fish's primary protection from bacterial and fungal infection is its body slime. That's why it is not advisable to handle sick fish—their body slime will come off on your hand. Adding salt to the tank water increases the water density, which in turn changes the rate of respiration through the fish's skin. The result is a rapid overproductivity of body slime. Fish are accustomed to some concentration of salt in their water, so it can't damage their weakened metabolism."

Mrs. Newman thanked me, but she seemed reluctant to let me leave.

"There's really no need to worry. Your oscars aren't suffering from a rare malady. I'm sure that you'll see a big improvement in their bearing by tomorrow morning. And, remember, if you don't see a real change, call me first thing."

"How did you get to know so much about fish?" she asked.

"Oh, I was a fish myself once!" I exclaimed as I closed the door behind me.

COLLECTORS

I confess to being a fanatic collector. I collect rocks, orchids, crystals, butterflies, shells, coral, stamps, coins, old magazines, string, begonias, and fish. And I love to hear all about other people's collections, whatever they may be. The most amazing collection I've ever heard tell about was described by my best friend's aunt. When she was a girl, back in the 1930s, she was invited to spend the night at the home of a school friend whose family lived in a town house in Turtle Bay. She stepped out of the elevator into the foyer and found herself in an underwater paradise. She was surrounded by floor-to-ceiling aquariums that spanned the walls, a very prestigious possession in those days. She stood there waiting for her friend, feeling dizzy as she followed the multicolored goldfish drifting through space, as though she had been transported to another realm.

Her amazement grew as her friend led her through the adjoining rooms, past a Rembrandt portrait that was covered by a velvet curtain and a dollhouse with toilets that actually flushed!

That night, she lay in bed, too excited to sleep, staring with fascination at the tremendous bureau across the room. It had a great many drawers of different sizes, and she knew she just couldn't fall asleep until she had peeked into them. She tiptoed to the chest, gingerly opened a drawer, and drew back in terror as dozens of colored feathers billowed into the air. She tried to catch them and stuff them back where they belonged, then opened another drawer. Feathers of all colors and sizes lay pressed between layers of tissue paper, feathers of such rarity that they could easily have floated through time from the Arabian Nights. Every drawer in the massive wooden chest was full of feathers.

The next morning, she confessed that she had peeked and apologized if some of the feathers might have escaped or been rearranged. Her friend's mother reassured her, explaining that everyone who slept in that room was bewitched by her feather collection.

Fish aren't feathers, but they do attract collectors in the same way that coins or stamps or antiques or plants do. There is enough zoological information available so that collecting fish can be enjoyed simply for their beauty and sophisticated behavior.

Collecting almost anything can relieve loneliness and stamp out boredom. One of the loneliest people I have ever met inadvertently started my collection of African cichlids, which are now my pride and joy. When I feed them or count their offspring, I remember Wallace, thank him for his gift, and hope he's all right, wherever he is.

This is how it happened: One afternoon, a man pulled up outside the shop on a motorcycle and came in. He was carrying a knapsack and wearing sunglasses and tattered clothes. He was gaunt and looked worn out, as though he had missed many nights of sleep. He came over to the tank where I was arranging some banana lilies and said that he had heard about me from friends. His voice was melancholy. His doctor had insisted that he leave New York, he explained, so he was pulling up roots and moving to Arizona, taking only as much as he could carry on his motorcycle. He pulled a plastic bag of African cichlids from his knapsack, and said he wanted to give them to me.

I must have seemed skeptical at first because he hurried to add that he didn't want any money for them, even though they represented a considerable investment. But he didn't want me to sell them, either. He asked me to take them home and keep their community intact. I was surprised and a bit confused, but I said I would adopt his fish.

He glanced around the shop. "I'm going to leave tonight, before it gets dark. I guess I feel pretty sad about leaving New York," he said quietly, "but I'll be happy to get out of the city. I want to go someplace where I won't feel so alienated, somewhere close to nature."

Wallace hadn't found anyone who wanted his aquarium equipment, so he told me I could have it all, too, if I came by that evening.

It was gray and cold as I hurried to the address he had given me. It turned out to be a welfare hotel tucked in between two brownstones near Riverside Drive. Old newspapers and furniture, which I assumed were the remains of Wallace's New York life, littered the street. I hurried down a long, dark hallway, trying not to notice the derelict who sat in the stairwell, looking like a caricature of an opium smoker. Nervously, I rang Wallace's bell.

"You'll have to wait. The door's blocked!" I heard shuffling on the other side. As I waited, I kept one eye on that derelict, who now seemed to be drifting euphorically in my direction. When the door finally opened, I stumbled in and gasped at what I saw: a room that looked like a victory garden gone to seed. Plastic globe terrariums decorated every shelf. Dried-out philodendrons clung to the window frame with a death grip.

Tropheus moorii

The only thing still green was the cactus. The half-dozen aquariums, which outnumbered the pieces of furniture, were half full and green and slimy with algae.

"Take anything you want," said Wallace despondently, waving at the room. "You already have my fish. I've lived here for two years, and they were my only friends. This place has started to make me think of Death Valley. I'm ready to go."

He gave me time for a good-bye handshake and a good-luck wish; then he vanished. From the window, I watched him start his motorcycle and ride off in the direction of the George Washington Bridge.

There I was, alone, surrounded by stacks of two-year-old newspapers, a mattress, and hundreds of dollars' worth of heavy aquariums and equipment, with no way to move it. I was in need of a friend with a crane or at least a very good sense of humor. I decided to call Robert, who is a prince among my dearest friends and crazy enough to be able to appreciate truly bizarre situations. Still, I couldn't quite bring myself to go into any detail over the phone.

"Listen, I have this little favor to ask. It won't take long at all—"

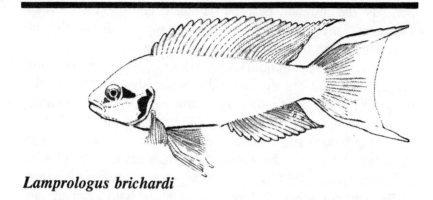

Lamprologus brichardi

A woman on the fourth floor was screaming so loudly that I could hear her in the lobby. Robert arrived, looking very agitated. He turned pale when he caught sight of the slimy, smelly fish tank as big as a bed. Still, he helped to empty it so that we could use it as a packing crate. By now, people had gathered at the door and were peering in at us, curious and amused.

"We can't do this," muttered Robert.

"We can. We have to."

Down the hall, an old man was coughing incessantly.

"Go get a cab," I said.

"Oh, sure! Go get a cab! What am I going to say? 'Oh, taxi. We're moving the Dead Sea upstairs. Wanna help?' "

"Just try—please."

Robert went, hailed a roomy Checker cab with the youngest driver he could spot. "We have a few aquariums up there. We'll make it worth your while."

"Aquariums? How many?"

"Well, just one—one big one—we're not going far—"

The driver ended up helping us carry the endless collection of aquaphernalia out of the room, down the hall, past the derelict, past the cougher, past the screamer, and into the elevator. Our arms were trembling. We kept trying to reassure the cab-driver that everything was going to be fine.

At home, I spent hours cleaning and disinfecting the tank. First, I siphoned out the remaining algae sludge and shoveled the gravel into a plastic trash can for rinsing. I made a cleaning solution (a handful of ordinary uniodized salt in 3 gallons of warm tap water) and scrubbed the glass until I nearly fell in. Scraping algae from the walls of an aquarium is difficult with-out the proper tools. I use a single-edge razor blade for scraping and a handful of crumbled nylon tulle bound with a rubber band as a scouring pad.

When the tank and equipment were clean, I put a layer of washed dolomite over the under-gravel filter, arranged my col-lection of cured corals and rocks, filled the tank with tap water, set up the motorized outside filter and heater, and finally plugged in the lights. I knew that the size of an aquarium helps to determine its personality. Yet, as I stepped back from the surprisingly massive tank, I was struck by the sheer magnetic presence and intense change of atmosphere that it had instantly brought to the tiny room. Today, the room must have the same effect on visitors that the aquarium hallway in that Turtle Bay town house had on my friend's aunt. It is the aquarium of my dreams, large enough to create a total complex community, large enough to grow fish to full size. It is my most successful tank because, being the largest, I find myself watching it the most and paying close attention to maintenance checks. It has remained a peaceful and beautiful environment for over three years.

Finally, I was able to reinstate the fish and take a good, close look at them. In spite of the trauma of their move, the African cichlids were in surprisingly good health. I became entranced with them at once. Their appearance was fascinat-ing; their faces, expressive; their colors, diversified. I was amazed at how attentive they were. Within their first hour in their renovated home, each fish drifted slowly to the front of the tank, but each would bolt with nervous excitement when I drew near. They seemed sad, and I guessed that they were looking for Wallace.

How familiar each face is to me today; I know each fish intimately. They are all individuals. Some are bullies; some, coquettes; others, hard workers. But I had no idea of this that first night. I stayed up all night with them, and went to my charts, trying to identify each one and reading all that I could find about my new charges.

I discovered that they were mostly species of the genus *Pseudotropheus,* one of many *mbunas,* a native word meaning "rock dwellers." They come from the great African lakes, which have been known to us for about 100 years. Lakes Malawi, Victoria, and Tanganyika may have over 200 species of fish, most of which are found nowhere else in the world. Thus, these fish are considered endemic, meaning they belong exclusively to a given location. The lakes are speckled with hundreds of islands and surrounded by streams and rivers, each with its distinct community of subspecies and crossbreeds. Each new exploration invariably yields unfamiliar species. The varieties best known to hobbyists inhabit the thirty-to-fifty-foot deep waters along the algae-covered rocky shorelines of the lakes.

My new cichlids were all of similar size and shape, but the variety of colors and markings was dazzling. Some were powder blue; some, orange and violet; many had vertical stripes. One had horizontal stripes, unusual for the genus *Pseudotropheus,* which characteristically have vertical stripes.

That horizontally striped beauty was the first I was able to identify. It is a Nyasa golden cichlid *(Pseudotropheus auratus).* This was the first African cichlid I ever met. I had received a bagful of juveniles from a client when I first worked at the shop.

They had made a strong impression on me because they were very active and made a brightly colored display. My new *auratus* is bright golden yellow, with three broad horizontal black stripes, edged in iridescent blue, that run from its nose through the eye, along the back and the edge of the dorsal fin, to its tail. These fish are black and yellow from birth, unlike their cousins, who gradually reach full color intensity as they grow. Territorial male *auratus* have predominantly black sides and belly with a clear yellow dorsal fin, almost the exact reversal of the original pattern, and flecks of blue all over that are brightest on the operculum (gill plates). *P. auratus* was first imported to this country in 1965. Its sturdiness and willingness to breed make tank-bred specimens easily available to collectors.

Rival to the *auratus* for Mr. Popularity is the Nyasa blue cichlid *(P. zebra),* a fish with many of the same attributes. They were among the first mbunas collected and catalogued by Sir John Kirk in the mid-nineteenth century. My blue cichlids are vibrant blue, with six to eight blue-black vertical bands, blue fins, and numerous orange egg spots on the anal fin and at the rear of the male's dorsal fin. These fish have surprised collectors by changing from brilliant blue to an unstriped gray when

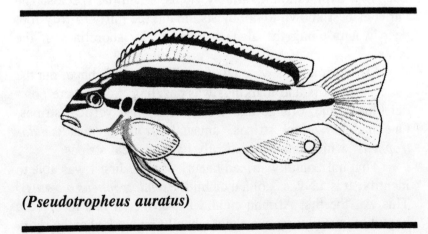

(Pseudotropheus auratus)

captured. And, in fact, they can change color instantly in the aquarium, warning tankmates of their moods. When spawning, their color may change to powder blue, with clearer dark bands. Thus, *P. zebra* has three color phases, whereas *P. auratus* has only two. Because they tend to bully other fish, they must be provided with personal territory. If kept in a tank with fish of equal or smaller size, blue cichlids will be the monarchs of the aquarium.

Because of crossbreeding and variation both in nature and in the confines of the aquarium, a great many varieties of *P. zebra* are available, ranging in color from pale blue to tangerine to mottled beige. They breed and crossbreed avidly, making themselves irresistible and profitable in the home aquarium. Their talent for throwing morphs (new color varieties), which will probably be exploited soon by fish hybridizers, makes a community of *P. zebra* fascinating to breed. You never know what the babies will look like.

The lovely apricot-colored cousin of *P. zebra*, *P. lucerna*, is a slightly larger fish. It should be kept with *P. zebra* to discourage rampant aggression and to function as a bouncer. This fish is a personal favorite of mine. I received three ½-inch

(Pseudotropheus zebra)

babies a year ago in trade for some kribensis I had bred and
raised. I was promised fabulous results when they reached
maturity, and I was not disappointed. The male *lucerna* now
measures over 4 inches from mouth to tail. His vertical bars are
barely visible beneath the translucent mauve glow that seems
lacquered to his sides, and his golden fins and tail shimmer with
blue highlights. His clear, dark eyes, larger than those of most
mbunas, give him an intelligent, sophisticated air. He is the
undisputed yet compassionate sovereign of the tank, growing
larger and more beautiful every day. He is most responsive to
my presence, hugging the glass closest to where I sit and chas-
ing away competitors for my affection. He allows me to stroke
him and even lift him out of the water between my fingers. In
recent months, this delightful creature and his attractive mate
have presented me with two broods of lavender babies that flock
to the surface when I am near, just like their parents.

The most amusing fish in the tank is a male *Labeotropheus
fuelleborni,* named for its comical, rounded, hoglike nose. De-
spite his goofy smile and his shyness, he has proved to be quite
intelligent. Leo, as I call him, is similar to the blue cichlid in
coloring, with light and dark blue bands and a bright orange

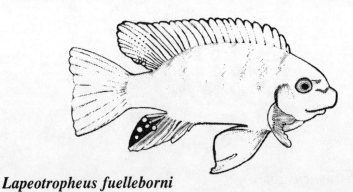

Lapeotropheus fuelleborni

dorsal fin with red-orange highlights on his fins and across his gills. (*L. fuelleborni* can also have uniformly deep blue bands.) His strangely shaped mouth helps him chew algae, his staple diet, from rocks. Consequently, I try to feed him a vegetable food supplement, such as boiled spinach, once a week. From the moment I laid eyes on Leo, it was love at first sight. After all, who could resist a personable little fish with a Jimmy Durante nose.

As I got to know my Africans, it dawned on me that these fish are more than charming. They are collectable. The first imported wild specimens to be kept in aquariums were quite delicate, expensive, and susceptible to pH and water-hardness factors. The only people who were interested in them were devoted and excited hobbyists. But as increasing generations have been bred in tanks, they have adapted perfectly to aquarium life. Africans are so new to aquarists that many of them still do not have common or colloquial names. And because of the wide variety within genus and species, positive identification can be difficult, confusing, and challenging. Only a few of the hundreds of varieties of mbunas are available today, but their popularity has grown so spectacularly within the last ten years that dozens of new varieties and subspecies are being collected and rushed to aquarists around the globe, and we can certainly look forward to many more.

A tank of Africans is magnetic. Unlike their South American relatives, they adapt famously to mixed communities. If you have a spacious tank, you can keep most varieties of Africans together, small fish with large.

Africans will breed and raise their young right in the aquarium, which I only discovered about three months later. I was on the phone, chatting with Marian. One of the cats in her office had fallen into the fish tank, causing some havoc among her staff as well as her goldfish.

"Excuse me," I remember saying, "but my fish are breeding."

"Oh, do tell how," she whispered.

What I saw and described to Marian was remarkable.

"They're mouthbreeders," I prefaced, "which helps to protect tiny newborns. The male is a blue cichlid, with intense electric breeding colors. The female is red but a member of the same species, *Pseudotropheus zebra.*"

It was their unusual color and frantic antics that had caught my attention. All the other fish were gathered at one end of the tank as the pair went through their mating dance on a flat rock shelf at the other end. The male chased the female at amazing speeds through the coral steeplechase until they both came to a startling standstill over the rock. He flaunted his anal fin, with broad fanning gestures that resembled the tense advances of a matador, and the chase continued. Again, he ran her to the breeding site; again, they froze. Again, he flayed the anal fin, with its seven gleaming golden egg spots. Both fish began to tremble as the first three or four eggs emerged from the female's ovipositor. She quickly scooped them into her mouth. Suddenly, the two fish changed places. Seeing the male's egg spots, the female, thinking they were certainly eggs that she missed, tried to snatch them up but got a mouthful of sperm instead.

"This is likely to continue for hours," I said. "I'll call you back."

Marian called me a voyeur, laughed, and hung up.

The next morning, the female lurked timidly behind the coral—unusual behavior, especially when I'm pouring in fish food for their breakfast. Afraid that she might be picked on, I netted her and gave her a private maternity tank. A closer look revealed the reason for her behavior. Her buccal sac (throat) was

greatly extended. When incubating young, mouthbreeders re-
fuse to eat for a period of three to four weeks, until the babies
have grown large enough to fend for themselves.

Mouthbreeding is a sophisticated adaptation for protection
of the young. I've always wondered how behavioral and physical evolution works. Does a fish respond behaviorally to physical adaptation? Or are these physical changes instigated by
behavior? At any rate, both forms of evolution are beautifully
illustrated by mouthbreeders.

Mbunas have evolved sophisticated qualities that separate
them from other cichlids. For instance, they are one of the few
fish born with preinflated air bladders. All fish depend on an air
bladder to navigate and to maintain balance. By expanding and
contracting this bubble, fish compensate for varying water pressures at different depths. Most newborn fish must swim to the
surface for a gulp of air to fill the bladder, but the mbuna is born
with a sealed preinflated air sac that enables it to remain in the
mother's buccal sac until it is old enough to be released. Then it
stays at the bottom of the tank, close to its mother or chinks in
the coral for protection.

The fact that most Africans breed readily in the aquarium
is good news for collectors. Many varieties are now available at
lower-than-reasonable prices. Recently, I purchased a dozen
1-inch-long *Lamprologus brichardi,* a gentle gray fawnlike
cichlid with graceful white tipped fins and a lyretail. I paid less
than $1 apiece, whereas five years ago, a mature pair could not
be had for less than $50.

Not long after I adopted Wallace's African cichlids, Herman, a hobbyist for many years, strolled into the shop carrying
his school of angelfish in plastic bags.

"It's taken me a long time to admit it," he said, "but I'm bored to death with these. They just grow and lay eggs and grow some more, and stare at me. I want a fish I can relate to, a fish that will be a challenge to breed, one that no one else is breeding. A shy fish, maybe."

"A shy fish," I mused. "I'll have to think about it. But in the meantime, why don't you come over later and see my new tank."

Herman left his angelfish with me, and I returned to my business.

During the workday, I thought about Herman's request for a shy fish—not a colorful or swift fish, but a fish with a unique personality, a rare fish that would appreciate Herman's tender loving care. I was sure that he would love the African cichlids because they are extremely intelligent and because they display interesting breeding behavior, but I wouldn't exactly call them shy. I looked through my books and charts and finally came upon a fish that I thought would be perfect.

That evening, after I had shown Herman my Africans, I told him about the *Julidochromis marlieri,* a timid little fish

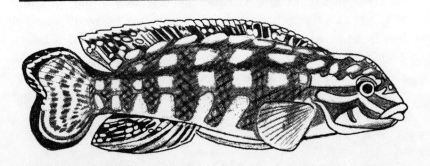

Julidochromis marlieri

with a severe glare and the bearing of a Hovercraft. I explained that although the julie was actually a cichlid, it was atypical in personality. I told him that if he wanted to breed julies, there would be no need to provide them with a 4-foot-long tank. Most African cichlids require running room essential to their courtship and mating.

We took our time visiting many wholesale distributors and private breeders in the area in search of Africans Herman might like. As I had expected, he was immediately attracted to the comical *Julidochromis*. They are shy and slow-moving and have a special appeal. Various species (meaning any group of fish that is able to interbreed and bear young), including *J. ornatus* and *J. marlieri,* like to hover close to coral and the aquarium bottom. *J. marlieri* are the largest of the group, with checkerboard brown and ivory bodies, highlighted by iridescent blue on their fins.

"Specimens of *J. marlieri* are still scarce," I told Herman, "so you can breed them for profit. Most African cichlid species are mouthbreeders and easy to breed. But the *Lamprologus* and the *Julidochromis* are exceptions. Both are very secretive about their breeding, and they need shelter—a conch shell is good—to give them a sense of security and a place to lay their eggs. But remember, julies produce small broods. And you need to keep an eye on them because the young may fight among themselves, although the adults will not harm them.

"I like them," he said. "They remind me of leprechauns."

"Choose the pair you like best, and we will see how they get along in your tank."

Herman selected two *marlieri* that seemed to have playful but shy dispositions. He was able to pick a pair because the females are larger and have brighter noses than the males.

Herman was delighted with his julies. In fact, he became so interested in the Africans that he wanted to add some other species. But before he could buy another fish, Herman called me to say that he thought his julies had begun to breed.

I went over right away to see for myself. The tank was empty except for a large conch shell.

"I don't think this is funny. Where are they?"

"They're in the shell," he whispered.

"How cozy for them," I said. "How do you know they're breeding?"

"I just know it. One will come out and take a quick look around to make sure no one's watching them. What else could they be doing in there?"

He was right. Within a month, eight adorable mini-julies emerged from the conch, staying very close to Mom and Pop.

Since the time when I got my African aquarium and helped Herman stock his, I have added various other fish to my cichlid tank, including scats, monos, loaches, and armored catfish. Black red-fin sharks *(Labeo erythrurus)* and leopard catfish *(synadontis)* add variety and help keep the tank clean. Amid the

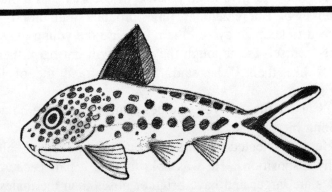

Leopard catfish *(Synadontis)*

dancing pastel African cichlids in my home wafts a dragonlike fish, prehistoric and mythical. He is actually an armadillo catfish *(Hypostomus plecostomas)* from Venezuela. He appears from time to time, as if by magic, sucking on a rock, hanging vertically against the aquarium glass.

My African tank has become more than a collection of fish. I think of them as a family—an unusual family, to be sure, but nearly a human one.

When it comes to collecting fish, many people prefer to find them in their natural habitats. One day, I received a call from a couple named Worthington. They were having trouble with some fish they had brought back from freshwater ponds and streams along the East Coast. They wanted my advice, so I scheduled a house call.

After I arrived at their apartment, my attention was immediately captured by a 100-gallon tank that spanned the living room wall. They introduced me to their collection: Cat Ballou and Cat Stevens, catfish they had brought back from Delaware; Fric and Frac, an inseparable pair of black bass they had pulled out of the Wallkill River; and an assortment of speckled sunfish, perch, and pike. All appeared to be living in peace and harmony.

The Worthingtons explained that just recently the fish had begun acting sluggish. They were clearly terrified of losing their adopted family.

Their observations were certainly accurate. The fish hung listlessly in midtank, wiggling their bodies without actually moving around.

"When did you set up the tank?" I asked.

"Last spring," said Mr. Worthington.

"How often do you change the water?"

"Every two weeks. We're very careful about that," said Mrs. Worthington.

"In that case, water quality isn't likely to be the problem, but I'll make some tests anyway." I checked the pH level; it was neutral, just as it should be.

As I stared at the tank, it occurred to me, quite suddenly, that this was winter, the time of year when the temperature of fishes' native waters drops some 30 degrees, the time when they go to the bottom of the lake in the fish equivalent of hibernation.

I told the Worthingtons to turn off the heaters, both in the tank and in the room. Mrs. Worthington looked somewhat distressed—after all, it was a cold day in January—but her husband assured her that they could keep the kitchen and bedroom warm with electric heaters.

"I'd also like you to cut back on the feedings of chopped chicken hearts."

Several days later, the Worthingtons called to report that the fish had returned to their normal habits. Everyone was very happy, even though they were also very cold.

Most of my clients like the idea of owning fish that come from faraway places, so they are surprised when I remind them of the lovely native American fish that can be collected near our homes. Many forms of fish and wildlife inhabit our marshlands. They need this protected environment if they are to breed and rear their young, assuring the survival of their species. But future generations may know of these animals only from pictures because, sad to say, estuaries and swamps are generally the first environments to be destroyed in the name of progress. We seem to have forgotten that these wetlands hold the key to maintaining a healthy balance between life on land and life in the water. They are the breeding grounds for crustaceans, al-

gae, and other essential food sources on the lowest rung of the
food chain.

I often use my vacation time to hunt for wild specimens in
native waters. Not long ago, I took a trip to the Florida
Everglades, where, after adjusting myself to the presence of a
jumbo snake and alligators, I collected specimens of the genera
Gambusia and *Rivulus*. These attractive live-bearers search for
food in small, active schools. They are carnivorous and help to
lower the mosquito population considerably, which has earned
them the nickname "mosquito fish." *Gambusia* bear a very
close resemblance to wild guppies, but don't let their looks fool
you. These are aggressive little fish, best kept in their own
aquarium.

Brackish waters are profitable hunting grounds. The
freshwater source is usually a cold mountain stream, free of
harmful minerals and pollutants. As this water merges with the
ocean, erosion carves gullies, caves, and pools in which plants
thrive and both freshwater and saltwater fish like to spawn.
Baby fish are easily collected in these areas, and because
brackish-water fish must be highly adaptable to varying salt
concentrations and temperatures, they are also able to adjust to
aquarium conditions with little difficulty.

I have hunted the feisty stickleback *(Apeltes quadracus)*
all along the Atlantic coast, from Maine to Virginia. They are
found in shallow, brackish creeks and among reeds and bul-
rushes in estuaries throughout the temperate zones of the north-
ern United States. The stickleback leads an interesting life. Like
the pygmy sunfish, it is one of the few fish that constructs a kind
of bird's nest. The male makes a depression in the sand and fills
it with bits of vegetation that he binds together with saliva.
Then he uses these self-made building blocks to construct his
nest. This complex little structure, which may be as large as 2
inches in diameter, looks like a golf ball with a tunnel through
it. It is quite strong because it is fortified with sticky secretions

from the male's kidney. The finished nest is anchored beneath the sand level, and it is often attached to a rooted plant for greater strength.

When the nest is completed, the male assumes bright red markings on his greenish body and goes in search of a mate. He drives a female stickleback into the nest, where she deposits all her eggs. After fertilizing the eggs, the male turns on his mate, chases her from the nest, and looks around for another ripe female. Often, he rounds up a harem, each female depositing her eggs and fleeing, until the little nest is filled to the brim.

Then the male stakes out a position in front of the nest's opening and flutters his fins to keep water circulating through the tunnel and over the eggs. He stands guard for fourteen days, until his babies hatch. He will protect them against marauding fish twice his size and becomes enraged at the sight of another red-bellied male stickleback.

Scientists have studied this protective behavior and have been able to induce the same aggressive response in male sticklebacks by confronting them with a dummy fish. In fact, the sticklebacks were far more eager to defend their territory against the fake fish, which had a bright red underside, than against a live male fish whose belly was less red.

Because of their aggressive nature, sticklebacks are not suited to community living; they should have a tank of their own. The minimum size that I advise for sticklebacks is 5 gallons. They prefer their water cool (between 60 and 70 degrees), and they like a bit of salt (1 tablespoon of kosher salt per gallon). They require frequent feedings of live worms and shrimp.

Catching the inhabitants for your own aquarium can become a pleasurable obsession. But getting those fish home can be difficult, frustrating, even downright exasperating if you haven't made shipping arrangements ahead of time. However, if you make the effort to contact them in advance, you will find that the officials of the agricultural inspection offices at airports and airline personnel are most helpful and cooperative.

While waiting for a flight from Miami to New York last year, I spotted a woman and her two young sons surrounded by four suitcases and five large cardboard crates marked "Tropical Fish—Live—Handle with Care." I approached them with a smile of understanding, reaching for a plastic bag of baby discus given to me by a Miami fish breeder. We became friends instantly.

"The boys were very lucky this trip," their mother sighed wearily. "Not only did they catch one each of every creature alive off the coast of St. Thomas, but we've almost got them home." She was holding her head as if it was pounding.

The younger boy spoke. "We got anemonies, pipefish, crabs, and coral shrimp, and Richard caught twelve kinds of reef fish with his slurp gun."

At this, Richard grinned coyly.

"But they had no room for the boxes on our plane last night, so we missed our flight. Back home in Boston, we have a hundred-gallon saltwater aquarium. We made it ourselves."

"Well, if they won't take the crates on the plane today," added their mother, "I'm just going to leave the fish and you two boys here while I go back home to your father."

Just then, a steward made his way over to us. He was accompanied by two redcaps, whom he instructed to load the fish boxes onto a wagon. "We're very sorry for this inconvenience. Your fish will be taken care of, and we'd like you all to travel first-class."

Everyone was delighted, including me, and the four of us happily sipped champagne and talked and laughed our way back to Kennedy Airport.

A friend named Sylvia travels around the world, collecting fish wherever she goes. The fish she brought back from a trip to India included eight 6-inch scats *(Scatophagus argus),* and we have spent a great deal of time enjoying their entertaining ways. Their genus name means "garbage eater," and they can be found near sewage or garbage dumps, which is just where Sylvia netted these beauties.

Scats are funny fish, with toothy grins and dalmatianlike spots. They gobble down an amazing quantity of anything you choose to feed them, which makes them the answer to a Jewish mother's prayers. They are always so anxious to be fed that they try to swim right through the aquarium glass whenever their owner approaches, wagging their tails like playful puppies. Within nine months, they can quadruple in size, and they will continue to grow for years, until they shine and bulge like spotted silver garbage cans.

Scats are similar in appeal to South American cichlids. They are attractive, become quite tame, and are always active. Furthermore, they are hardy and will live for a long time. Scats need room, so it is best to raise a school in an aquarium of at least 30 gallons. Otherwise, the only trick to keeping scats

Scat *(Scatophagus argus)*

healthy is to maintain a level of a bit more than 3 tablespoons of salt for every 10 gallons of aquarium water.

Scats are not overly aggressive, but they can defend themselves among larger fish. Sylvia keeps her scats in a 55-gallon tank along with two shiny silver monos *(Monodactylus argenteus)*, an ugly *Synodontis* catfish, two green puffers that have grown to a whopping length of 6 inches, and a pair of round-nosed red-top African cichlid *(Labeotropheus trewavasae)*.

Sylvia brought a puffer *(Tetraodon schoutdeni)* back from a trip to Southeast Asia. Puffers are related to the American

Silver Mono
(Monodactylus argenteus)

blowfish. If they feel threatened, they inflate their rubbery bodies until they swell to many times their original size. They can grow 7 inches in nature, and they are such voracious eaters that they seem to get bigger as you watch them. They have stubby little fins and tails and no ventral fins. This restricts their movement and gives them a sluggish, comical gait. They have metallic green spots and a white stomach.

Because they come from brackish waters, they can be maintained in either a freshwater or a saltwater aquarium. At first, they are shy, but when they learn to expect you to feed them, they rise to the surface and beg for more. I usually have a few baby puffers in the shop. I've watched them closely and learned that it would be a mistake to be fooled by their adorable baby face and deliberate plod. More than once, I've caught a puffer sneaking up behind its tankmates and biting their tails.

One day, a befurred matron alighted from her Rolls-Royce, instructed her chauffeur to wait, and walked into the shop accompanied by a naked chihuahua and a small boy. She removed her son's suede jacket and requested a tour of the tank room. I led Junior around by the hand and pointed out his choices for starting a fish tank. It's not easy to communicate with a world-weary six-year-old who uses four-syllable words and speaks with a broken-jaw accent. I knelt beside him, watching as he became mesmerized by a tank of puffers.

"Mummy, this is the remarkable little fish I wanted to see. Buy him. Buy him."

"Don't be hasty, Gregory. Let the man choose a fish for us."

"But this is the balloon fish. Look how he swims. He's so cute. Look at his big eyes. He knows me. I want him."

"It's a puffer," I explained, "and is best kept by himself."

"I want to touch him. I want it to blow up like a fat balloon. I want to touch."

I scooped out the inch-long fish and dropped it into Gregory's hand. "Be careful. He's slippery."

We waited for the little fish to triple in size. Instead, we watched in horror as the adorable puffer bit Gregory's tender hand. He screamed and threw the fish down onto the floor and began to cry. The dog started to yelp and came after my foot. Gregory's mother grabbed them both and rushed to the waiting Rolls, muttering something about my irresponsible attitude.

I had handled puffers before, gently prodding them to inflate. But this biting business was new. Later, I went back to my fish encyclopedia in search of an explanation. The puffer has a strong set of teeth that are fused together in a hard, sharp ridge, rather like a parrot's beak. These teeth are useful in the aquarium because puffers are able to eliminate and eat snails, crushing the shells and chewing the tough flesh with their rabbitlike teeth. Meanwhile, in the tank room, I picked up the rubbery puffer, now the size of a Ping-Pong ball, and scolded him. He seemed to grin and say that he was better off in the shop than in any chihuahua's home. I sighed and put him back, thinking maybe he was right.

My holidays are never dull. I rarely make reservations, and I always travel light: dungarees, snorkel, mask and fins, and a dependable net. I've found that the best way to enjoy myself in a foreign land is to get in touch with the countryside, to go on nature expeditions.

One season, when the Christmas rush at the shop was over, I decided to escape from the city and go someplace where I could collect coral, rocks, plants, and fish that would remind me of my holiday throughout the rest of the year. It is always hard for me to leave my fish alone for more than a weekend. One or two always seem to die out of spite during my absence. But I made a half-dozen friends responsible for my tanks and comforted myself with the knowledge that we all shared the same respect and appreciation for tropical fish.

Puerto Rico was my first stop. I roamed the beaches for days, scanning tidal pools for the sea urchins, small fish, tiny crabs, and shrimp that hide beneath hunks of volcanic rock. One afternoon, a group of kids joined me, and together, we found an oval pool carved in the rock breakers, plugged up the drain hole with smooth stones, and stocked the pool with all we could catch. The kids had paper cups and bottles, and we all took turns using my net. Soon the pool was teeming with life: schools of little yellow-and-black-banded sergeant majors (*Abudefduf saxatilis*) moving in tight formations and little crested gobies (*Lophogobius cyprinoides*) leaping about like space-age frogs. It was more exciting than any aquarium because it was natural and it was free. For days after, whenever I revisited the tidal pool, the fish were there, and so were a lot of the same kids.

The goby is one of the most abundant and interesting native fish of Puerto Rico. Closely related species are found in many parts of the world, from the saltwater tidal pools of Puerto Rico and all tropical waters (meaning bounded by the tropics of Cancer and Capricorn) to the brackish waters of Borneo to the freshwater mud flats of Japan and the Asian mainlands. The smallest species of fish are gobies; some rarely reach a mature size of 1 inch. These tiny fish skip and jump from coral to gravel and offer a real challenge to the paper-cup fisherman. I was particularly eager to take one home because even the smallest goby adapts easily to a saltwater aquarium. They are gentle and shy and will even coexist with the delicate sea horse, which makes them wonderful additions to most marine tanks.

One of the most curious of the gobies is the bumblebee goby (*Brachygobius xanthozona*), an inch-long yellow-and-black-striped oddity that buzzes about the substrata with winglike fins and beelike maneuvers. Shy and demanding, these tiny creatures are not really suited for a community tank. Give them a 5-gallon tank of their own with plenty of hiding places, and season their water with 1 teaspoon of salt per gallon. Your reward will be an interesting and unusual display.

When I returned home, I set up an aquarium with the booty I had brought back. I had a 20-gallon saltwater tank aged and ready for my new collection of anemonies, feather dusters, shrimp, hermit crabs, and gobies. The change from natural seawater to artificial marine water must be accomplished gradually; the animals must be placed in glass bowls or plastic buckets, and aquarium water must be allowed to drip in slowly, mixing with the sea water. I tied a knot in a length of air-line hosing, placed one end in the tank, sucked on the other end to start a siphon, and regulated the flow to 1 drop every 3 seconds by tightening (or loosening) the knot. Within a 2-to-3-hour period, the fish had adjusted to the water that would be their new home.

In many ways, the most exotic collector's fish are the killies. Every year, in isolated areas of East Africa, the woods fill with shallow pools and puddles after the seasonal rains. As if by magic, these tiny pools glitter with brightly colored fish. Where do they come from, and where do they go when the forest is dry?

The killies have adapted to their environment like no other living fish. In order to survive, they must be able either to live on dry land or to leave eggs that can remain viable through the dry season. They produce eggs that sink into the muddy peat and remain buried for a month or two as water evaporates and the adults perish. When the rains come again, the eggs hatch almost immediately. They grow rapidly, maturing within weeks and breeding prolifically, as if they knew what fate had in store for them. Small wonder that they are known as *annual fish*.

Killifish

Aside from this distinction, killies are dazzlingly beautiful and fascinating to watch. They have long appealed to the dedicated hobbyist. They mature at 1 or 2 inches and grow upwards of 3 inches, but they offer more differentiation in color and shape than any other small aquarium fish. Many species resemble living jewels, sparkling with metallic blues and vibrant ruby reds and violets. Some sport striking lyretails and flashy dorsal fins. They dart about, flirting and taunting each other, sometimes even caressing, playing sensual touching games. They signal to each other with their flaglike fins and swim very close to each other, almost as if they were dancing a tango, pausing now and then to steal a kiss.

Because their native habitats provide them little room, killies can be kept successfully in just 1 or 2 gallons of water. However, most members of the genera *Aphyosemion* and *Nothobranchius* are quite pugnacious, so each pair should have their own small aquarium. What an ideal tank to fill that little cubbyhole in the kitchen or hallway that you thought was too small even for a goldfish bowl.

Killies require live food, such as brine shrimp and daphnia (minute crustaceans). Their diet is best supplemented by freeze-dried worms or frozen shrimp. You must be careful not to overfeed them and to keep their tank clean. Killies are hardy and very active if their water conditions are right. But if they aren't given the soft, acid water they prefer, they will let you know by refusing to eat. A filter is neither necessary nor advisable for a tank of killies. And no heater is required; in fact, killies thrive in cool water.

Keeping killies is as easy as keeping a goldfish bowl. There are scores of species available. Occasionally, you can get them at aquarium shops; more often, you simply purchase the eggs through the mail (write to any killy association for a list of suppliers, see page 296) and hatch them in your own aquarium. But if the novelty of this tiny jewel of a fish does not appeal to you because of its brief life span (8 or 9 months), there are related species of equal charm and beauty and greater longevity.

If you have collected doorknobs or postage stamps, hats or thimbles, and you are ready to throw yourself into a new field, I suggest you buy a pair of African cichlids or killies. An unusual species may yield enough offspring to use as barter for an entire collection of related fish. On the other hand, you might want something as curious as a puffer, a scat, or a stickleback. No matter which you choose, and no matter what your initial reason for collecting may be, chances are you will be enthralled and captivated for a long time to come.

SOUTH AMERICAN CICHLIDS

I always urge my clients to take action immediately if they notice any signals of distress, such as a fish gulping for air or refusing to eat. But in most cases, people wait too long, and by then, the damage is irreparable. As a result of one such call, I found myself literally buried in my work.

Jack English phoned me at the shop and asked if I would come and convert his saltwater aquarium to fresh water. He sounded discouraged, but I thought that all I would have to do was make a few water tests, give him some reassurance, and sell him a few more fish.

I arrived at Jack's home in Gramercy Park at noon, carrying my little bucket and siphon hose. I rang the bell and he answered at once. He was wearing a red and black kimono. As the door swung open, I caught sight of a huge murky aquarium reflected in the expanse of mirror behind the fifteen-foot bar. The room smelled like the ocean, and I began to realize that this would be no routine house call.

Jack's aquarium, which was situated opposite the bar, spanned the length of the hallway from the front door to the living room; it was fifteen feet across, four feet deep and seven feet high. Water gurgled down the side of the tank as it overflowed the outside filter, leaving an icing of salt crystals on the glass and on the wooden base on which the tank rested. I glanced at my bucket and siphon and then back at Jack, who was behind the bar mixing bloody marys.

"Here, have a drink before you begin." He handed me a giant red goblet. Normally, I don't drink when on the job, but that day I accepted—gratefully.

"I lost the last grouper on Friday," he grumbled. "I thought about having it for dinner, but I changed my mind. I'd built up this animosity toward it after it killed off everything else in the tank."

"Too bad. Groupers are really decent fish." I made no effort to hide my aggravation. I felt I had to make it clear to Jack that his aquarium had failed because he had not taken an active interest in its welfare. I remembered making a house call when this huge tank was happy and full of four or five different kinds of grouper (the saltwater oscar). That had been only three months ago. They must have been abused indeed to have died so quickly, for groupers are hardy fish.

Groupers are a diverse family of very large fish; many reach a body weight of more than 1,000 pounds. They are found in most warm waters of the world, notably in the Indo-Pacific region. They are very intelligent and quite unafraid of divers. They are also very photogenic. These are the hulking fish that you've seen so often in underwater documentaries. Groupers are also one of those misunderstood fish that often undergo a change of sex midway through their life.

Jack lived in a garden apartment, so emptying the tank was no problem. "Give me a garden hose and some music," I said, "and leave me alone with this tank for at least an hour."

I siphoned out 400 gallons of salt water into the garden drain, finished my bloody mary, and sat down to think about how to clean that tank.

I asked Jack for enough rope to hang myself but used it instead to hoist the chair-sized hunks of coral out of the tank and carry them to Jack's sunken Roman bathtub for rinsing. It took me hours to rinse off the sludge of algae and decaying food, and I had to be careful not to drip it on the antiques, especially the Viennese font, that decorated the duplex. I had resigned myself to an all-day undertaking.

The under-gravel filter was covered with crusted dolomite, a crushed limestone used as gravel when high alkalinity is desired. Improper circulation and filtration had caused it to harden into a solid block. Reluctantly, I climbed into the tank and used a shovel to excavate the top layer. Then I hauled the filter to the tub to rinse it clean under Jack's shower.

Next, it was back into the tank, this time with a metal spatula, to attack the algae that covered its walls. It would have been easier to scrape barnacles off the hull of the *Queen Mary*. My clothes and hands were green and slimy. Five hours had passed by now, and I decided that my work for the day was finished.

Jack and I sat down and, over another round of bloody marys, discussed his plans for the aquarium. He had no idea what kind of fish he wanted to put in it, but he knew that he wanted a lot of fish, fish that would be interesting to watch.

"I like a fish who puts up a good fight once in a while, you know?" he said, looking at me as though he felt the same way about people. While I was working, he had changed from his kimono to a pair of boxing shorts and had been hitting a punching bag that hung from the middle of the dining room ceiling.

"First let's worry about cleaning up the tank and equipment, then we'll get you some fish. I hate to convert a tank from one water system to another. You see, very different bacteria, both beneficial *and* harmful, are found in each kind of water. Certain organisms may cause no trouble at all in fresh water, but they will wreak havoc in a saltwater tank. This kind of problem is less likely in changing from salt water to fresh, so you are probably safe in converting your tank. Still, the best way to set up any aquarium is with clean equipment. I know it's time-consuming and bothersome, but it's the only way.

"To start with, let's get some fresh water filtering through your tank." I connected the power filter. "Let it circulate this way for a couple of hours. Then fill it up to flush out all the loose debris, and drain it once again. After that, you can replace the gravel and the coral." At that moment, the gravel sat out in the garden in three garbage cans getting a good rinse of its own while the cleaned coral remained piled high in Jack's sunken bathtub.

On the way home, I wondered what kind of fish would suit Jack English. He had a very large investment in that tank, so I knew he would take good care of the *right* fish. Obviously, saltwater fish were a mistake. They require a great deal of time and devotion, and Jack didn't have that kind of patience. Many people don't. I had just heard a story about a businessman who bought $1,500 worth of saltwater fish and lost them all overnight. They are tricky creatures.

When I got to my apartment, I made the rounds, greeting and feeding my friends. I watched as my overgrown Jack Dempsey hogged all the food and picked on the smaller convict cichlids in my South American tank. I decided to get rid of the Jack Dempsey, and then flashed on Jack English in his boxer shorts. And then I had my answer. The next day, I invited Jack to my apartment to see the tank of South American cichlids I had just set up. (I never recommend any fish that I have not experimented with myself.) I was finding these cichlids just as interesting as their African relatives, and I had a hunch that they and Jack English would be ideal for each other.

The cichlid family is vast and is represented as spectacularly in South American waters as it is in African ones. The presence of these fish in the rivers of two continents lends strong support to the theory that the two continents were once connected and that over the eons they drifted apart. Be that as it may, African and South American cichlids are close in temperament, although the South Americans have the edge when it comes to belligerence.

Many South Americans come from the Amazon River basin. They are all interesting, intelligent, and hardy. When they are small, these fish make a happy addition to any freshwater community. They are extremely sensitive to your presence and are always first at dinnertime. In fact, they spend a good deal of their time at the surface waiting for food. It is small wonder that they grow faster than any other fish in the tank. And as they grow, they begin to pick on the smaller fish. The aquarist is then faced with a major dilemma: Let them eat every other fish in the tank? Put them up for adoption? Or create an environment especially for them?

Many people trade their South Americans. They didn't know when they bought them that those lovely babies would grow up to be fighters. The trade is no problem; large cichlids are always in demand. But the experience can be a distressing one. For this reason, I sell the babies with a stern warning that there is no way to keep them small and peaceful. Sometimes it is difficult to get people to take this warning seriously because cichlids never seem very aggressive in a shop aquarium. Actually, they don't have much choice except to get along with their neighbors in such overcrowded conditions. No individual fish has enough room to stake a territorial claim. But when you bring home one or two, the bickering begins.

South Americans must be kept with fish of equal size and aggressiveness, and, as with other groups of fish, are best kept in a community of fish of similar geographic origin. Even then, a male often becomes overly territorial. He may even kill the female before he is ready to breed. In general, however, their aggressive behavior follows a definite protocol. A male will attack another male of his own species first, then a male of a directly related species.

One of the outstanding characteristics of cichlids is that they apparently can see colors, and colors play an important role in their communication with each other. They are able to change colors, like chameleons, indicating how they feel or how they relate to other fish in the tank. Dominant males are the most vibrant, whereas subordinate males adopt colors and patterns that assure the tank bullies that they offer no threat. Interestingly enough, the color communications of African and South American cichlids are dissimilar, and this can lead to confusion, misunderstandings, and fights. This is the main reason why South Americans and Africans should not be kept in the same tank.

Jack English met me at the shop the next evening, and we headed for my apartment for a look at my South American tank. I was eager to see my breeding pair of rainbow cichlids (*Herotilapia multispinosa*). They had begun to show breeding signs, so I had given them a private tank with plenty of rock caves for spawning and daily feedings of live tubifex worms to put them in prime condition.

"All South American cichlids are substratum spawners," I explained. "In nature, the males dig pits in the muddy or sandy bottom; in an aquarium, they will rearrange the gravel. But if the bottom of the tank is bare, they will spawn in caves, on rocks, or even among large leaves. By the way, if you're interested in large spawn, you should separate the parents from the eggs by removing them to another tank. This will condition them to produce a larger number of eggs next time. In most cases, rainbow cichlids are the perfect fish for the novice—they breed quite readily."

"How do you know they're going to breed?"

"Rainbows are a dull gray color until breeding time; then they take on a dark golden hue that they will keep for the rest of their lives. Mine have started showing their colors. And I wasn't at all surprised when the male began his courtship behavior almost as soon as I put them in their own tank. But the female wasn't ready. For the past week, he's chased her around the tank and through the rock tunnels in the same figure-eight path. I wonder if she's had a change of heart yet."

When we arrived, I turned on the lights, and we went directly to the rainbows' breeding tank. The atmosphere was strangely peaceful. The male was digging his pit, spitting mouthfuls of gravel onto the protective wall he was building around the breeding site. The female was nowhere to be seen. I peered into the caves and among the plants, but I couldn't spot her. I was upset, afraid that something had happened. Finally, I reached in and started ripping the tank apart, expecting to find her pinned under some coral. But no, she was really gone.

In confusion, I turned away from the tank—and then I saw her. Under my bed, more than ten feet away, lay the motionless, dehydrated female rainbow.

"He must have driven her to such distraction with his passionate advances that she just had to make that wild, olympic leap to get away from him," I said quietly.

I picked her up, and although she didn't move, I could feel the strength of life in her body.

"Is she dead? Is she dead?"

I shook my head. Holding her loosely, I guided her into the hospital tank, a clean, fresh 5-gallon tank that I keep ready for just such an emergency. I watched her for a moment; then I spoke to Jack, but I was really thinking out loud. "I've heard stories of artificial respiration saving larger fish. There's nothing to lose by trying it."

He stepped closer and leaned over to watch as I picked her up.

"You can't be serious? Not mouth to mouth?"

I cradled her in my curled fingers and manipulated her mouth open with my little finger while slowly moving her back and forth to force a stream of water into her mouth and through her gill chambers. I stroked her body to remove the encrusted dust and to give her a chance to secrete more body slime, which she would need to help her to survive. After three minutes of this, she extended her gill plates and took her first breath by herself. I continued to guide her through the water in this manner until she was breathing with some regularity, and then I let her rest at the bottom of the tank.

"Five minutes later and I would have lost her," I sighed.

"I sure wish I'd known about you sooner," Jack said. "You could have saved my groupers."

"Look, this doesn't always work, but it's always worth a try if a fish leaps out of the tank or just stops breathing, for any reason. Sometimes, at the shop, I drop a fish or two on the floor, and although it usually doesn't seem to hurt them, occasionally it does. Often, a fish will jump out of the tank by itself and flop around in the dust for the better part of an hour, and still it can be revived. I think she'd been out quite a long time, though."

"I can't imagine holding a fish like that."

"Well, of course, you shouldn't handle a fish unless you have to, unless you're going to transport it or isolate it. Any handling can cause undue stress that will leave the fish vulnerable to disease. But you mustn't be afraid to catch a fish with your hands. Be very gentle; that's important. If you use a light, firm touch, and if you do it confidently, it causes less damage and trauma to the fish than a net. A fish can catch its rays and spines in a fine net. Just the other day, a client brought in a spiny catfish that was so entangled in a net, I had to cut the net apart to free it.''

The female rainbow looked comfortable, so we left her and went to the living room, where I introduced Jack to the rest of my South Americans.

"I stocked my tank with a pair of each species, but South Americans are actually easier to keep healthy if you have only one of each kind. That eliminates the problems of sexual aggression and rampant territorialism. And I set up their aquarium with everything they could desire in the way of comforts: a three-inch bed of gravel, rock caves, pieces of driftwood, plenty of sturdy swordplants. The only filter necessary is that outside power filter.''

The prettiest fish in my tank is a male blue acara *(Aequidens pulcher)*. He is covered with glittering blue and green spangles and has a maroon shine to his fins. He is a perfect gentleman and a real beauty, and when in a good mood, he is absolutely radiant as is his rosy-hued relative the *kribensas*.

The oldest member of the group is a big black marble angelfish *(Pterophyllum scalare)* who prances around the tank like a mad prince. The flag cichlid *(Cichlasoma festivum)* looks a lot like an angelfish, and it has the most delicate appearance of all the South Americans, with a long, pointed nose and a small mouth.

"This cichlid was imported to Germany in 1908 and was successfully bred in an aquarium just three years later. Like any other fish, *festivum* is best purchased young. The key to spotting a superior specimen, even when it is only a few months old, is to be sure it shows some iridescent coloring. Such a baby will grow up to be a fabulously colored adult, with peacock green lines decorating its face in an intricate design that resembles brocade. The *festivum*'s most unusual characteristic is a

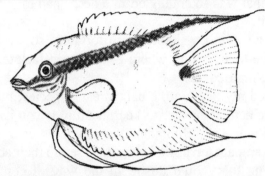

Festivum *(Cichlasoma festivum)*

diagonal black mask extending through the eye and all the way to the dorsal fin ray. These fish are shy but entirely personable, and they make good tankmates for angels and discus."

The horsefaced *Geophagus jurupari* are very charming fish. They use their huge, shovellike mouths to scoop up gravel in search of food bits their companions have overlooked. They are one of the few South Americans that are mouthbreeders. "Mine are still quite young, but the shimmery turquoise coloring and mosaic markings typical of these species are already beginning to grow more vivid."

While we watched, the fish swam up to the glass and watched us. They seemed to be flirting with us, begging for food, and in general, asking us to play with them.

"You can see why I say that these fish quickly become members of the family. They're the kind of fish you can really talk to. They're so bright and aggressive that it's often impossible to catch and remove them from the tank because they know you're after them. If you catch their eye for a split second while you're holding a net, they know a predator is threatening them. They're such masters of their terrain that they can make

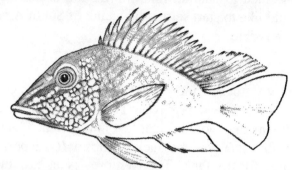

Geophagus *(Geophagus jurupari)*

themselves uncatchable. Many fish will give you only one or two opportunities to catch them before they realize you are after them and disappear. That's why a fast swipe with a six-inch net is better than laboring with a smaller net. You should wet the net in advance because if the net scratches away the fish's protective body slime and there is bacteria in the net, you may infect the entire tank. The best thing to do is dip the net first in a mild solution of methylene blue to sterilize it. And always rinse the net under tap water when you are through, and allow it to dry. Some manufacturers actually make green nets, claiming that they're less visible to the fish. But this is nonsense. It's not the sight of the net that makes the fish aware; it's the movement of the water.

"You have to realize that if you are going to have South Americans, you will have to feed them live food. Some people can't stand the sight of one fish consuming another. But nature often demands that one fish eat another, so an aquarist must decide whether he can cope with this on a regular basis. Any of the large South American fish, such as the oscar, the arowana, and the snakehead, must have a supply of feeder fish."

Jack seemed to take all this information in his stride and said he would like to start setting up a tank of South Americans as soon as possible.

Before we stocked Jack's tanks, I removed the coral and added lots of massive rock caves. Then we searched for very large specimens that wouldn't get lost in the tremendous tank.

Jack's first fish was my Jack Dempsey *(C. biocellatum)*, now too large for my tank. The Dempsey is an extremely aggressive fish, as gorgeous as it is feisty. Mature specimens are entirely covered with a mosaic of turquoise spots that shine with the radiance of a stained-glass window. If they weren't so beautiful, no one would bother with them because of their mean nature—no one but Jack, that is. He gets a tremendous kick out of riling up his Dempsey by holding up a mirror and watching it try to shadowbox with its reflection—shades of its namesake.

Next, we added a group of eight 6-inch convicts *(C. nigrofascriatum)*, the most human-looking of the South American cichlids. The young are pugnacious (as I learned long ago)

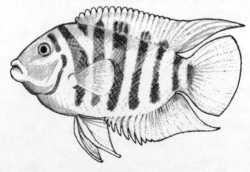

Convict *(Cichlasoma nigrofascriatum)*

and will try to gobble down anything that moves, including a drop of water running down the tank wall. They sport ten dark stripes on their steel gray bodies, and they wear a little black mask and have intelligent eyes. This is one of the few species in which the female is prettier than the male. Males have long, flowing fins, but females glisten with a gold blush on their sides.

The most dramatic members of Jack's new community were the beautiful firemouth cichlids *(C. meeki)*. Its chiseled profile, pointy fins, and bright red throat make this a stunning fish. And firemouths are even more stunning when kept in small groups. This is an excellent candidate for a cichlid community because it will neither bully timid tankmates nor be pushed around by more aggressive neighbors. It will get along well with everyone.

Actually, Jack's new tank of South American cichlids does not look very different from his old tank of groupers. But he has had great success with his freshwater tank because he has finally found fish he can enjoy, and even, in the case of that Dempsey, identify with. His fish have grown to monstrous size,

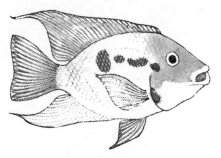

Firemouth (*Cichlasoma meeki*)

and the firemouths have actually raised a family right in the community, which pleased Jack no end. What had once been a source of aggravation is now a source of delight, and it's wonderful to see him enjoying it so much. He has recently taken to climbing into the tank and swimming around with his pets—which take bits of sirloin steak from his hands.

SALTWATER AND INVERTEBRATES

As soon as school is out in early summer, the shop bulges with young people. Elmer came in one bright June afternoon, looking even more preoccupied than usual. Elmer is one of my favorite clients; I enjoy his visits. He is fifteen, wears braces and glasses, and knows more about natural science than almost anyone who comes into the shop. At first, I was puzzled by the fact that Elmer always seemed to be riding a different bicycle, but I soon discovered the reason. Elmer is very absent-minded, and he usually forgets where he leaves his bike. But that does not bother Elmer; he keeps a collection of bicycle parts in the basement of the building he lives in, and he simply builds a new bike from scratch every time one is misplaced.

"Hi," said Elmer, "I've sold my aquarium. I'm going to start all over." Elmer tends to say a lot all in one breath.

"Whoa," I said. "Sit down and explain."

"I traded my twenty-nine-gallon tank and all my sword-tails and all my equipment for *cash*. I've been babysitting all year and saving everything I made. I'm going to the shore for the summer, and when I come back in the fall, I'm going to start a saltwater tank."

After taking a minute to adjust myself to Elmer's news, I said, "Okay, I'll help however I can."

"The trouble is"—he frowned as he peered at the new shipment of hybrid swordtails swimming frantically in an isolation tank behind us—"I've been hearing all this stuff about how hard it is to maintain a saltwater tank."

"What have you heard?"

"Well, I went to one saltwater place, and the man said, 'Don't start small, or your fish won't survive a month. Saltwater fish are delicate. You need three test kits, an ozonizer, an ultraviolet sterilizer, a protein skimmer, multiple filtration, and my help.' "

We both laughed.

"I suppose that's true if you believe it's true."

"Well, is it true? What do you think, Scott?"

"Equipment is a substitute for commonsense care and an understanding of natural life-support systems. You know yourself that one form of life is dependent on another. Take fish and bacteria, for example. In the closed environment of an aquarium, waste materials must be broken down into nontoxic organic compound; otherwise, the fish will suffocate in their own chemical wastes. Beneficial bacteria convert these compounds to elementary nontoxic gases. But it's not so difficult to establish these helpful bacterial cultures as some people would lead you to believe."

"I suppose you're right," he sighed, "but it *is* confusing when you hear so many different opinions."

"Well, there are all kinds of opinions about saltwater fish. Some people wouldn't touch them with a ten-foot pole; others wouldn't have anything else. You can buy certain chemical mixes and bottled trace elements that make perfectly suitable artificial seawater. With the right water conditions, it's much easier to maintain marine fish. I don't believe that lots of equipment is the secret of a successful saltwater tank. After all, pumps and filters don't run the oceans. And it's important to remember that even the most delicate fish possesses some degree of adaptability to gradual changes in its environment."

I told Elmer that I had just completed setting up my own saltwater tank—my first. I had gone about it with a great deal of care and concern. He was eager to learn everything he could before going on his hard-earned vacation, so that evening, he visited my apartment.

I had chosen a 20-gallon tank, which I equipped with an under-gravel filter and an outside power filter. I added 30 pounds of lightly rinsed dolomite and then filled the tank with water. After the tap water had filtered for a few hours, I added enough marine mix to give a salinity density of 1.025, which I measured with a hydrometer. Next, I added well-washed rocks, shells, and coral to create an arch above the gravel floor, leaving as much gravel exposed as possible for those animals that move along the bottom of the sea, such as anemones, crabs, and shrimp.

The key to the success of a marine tank lies in the establishment of a biological filter. Unlike a freshwater aquarium, a saltwater tank accumulates toxic levels of waste materials in very little time. As in nature, denitrifying bacteria break up and consume these waste products. The under-gravel filter traps all organic materials within the dolomite, where these helpful bacteria thrive. Consequently, the dolomite becomes the actual filter medium. A 1-inch layer added to the outside power filter will provide an even more efficient biological filter that will rarely need cleaning. Don't treat a marine tank with antibiotics; the medication may cure the fish but it will destroy the organisms in the biological filter.

Equally important is the introduction of algae into the marine tank. These same bacteria live amid the algae, which also take nourishment from nitrogenous wastes. Algae acts as an indicator for nitrate and nitrite levels. If the algae begins to darken, it is dying. Make an immediate water test. I used a starter culture of algae that I got from the shop. As the lush green carpet began to spread, I kept the fluorescent light on for 14 days and nights, and also placed a 30-watt incandescent lamp over the tank. I measured the specific gravity (salinity level) with a hydrometer, keeping the reading as close to 1.025 as possible.

Then I added the first occupant, a bold black and white four-stripe damselfish *(Dascyllus aruanus)*. The damselfish is very hardy, able to withstand the buildup of nitrogen wastes as nitrifying bacteria accumulate. Once every two weeks for the next few months, I added to my saltwater collection: a vividly colored blue devil, two purple Atlantic anemones, and their symbiotic partner the sebae, or black clown fish *(Amphiprion xanthusus)*, painted in deepening tones of amber and ornamented with white bands outlined in black. Two little orange-and-white-striped percula clowns *(Amphiprion percula)* wiggled through the coral arches like rubber puppies. Finally, I chose a velvety deep maroon clown fish *(Premnas biacueatus)* to round out the community.

Clown fish and damselfish are the easiest marine fish to keep healthy, and they are a visual feast, their vivid colors rivaling any of nature's creations. They accept all kinds of food, but you must resist the temptation to feed them live brine shrimp. Marine parasites are common among these shrimp, and although they pose no danger in a freshwater aquarium, they can cause a disaster in a marine tank. I feed my fish squid flakes, raw clams, and freeze-dried shrimp. In return, they carry on happily, like clowns in the center ring of a circus.

I was surprised to see Elmer back in the shop in August. He explained that his money had run out. But he was so excited, he didn't seem to mind.

"Wait till you see what I brought back. I'm into a whole new field!" He was beaming. He asked me to come and see what he had collected and to help him set up a new tank.

Clowns, Damsels, and Anemones

The next morning, I found him in his room in his parents' nearby brownstone. He was leaning over a large plastic tub.

"Let's see what kind of animals you have in there." The container looked like a miniature tidal basin. Its inhabitants, a mixture of invertebrates, crawled about, appearing and disappearing in the sand. I have always been fascinated by these tiny animals that hug the ocean floor. It's hard to believe that these exotic and highly varied creatures without backbones are all related, but they are. They range from the sluggish, deliberate snail to the erratic, lightning-fast shrimp and crayfish. They possess mythical qualities, almost seem to be figments of a timeless imagination.

"What do you think?" Elmer grinned at me.

"I think you're a very good hunter," I said.

As I inspected each of Elmer's creatures, I told him that the crustaceans offer an endless variety of shapes, sizes, habits, and personalities. They can be kept in a tank with fish, but a special invertebrate tank can be a preoccupation unto itself because these forms of life are not easily studied in their natural habitat.

He had two small hermit crabs, which are found at beaches and in bays all over the world. Their sly habits and gregarious nature make them an entertaining addition to any marine aquarium, and because they are hardy scavengers they will help around their house, too. As they grow, they acquire abandoned shells for their new mobile homes, and they will be happy to move into a lovely seashell if you put one in the tank. They will eat just about anything but are too small to threaten their tankmates.

A pair of fiddler crabs (members of the genus *Uca*) were dancing on tiptoe and moving from side to side. Then they

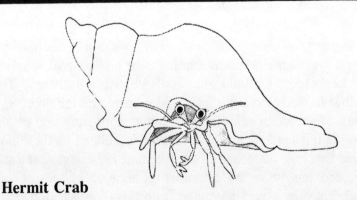

Hermit Crab

dashed to the little tunnels in the sand that Elmer had provided for them. "There are hundreds of species of fiddlers," I said, "from tiny ones with delicate shells that look ceramic to bright, stocky crabs from tropical seas, to spider crabs with long, wiry legs. Often a sponge or an anemone will attach itself to a crab's back and get a free ride to a fresh source of food. There are even varieties of tropical land crabs that grow as large as baseballs and climb trees. They make fabulous terrarium pets."

Elmer was especially proud of the Atlantic anemones he had brought back. They were white, pink, and lavender with orange trunks.

"These extremely beautiful animals are often mistaken for sea plants and flowers. Their pastel-colored tentacles absorb water, inflate like long balloons, and undulate with the current. Anemones and other coelenterates are filtering animals. They use a suction plate on their underside to attach themselves to a rock or coral. As they pass water through their trunk, they extract plankton and tiny animals from it. They enjoy crushed shellfish periodically and should be fed by hand. All you have to do is touch the meat to the anemone's tentacle. It will engulf its food like a Venus's-flytrap.

"Pacific anemones are also fascinating aquarium animals. They come in a wider variety of shapes and sizes and vivid colors than Atlantic anemones, and are much more likely to form a symbiotic relationship with clown fish. The best place to maintain and display them is a long twenty- or thirty-gallon tank that provides them with a large gravel bed area. They need this space because their body membrane expands and contracts as water passes through it. One minute, they may look as small as a nickel; the next, they will be as large as a grapefruit. They use their venomous tentacles to stun their food, whether that food is alive or prepared, but they are harmless to man."

I also told him that he might be interested in adding some shrimps to his collection of invertebrates. Many of them live in the warm waters of Florida, and they are just as plentiful and varied as the crabs. Their delicately painted bodies and long appendages are quite agile. As they navigate, they resemble tiny lunar excursion modules. Their effectiveness as scavengers is directly related to their size, and they are quite harmless to all tankmates. They have a bizarre habit of shedding their entire exoskeleton (which is what a shrimp's shell is called) in one piece once a month. It is startling to see a shrimp busily looking for food while its former self watches, a motionless phantom, from a nearby rock.

"I'd like an octopus," said Elmer, "but I'm not sure how it would work out."

"Well, the first time I went snorkeling in the Caribbean, I followed a pair of octopi that were gliding around some jagged rocks right along the shore. I was amazed by their gentle, affectionate behavior. And their gracefulness made me want to bring them home, but I knew that keeping them happy would be a very big challenge."

"Why is that?"

"The octopus is as delicate in temperament as it is in appearance. It requires quite a bit of special attention. It is sensitive to nitrogen waste materials excreted by other fish and even to its own wastes and sepia, the dye that is released when the octopus is frightened. Its aquarium should be as large as possible and should have good aeration, filtration, and circulation. If the octopus is not comfortable in the aquarium water, it will do its best to escape. It prefers a diet of live crabs, which it crushes and sucks clean, but it can be taught to eat dead crabs or goldfish."

"Sounds like more than I want to take on right now," he said wistfully.

"Put some clams and scallops in your tank. They aren't very exciting creatures, but they help to filter aquarium water. I think you should try to get some flame scallops. They sport a crimson fringe of tentacles that add a decorative touch to the tank floor.''

I advised him against putting snails in the tank. "They are overrated as scavengers and often die from lack of food. If their deaths go unnoticed, their decaying bodies will pollute the tank. They are best suited to but still not recommended for a small invertebrate aquarium, where you can keep track of them. In fact, you must keep a close watch on all your invertebrates. If one of them dies, remove the corpse immediately. Dead matter can pollute your entire tank in a very short time.''

Elmer seemed to be losing patience with my lecture. "This is all very helpful stuff to know," he said, "but these guys need a real aquarium right away. What kind of tank do you think they should have?''

"A small aquarium is best for invertebrates. There is no reason to start with a tank larger than five and a half gallons, which will hold four gallons of saltwater.''

Elmer disappeared into a closet and emerged a minute later carrying a small all-glass fish tank. "How about this?''

"It's perfect. There are three main things to remember when you're setting up a small saltwater tank: You must have good-quality fresh water, good-quality marine mix, and only healthy specimens. If you are using good water and good salt and your fish are dying, you should get new specimens from a different place. You'd be surprised at the things that are done to fish that make them unhealthy. For example, in the Philippines, they sometimes use sodium cyanide, which is a poison, to catch fish. They put it into the water to slow the fish down so that they are easily caught. Fish caught this way often die a week or two later.''

Elmer cleared his throat. No doubt about it, he *was* losing patience.

"Okay," I said, "let's get started."

Because the tank was so small, we decided to use bottled distilled water instead of tap water, which contains quantities of chlorine and fluoride. Most of the tank's inhabitants would be scavengers, so Elmer would need only a minimum of filtration; a simple under-gravel filter driven by a small vibrator pump would be sufficient.

I went back to the shop to get the filter and a few other things that I knew he would need. When I returned, we washed the tank and filter thoroughly with warm water. Then we poured in 4 gallons of bottled water and added 1½ pounds of marine salt, which we stirred quickly to help it dissolve. We put 2 inches of dolomite over the under-gravel filter. Finally, I turned on the air pump and added a small outside filter. I instructed Elmer to let the filter run overnight to clarify the water. After twelve hours, he was to remove the outside filter and add 1 tablespoon of a copper medication. Then he could put his invertebrates into their new home.

"Call me when you've done all that," I said. "I'll stop by tomorrow evening to see how things are going."

When I returned home that night, I found myself longing to see my sea horse. It had died about a month before, but I often imagined it alive again.

A most exotic and misunderstood creature is the sea horse. Although it doesn't look like a fish, that is just what it is. Imprisoned in its armorlike body, it looks like one of Mother Nature's practical jokes. The only functional parts of the sea horse's peculiarly shaped body are its mouth and tail. It moves about with difficulty, using its tail for leverage. It doesn't need a large space to live in, but it does need a coral or driftwood hitching post in its corral. Without a hitching post to grasp with its tail, it will become exhausted from continually trying to locomote. A sea horse needs live food, preferably brine shrimp. But because it is so restricted by its physical apparatus, it is a slow feeder. It should never be kept in a tank with fish because it will never get any of the food. However, a sea horse can live happily with such companions as hermit crabs, snails, anemones, feather dusters, starfish, scallops, and shrimps. And it is as sensitive as an angelfish to temperature fluctuation, light, and sound.

The female lays her eggs in the male's pouch, where they incubate for about three weeks. When the time comes, the male

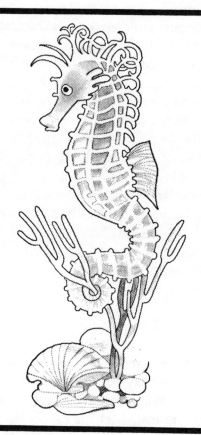

Sea Horse

goes through labor contractions until the pouch is forced open and out pop dozens of baby sea horses, one at a time or all at once. The tiny babies (only ⅛ inch long) are perfect replicas of their parents. They must be fed microscopic one-celled animals or newly hatched brine shrimp.

Mature dwarf sea horses from Florida are less than 1 inch long and often breed in captivity. Pregnant males (of all types) can be found or purchased. If you decide to buy a sea horse, you can expect to pay anywhere from $.59 to $15.00, depending on species rarity, color, and size.

Trying to describe a live sea horse to someone who has never seen one is like trying to describe a dream. There is something ancient, something mystical about the creature. The experience of owning a sea horse is more intense than that of owning any other kind of fish. Imagine sharing your life with a creature that seems to be part gargoyle, part unicorn.

There was a great difference between sitting in my room doing nothing and sitting there watching my sea horse. I felt that I was slipping into a time warp. Like all sea horses, mine was very shy but also very much aware of what was going on outside his tank. I had to be highly observant in order to develop a rapport with him. His mannerisms were so subtle and so ethereal that I came to think of him as a bridge between real life and fantasy. When I saw him release his grasp on his hitching post and begin to drift and undulate, I felt as if I had taken a deep breath, as if we were one. He seemed to become an extension of my reality, and I came to believe that he brought me luck.

My relationship with my sea horse added a comforting, liberating dimension to my life. His survival in the face of his fragility reinforced my belief that life *will* continue, no matter how precarious it may be.

When he died, I couldn't bring myself to replace him. I still haven't. Instead, I let his exoskeleton dry out, leaving a hardened little sea horse to remind me of my departed friend.

FANTASY
AND
ENTERTAINMENT

When I was in college, I studied theater and stage design. It wasn't long before I realized that a bare stage and an empty fish tank present the same possibilities for design. In both cases, you begin with a rectangular space; to it, you add both stationary and mobile objects, creating an atmosphere through the use of lights, colors, textures, shapes, and sizes. The artist is presented with the opportunity to create moods that will appeal to basic human sensitivities. There are a dozen different treatments that can be given to any script through costume, lighting, and scenic design. An aquarium presents the same three variables: the fish you choose as the leading characters and the ensemble, the decorations that serve as the set, and the various modes of lighting. There is one important difference, however. In a play, the script sets the definitions for the characters and their interrelationships, but when you're setting up a theatrical aquarium, you are free to be the playwright and the designer, as well as the audience. Each fish has its own dramatic qualities, and as casting director, you can choose to showcase any one quality or to combine many.

In my college dormitory room, I had a fish tank instead of a TV or radio. It was the stage for the dorm mascots: three bold, inseparable angelfish. Because they sported their swordlike silver feelers fearlessly and invariably defended each other against all odds, they became known as The Three Musketeers.

I set up a tank of bloodred swordtails and black mollies for a dorm neighbor. I added a chorus of rasboras and zebra danios, who paraded gaily to show off their smartly designed costumes, and the tank at once became musical comedy extravaganza. We used to put show music on the stereo and watch them dance.

Today, I have a tank designed for sheer fantasy. I began by painting the back and sides of the tank black. When I added black gravel, the effect was that of a bare stage framed by black

Plecostomus **catfish**

velvet curtains. Amazon swordplants and fine, leafy trails of hygrophila flourish in soil trays, a billowing mass of shimmery emerald- and spring-green leaf clusters. Through this feathery water garden waft a few brightly colored tetras, mothlike *Plecostomus* catfish, little red-tailed sharks, kuhli loach, and elfin bumblebee catfish, like the spirits in *A Midsummer Night's Dream*. One large, round coral cluster, stark white against the black gravel, provides shelter for all. The tank is equipped with only an under-gravel filter, but it needs very little attention other than proper feeding. The plants keep the water sweet; the coral maintains a high alkalinity. The sharks, catfish, and loaches clean the bottom of debris, and the *Plecostomus* uses its sucker mouth to eat the algae right off the glass, plants, and coral.

My fantasy tank sits on an 8-inch-high crate placed below my bedroom window. During the day, shafts of sunlight reach the tank, encouraging plant growth. And in the darkness, this aquarium is a heavenly night-light. Because black does not reflect light, only the plants and fish are illuminated, their movements casting rippling shadows across the moon-bathed floor and walls.

Although I am keenly aware of an aquarium's theatrical possibilities, it was a real challenge to be called upon to design an aquarium for one of Broadway's leading producers. I couldn't wait to meet him and get a look at his headquarters, so I paid him a visit the very day he called.

I jumped out of the elevator and waded through the deep pile carpet, past a hallway lined with dozens of my favorite theatrical posters, toward a lovely red-haired vixen who sat behind the desk outside the big man's door.

"Oh, yes, the fish doctor. He's waiting for you."

I followed her into the room. Speaking of sets! Sumptuous was the word. There was a huge mahogany desk with a thronelike carved chair behind it, almost an entire wall of shelves covered with silver bar accessories and leather-covered cabinets, a gentleman's bathroom with a fabulous collection of expensive toilet articles, all monogrammed. Behind the desk stood an unusual Plexiglas aquarium, obviously designed and constructed for the spot it occupied. No doubt it had been a wonderful idea ten years ago, when Plexiglas was first introduced, and I'm sure that it had been outrageously expensive. But now it was a white elephant. Both sides were so scratched that even crystal-clear water would have looked cloudy. I sat down in front of the tank and peered into the algae-green water at a sorry collection of listless gouramis. Among them were a giant thick-lipped gourami *(Colisa labiosa)* and a silvery moonbeam gourami *(Trichogaster microlepis)* that had grown to an enormous size. There was not much else of interest.

The door at the other end of the office opened, and Mr. Big emerged. I caught a glimpse of a twenty-foot-long table surrounded by overstuffed armchairs. I really wanted to ask him to make me a star, but suddenly I had just enough nerve to say hello.

He grasped my hand. "You're the medic they sent me? Don't look like a doctor to me."

"Well, my patients are pretty unconventional, too."

"What is this fish doctor routine, anyway? Are you licensed by the AMA?"

"I *am* the AMA—a master aquascaper."

"Well, you have a sense of humor, but this tank is no laughing matter. I can barely see the fish any more through this worthless plastic, and there's not much in there to look at anyhow. What do you think about that?"

"Fish reflect their owner's personality. Maybe you've outgrown those gouramis."

"Gouramis," he said. "That's what they are. I knew it was something Italian."

"Well, I guess it's time to recast."

"What's wrong with the Italians?" he persisted. "Why don't I like them?"

He thinks he has me, I said to myself.

"Why did you choose her," I asked, pointing to a poster on the wall behind him, "for that particular play last season?"

"She's a damned good actress—and she's my sister-in-law."

I smiled.

"But," he went on, "I guess it's her personality that makes her a winner."

"Well, the same goes for fish. Are you aware of the huge variety of fish personalities?"

For the first time, he was paying attention. "How could a *fish* have a personality?"

"What is personality? In people, personality is a hodgepodge of qualities, including appearance, temperament, and behavior. Fish are alive. You have to acknowledge that in order to enjoy them and in order for them to enjoy you. If those gouramis didn't have personality, you wouldn't have any feeling for them at all, like or dislike. My specialty is matching my clients with fish that are right for them."

"Okay, kid, give it a try. Casting's up to you. Talk to Millicent about the details. I'm going to the Coast for four days. Surprise me."

The door closed behind him. As soon as I could catch my breath, I leaned over the fish tank. "You're coming home with me, fellas, like it or not."

Millicent sprang up from behind her desk and grabbed my arm. "I have to talk to you. Every morning, I come in and feed those fish, and I have my coffee with them. They know who I am, I'm like their protector. He's been talking about flushing them down the toilet. That's because they like me more than they like him. He's jealous. What is he going to do to them?" She looked as though she might easily burst into tears.

"I'll give them to you if you'll marry me," I teased.

"It's a deal," she laughed, "if it's okay with my husband."

"If he won't let you marry me, I'll settle for lunch. Tomorrow. We have a big project to take care of and not much time."

"I'll pick you up at the shop at noon," she said. "But be ready to hop right into the car. I don't know how to park. Do you?"

I nodded yes.

That night, I began to worry about getting enough fish together in such a short time. I don't like to stock a tank all at once; I prefer to add a fish or two every few days. But this was an exceptional case. I was so distracted, I couldn't even remember what fish we had in stock. So at 2:00 A.M., I found myself trudging through the streets under eerie orange lights to open the shop. After looking around to make sure that I hadn't been followed, I went in, locked the door behind me, and plugged in the fluorescent fixtures over the tanks.

Just as there are eccentric people roaming the streets of Manhattan all night long, there are tropical fish that are active primarily during the night. In their native waters, they prowl the bottom, searching for bits of food and preying on unsuspecting fish. But in an aquarium, these curious creatures are both a novelty and, generally, a beneficial addition to a fish community.

The light revealed that only the scavengers were active. A tank that normally seems empty during the day was now very busy indeed as dozens of little striped clown loaches and elephant-noses scurried about. Gradually, the other tanks came to life as the lounging inhabitants began to rise from their gravel beds to see who had turned on the lights. Within five minutes, most of the fish in the shop had changed from their pale night-time colors to their normal daytime hues.

No light penetrates the depths of the sea, but fish have adapted. Like the firefly, deep-sea fish provide their own light through the use of bioluminescence, or chemical light. Nocturnal fish that dwell in shallow waters have developed equally remarkable adaptations in the form of highly sensitive feelers (called *barbels*) and extended mandibles. These enable the fish to substitute touch for sight. Generally, the longer a fish's barbels, the more adapted it is for nocturnal life. The scavengers are also protected by needle-sharp retractable bony spines concealed in their fins and behind their gills. All in all, these fish make unusual-looking additions to an aquarium.

Nocturnal fish require special consideration, but if they are well cared for, they will live a long time. And because they help with the housework, they certainly earn their keep. First of all, they need places where they can spend the better part of the day relatively undisturbed by their tankmates. Most of these night creatures are homebodies, and they appreciate rock caves and tunnels where they can be sure of privacy. Then there is the problem of feeding. Most nocturnal fish are usually resting when other fish are having dinner, so they must be fed separately. But this is really very easy to arrange. I drop a pellet or two of compressed fish food into the tank an hour or so after turning out the lights. They sink to the bottom and disintegrate slowly enough to ensure a proper share for all the night creatures. (These special pellets are readily available at hobby shops.) Even with these regular private feedings, however, certain nocturnal fish with mouths large enough will catch and eat small fish such as neon tetras or baby live-bearers. During the day, the community is peaceful, but at night, the hungry predators must eat. This is often the explanation for the mysterious disappearance of tiny fish.

I was sure that Mr. Big would appreciate nocturnal fish because they keep theater hours. Each has its own peculiar personality, from the gawky, dragonlike *Plecostomus* catfish, which resembles a prehistoric creature, to the gaily painted, comically oafish clown loach *(Botia macracantha)*.

I scooped up a pair of jumbo elephant-noses *(Gnathonemus petersi)* to begin Mr. Big's collection and placed them in a holding tank. The elephant-nose, which comes from Africa, is in a class by itself; it is perhaps the most curious of all aquarium fish. Its smooth black body is shaped like an anteater's. And it uses its movable nose (actually an extension of its top jaw) to poke around in the gravel for bits of food.

The timid elephant-nose is somewhat difficult to maintain. It needs a roomy, well-planted tank with a shelter (preferably a deep rock cave or a dark corner) that it can call its own, whether it has a tank all to itself or is a member of a community. And in deference to the elephant-nose's shyness, the tank should be dimly lit. This fish is rather sensitive to the quality of the water;

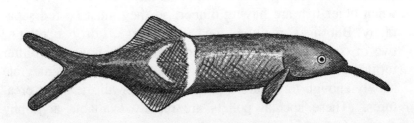

Elephant-Nose *(Gnathonemus petersi)*

it will do best in water that is kept at 80 degrees and has a pH of 7.2. An elephant-nose will take any chance it can get to jump out of the tank, so a cover is essential. If, in addition, you give an elephant-nose frequent feedings of tubifex worms, it will grow up to a whopping 12 inches in length and live for years.

In spite of its many special requirements, the elephant-nose is worth the trouble. It is even entertaining enough to warrant a tank of its own. After a period of adjustment, this cartoon of a fish will relax and roam its tank freely. It always makes me think of a baby dinosaur.

I had a hard time netting another nocturnal oddity, a cute little black ghost knife fish *(Apteronotus albifnons),* named for its long, tapering shape. It has a gossamer anal fin that extends from its gill plates to the tip of its narrow, pointed tail. This fin undulates, enabling the fish to swim forward and backward with amazing precision. Often a patch of ivory decorates the tail or runs in a thin stripe along the knife's back, or blade. The ghost knife has the face of a chocolate Easter bunny wearing an ear-to-ear grin, but it is carnivorous and territorial and therefore best kept with fish of comparable disposition. It is aptly named for its secretive and unorthodox behavior. It appeals to only a small percentage of aquarists, just as bats appeal to just a few pet owners. The ghost knife is dark and mysterious, awkward yet agile, just the kind of bizarre creature I hoped might appeal to the demanding Mr. Big.

For variety, I picked two angel catfish *(Pimelodus pictus)·* Their silvery bodies are freckled with large black polka dots, and their long, delicate barbels indicate that they are extremely nocturnal creatures. The spines in their fins are razor sharp, and when I netted them, they became so entangled in the nylon mesh that I had to cut them free.

In their small, crowded tank in the shop, these fish dashed about wildly. But I knew that once they adjusted to a home aquarium, they would resume some of their nocturnal habits,

Angel Catfish (*Pimelodus pictus*)

only venturing from their den at feeding time, until they readjust to a new environment. Their ethereal beauty and frantic, jerky movements make these catfish attractive scavengers in a community tank. But they have large, bony mouths that enable them to swallow inch-long fish in one gulp, and they are probably the biggest culprits in reducing populations of small school fish such as tetras, consuming one or two fish every so often. They should be kept only with tankmates that are too big to tempt them. They should not be handled too often because their sharp spines become easily ensnarled in the net. Sensitive to sudden changes in water quality, once placed in a tank, they are best left there.

I looked at the fish I had chosen through sleepy eyes. They were a good beginning, but I knew I was going to need a great many more. In the meantime, these fish would have a chance to get acquainted in the holding tank and become an established community.

I double-checked the custom 60-gallon showcase aquarium that was meant for my own store display. It had the same base dimensions as the Plexiglas disaster and was just the tank I needed for Mr. Big. I readied all my equipment for the next day's job and toyed with the idea of turning off the lights and curling up under the counter in order to avoid the walk home, but I knew that I needed to sleep in order to be ready for this important assignment.

I was back at the shop early the next morning. I painted the back and sides of the aquarium with black latex enamel. When it was dry, I took the two filters (powered and under-gravel), the heater, the pump, and the light and packed them carefully in the tank.

Noon arrived, as did Milly, at the wheel of a little orange MG convertible. She was wearing sunglasses and a flowing scarf. People had stopped to stare at her. I looked at the mammoth aquarium sitting by the doorway and back at the little sports car. Milly was busy enjoying the attention and oblivious to the difficulty I had securing the tank behind the seat.

I hopped into the passenger seat, and we pulled out with a screech, waving to our audience as we left.

"Put these on." Millicent handed me a pair of mirror sunglasses and a checkered hat. "Lunchtime is playtime when the boss is out of town," she said with a giggle.

"Let's get this tank installed before we get arrested," I urged.

"Why don't we have a picnic in the office!"

We stopped in front of a delicatessen. Milly produced a $20 bill and told me to buy some gourmet treats on her expense account. I was back in five minutes with a bag of smoked salmon and caviar.

"I thought you liked fish. How can you eat them?"

"I love fish," I said, "especially smoked. I eat fish. I breed fish. I watch them and cure them. I even wear fish," I said, pulling out two tiny silver fish that hang from a chain around my neck. "They protect me from the fish that haunt my nightmares."

"You're as crazy as I am." Milly darted back into the traffic. "I dream about those gouramis. I never thought I could feel so attached to slimy little creatures, but they are so beautiful—like they're painted with jewels. And they know when I'm about to feed them. I think of them as *my* fish. What are you going to do with them?"

"Why not bring them to your house?"

She beamed. "My husband never allowed animals in the apartment. He said that keeping any animal locked up in a city apartment was cruel and unfair."

"For the most part, that's true. Wild animals often become neurotic in captivity. But domesticated animals have known no other existence and can adjust to almost any conditions. Most tropical fish are born in the confines of an aquarium. If you give them proper space, food, and care, they show no signs of discomfort."

The office building was just ahead. Milly drove through a red light and up the driveway into the entrance, undid her scarf, and signaled to the doorman, who flew out of the lobby.

"This is the fish doctor, and he needs your help." They were so eager to help her, they didn't know what to do first. "Bring all this up to the suite," she said, pointing to the aquarium. I loaded two fifty-pound sacks of gravel onto a Tarzan of a doorman and watched him disappear into the service elevator.

The old Plexiglas tank was looking slimier than ever, so I siphoned 10 gallons into a plastic garbage pail and added the eight gouramis. Millicent was pressing behind me, urging me to be gentle. We moved the old tank and put the new 60-gallon one in its place.

"How can we make this look like a stage set? That's what the boss expects, and he's hard to please," said Milly.

"Imaginative lighting helps to make a play visually dramatic. Stage sets are almost always framed by black velvet curtains that reflect no light and seem to disappear into space." I was thinking out loud again. "Lighting can give special emphasis to shapes and shimmery qualities to colors. Just as the stage comes to life when the houselights dim, an aquarium makes a dramatic statement in a dark room. As the characters in your stage tank interact, the aquarium becomes a form of living theater."

As usual, my first step was to place the under-gravel filter into the clean, empty tank and cover it with a 3-inch layer of black silicon gravel. In this case, the type of gravel was very important. Fine silicon gravel not only has a rich, velvety texture but is also coarse enough to allow plant roots to branch out; it will not pack tight or cake. I banked the gravel twice as deep along the back tank wall as in front to give the same sense of depth that a raked or inclined stage provides. I planted long tendrils of corkscrew *Vallisneria* along the sides to resemble stage wings and used clusters of coral and massive quartz crystals to define the playing area. The black tank and white quartz contrasted with the shades of green in the crowns of Amazon swordplants and cryptocorynes. I added a pagoda paperweight from the boss's desk for an exotic touch. Then I filled the tank slowly and deliberately to minimize water clouding, and when the fluorescent hood was turned on, the aquarium became a mythical kingdom.

Milly had been watching silently. "If I wasn't sold on this aquarium business before," she said, "I sure am now. In twenty minutes, you've created never-never land. It's beautiful enough to keep me entertained, even without fish. Come on; let's go shopping. I want a fish tank, too!"

"Fine, we also have to find more fish for the boss."

"But first—lunch," Milly declared. She brought out a tray of food and opened a bottle of wine. "This is his private stock, and I'm sure he'd want us to have some." She dimmed the lights in the office, and we sat down in front of the tank, bathed in its romantic reflections.

While trying to decide how to cast this production, I remembered that financial backers in the theater are known as *angels*, so I decided to use angelfish as the leading players. Milly thought it was a good idea.

I explained to her that entire books have been written specifically about angelfish and discus, two closely related South American fish whose requirements are very different. Both fish are striking to behold, their laterally compressed, disc-shaped bodies marked with bold, dark vertical stripes. They are alert and commanding and breed in much the same manner. However, angelfish are one of the easiest aquarium fish to raise to maturity, whereas few discus are kept alive in an aquarium for more than six months. It is best to keep either fish in groups of six or more in a tank of at least 50 gallons of water. A school of large tetras and four or five scavengers are welcome coinhabitants in a tank of angels or discus.

We went from shop to shop, in search of angelfish for the new tank. I told Milly that when selecting a group of angels, it is advisable to find fish of equal size; this will minimize fighting within the group. There are many kinds to choose from, and if you mix them all in a large tank, you can develop a new strain of fish because all varieties of angelfish will crossbreed.

Angels come in a variety of colors and temperaments. But even within a given species, personality, temperament, and appearance can vary greatly. The babies are nearly identical, but as they grow, different personalities emerge. When they are about two months old, a pecking order evolves. The most aggressive fish (usually, but not always, a male) gets to the food first, so naturally it has a growth spurt. Its colors deepen, often showing the defensive red-eye coloration very early, as it be-

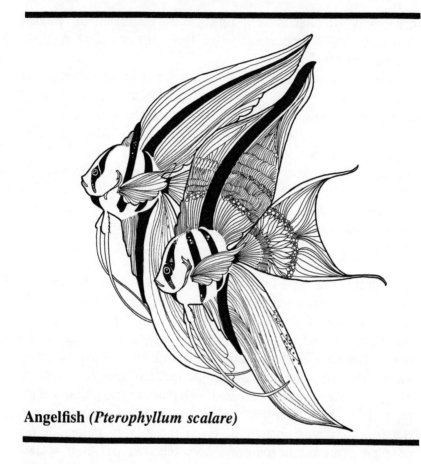

Angelfish *(Pterophyllum scalare)*

gins to protect its territory. You must take care that the tank bully doesn't prevent the others from eating. A bully can be exasperating for tankmates and for their owner. I once pulled a sassy marble angelfish right out of his tank to scold him and give him a gentle spanking, which succeeded in discouraging his roughhouse tactics—temporarily. Finally, I had to remove the bully from the tank altogether, whereupon another fish assumed the role of king of the mountain, and a new pecking order was established. The only health insurance for weaker fish is frequent feedings (two or three times daily) of high-protein fish food.

When angelfish were first imported from the Amazon in 1930, pairs were very expensive, and they were considered nearly impossible to breed, but now that angelfish are almost all tank-bred, most will breed prolifically. Well-conditioned angelfish will pair off at the age of nine months and will breed readily in a community aquarium. However, the eggs must be removed and hatched in a clean nursery tank in which the water is circulated constantly. (This can consist of something as simple as a gallon mayonnaise jar and an air pump.)

During the next two days, Milly and I were inseparable. We hit aquarium shops in Manhattan, the Bronx, Brooklyn, and even New Jersey. She drove, and I parked. In New Jersey, we found a 20-gallon chrome-frame aquarium for her home. Such tanks are becoming difficult to find now because most aquariums and accessories are made of plastic and glass. Milly's living room is decorated with chrome and glass, and the idea of having a tank that matched and would become part of the furniture was appealing. Even the silvery colors of her adopted gouramis fit the decorative scheme, and their sparkle and luster suited Milly perfectly.

One afternoon, I parked near a lot filled with the remains of a demolished building. We jumped out of the car and set about collecting hunks of bedrock. As I told Milly, this is a good way to procure aquarium rocks. Much of the city's substratum is composed of mica schist, a nontoxic rock with silvery flecks. Milly jumped around the lot amid the bricks, garbage, and cats, scavenging and laughing gleefully with each new find. She looked like a little girl dressed up in high heels and sunglasses.

We went back to her apartment to install her aquarium. It took over an hour to decide exactly where it should be located. Situating a fish tank in a room is an art in itself. Many factors have to be taken into consideration. An aquarium is visually different at different heights and creates varied moods and effects depending upon the furniture, existing lighting, and objects that surround it. Furthermore, an aquarium should not be moved once it has been filled with water because movement will cause a shift in weight that changes the pressure within the tank and occasionally results in a crack or a slow leak.

Milly finally settled on a spot in front of a mirrored wall. We rearranged a pair of six-foot étagères to flank the tank and spanned them with a glass shelf for houseplants. I covered the floor of the tank with a layer of smooth white beach pebbles. Then we added the found rocks, which we had washed very carefully. The mirror reflected crystal caves and made the shimmering world appear twice as large. When the tank was filled and the filters turned on, I added a gentle stream of bubbles that bounced up around the jagged rocks and sparkled in the mirror like diamonds.

"It's like having my own private puppet theater or fantasy world—or something!" squealed Milly. "I can't thank you enough."

Just as she reached out to hug me, a resounding knock came at the door. She jumped back.

"I'll bet it's my husband, dammit. Don't let him bother you. We've been separated for months now. He's not really mean, but he's got a temper, so don't provoke him. I'll do the talking." Then she said, "Just a second, Stan, I'm coming. Why don't you use your key?"

"I will," he growled, and the door flew open. Stan may have been dressed like a stockbroker, but he was big enough to play defensive linebacker for the Green Bay Packers. He stood in the doorway, a mixture of anger and curiosity.

"Relax, dear, and don't offend the fish doctor with any shouting. This man is a professional."

"You never were much for amateurs."

"Not since you."

It didn't take them long.

I busied myself trying to hide the wine bottle behind a speaker.

"What do you want, Stanley? As you can see, I'm busy with my new aquarium."

Stanley strolled across the room and inspected the tank. "Replacing me with fish, eh? I think that's very funny."

"You never let me make decisions. You never let me have pets or anything that belonged to just me."

They were talking as if I weren't in the room.

"Well, it took drastic measures for me to understand." Stanley's voice sounded gentler. "Can I talk to you?"

Milly turned to me. "Excuse us for just a bit. Can you finish up, and I'll drive you back to the shop?" They disappeared into the bedroom.

I finished cleaning up and hooking up the lights and heater. Then I sat, quietly watching the stream of bubbles, until Stan and Milly came back in, arm in arm and smiling.

"Tell him why, Stan. There was a reason he wouldn't let me keep tropical fish, Scott."

"When I was eight years old, my Uncle Bunny gave me two goldfish for my birthday. My mother put the bowl on top of the refrigerator where it would be safe. Every day, when I'd come home from school, I would run into the kitchen to feed my fish. But one day, my little brother decided to play 'Sea Hunt,' and he climbed on a chair and went spearfishing in my goldfish bowl with a fork. When I saw the dead fish, I beat my brother so hard that he cried and I got punished. After that, I couldn't look at fish in bowls any more. I really loved my goldfish."

Milly had tears in her eyes as she gazed at Stanley. I picked up my bucket, and let myself out as they turned toward each other. Maybe the gouramis had saved their marriage.

I didn't have long to finish the boss's tank. Milly and I collected fish and brought them to the shop, where I isolated them for observation (to make sure they were perfectly healthy) and then introduced them to their new neighbors in the holding tank.

All of a sudden, it was time to move them to their new home. First into the tank were the scavengers and nocturnal fish; they needed this head start to find their own territory. One dozen of them went streaming in and quickly disappeared. Next, I added six large angelfish, a pair each of silvers, blacks, and marbles. They glided into the tank with an aristocratic flourish. These fellows knew at once that they were the leading players. I also added a pair of fantail goldfish because their butterfly flutterings are reminiscent of a ballet dancer's. The ensemble of dozens of cardinals and rasboras was resplendent against the black backdrop.

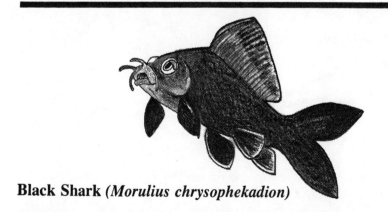

Black Shark (*Morulius chrysophekadion*)

I drew the office curtains, turned out the lights, and switched on the incandescent spotlight above the tank to take a careful look. Milly came in, and we both watched in silence. The angelfish soared blissfully, sparkling as the shafts of light bounced off their silver scales. As the water cleared, more fish emerged from the shadows to explore their new environment. The elephant-noses had adopted adjacent caves and established territory; now they searched the gravel with their movable snouts, occasionally butting their heads the way dolphins do. Half a dozen black sharks and catfish nosed out every inch of tank space. The silvery angel catfish sparkled and scurried along the bottom as tight schools of cardinals twinkled above them. I had even added a few pairs of my own bloodred and marigold swordtails, and their quick, streamlined movements blended in perfectly. The black walls and gravel successfully framed the tank's contents, and the fish and plants seemed to be lit by individual spotlights. The resulting panorama was dramatic and full of activity and surprises. I knew that such a diversity of creatures would make for very interesting relationships within the community.

Glass Catfish *(Kryptopterus bicirrhis)*

"He's going to go crazy over this, Scott," whispered Milly. "I can't wait to see his face tomorrow morning."

I gave Milly a can of fish food and instructions for daily feedings, left my bill with best wishes for a long and successful run, and dragged myself home for a well-deserved good night's sleep.

When I opened the shop at noon the next day, the telephone was ringing. It was Mr. Big.

"I've been calling all morning," he snapped. "Don't you believe in working a full day?"

"I've been up nights with your nocturnal fish," I answered.

"Well, I called to congratulate you on a job well done. Who'd have ever thought that this old grouch could find happiness with a couple of ugly elephant-nose submarines? I am thoroughly charmed by your whole concept of design. I've not gotten a thing done all morning because I can't bring myself to turn on the room lights and risk alienating my fish.

"I want you to visit here once every week, just to help me learn how to care for them. In return, Milly can get you a pair of tickets for whatever Broadway show you'd like to see. How's that?"

"It's a dream come true," I said. "I'll see you next Thursday."

"And we can discuss the five-hundred-gallon tank I'd like designed for my town house. So long, AMA."

I hung up the phone and went about my chores, delighted by the knowledge that Broadway's Mr. Big and I had something very special in common.

BREEDING

I plunged into the early-morning crowd, letting it carry me underground. Then I dug out a token and squeezed myself, along with my doctor's bag, my bucket, and a plastic bag containing a fish, through the turnstile. There were no seats on the subway, so I swayed, under the scrutiny of thirty pairs of eyes, bucket hand on the strap, fish hand on the doctor's bag, then fish hand on the strap, and so on.

"Whatcha got in there?" A teen-ager disguised as a hoodlum was peering over the edge of the bucket.

"Oh, just some odds and ends." Usually, I enjoy answering the inevitable questions about my portable aquarium, but not today. I was barely awake, and I felt as grumpy as I must have sounded.

"Whassat in there?" my friend persisted. He crouched down to get a closer look at the discus, who stared back timidly from his bag, frozen with fear.

"What does it look like?"

"Looks like a fish."

"See! You knew it all the time."

It was going to be one of those days; I could feel it in my bones. Mrs. Newman had called at seven, beside herself because her oscars had white spots again. I had promised to pay them a visit before the day was over.

I decided that I needed some air, so I got out of the subway and walked across the park to my first house call. In the park, things were a lot more pleasant. People smiled, pointed at the discus, and stopped to talk. One elderly woman, who was busy feeding pigeons, exclaimed, "Why, isn't that a pompadour fish? Where are you taking him?"

"I'm taking him to get married."

She blinked in disbelief.

"I wouldn't lie to you, madame."

It was, in fact, true. I was taking one of Mr. Jefferson's prize male discus to meet one of Mr. Templeton's females.

Mr. Jefferson is not exactly one of my favorite clients. He is an industrialist, extremely high-strung and invariably intoxicated by lunchtime, which is one of the reasons I had started early today. He insists that I make a weekly visit to service his crystal-clear, problem-free tank.

I never know what to expect from him. For example, he was extremely disturbed when, soon after his aquarium was set up, two of his school of seventy-two cardinals died. He called me and demanded my presence and an explanation.

I looked at the fish, then at Mr. Jefferson. "They're dead," I said.

"Even *I* can see *that*. I'm paying you to tell me why. And what are you going to do about it?" He was shouting.

"Mr. Jefferson," I said, "it is in the nature of every living thing to die. Isn't it wiser to dwell on the novelty of life and to savor its mysteries before it is gone? And remember, death makes room for new life."

I didn't even fully realize what I had said, but it was

enough to send Mr. Jefferson out of the room without another word.

Today, however, Mr. Jefferson's anxiety was warranted. His tank was anything but peaceful. Both discus had changed dramatically. Their eyes were a blazing red, and vibrant dark blue striations marked their bodies. They had begun to fight. I had surmised that both fish were males because they had the slightly bumpy forehead and pointed dorsal and pectoral fins that are characteristic of the male discus. Now that they had assumed their intense breeding colors (which are brighter than the females), it was clear that I had been correct. I netted the larger one, placed him in a double plastic bag, and left Mr. Jefferson with the promise of a more suitable companion for his other discus.

I made my way across town to Mr. Templeton's leather goods factory. Mr. Templeton takes an active interest in his pet discus, who live in a 50-gallon tank that sits on a counter right behind his desk. The tank is well planted with foot-high Amazon swordplants, which I had first potted in soil. On the desk, a collection of aquarium books is wedged between handbags and cowhide samples.

Mr. Templeton was happy to participate in the discus experiment. I put Mr. Jefferson's male into his tank and took one of his females to join Mr. Jefferson's other male.

All we could do now was give the new couples time to get to know one another and hope that something would come of our efforts. It is rumored that discus matchmakers have died waiting.

The *Symphysodon discus* comes from the Amazon River tributaries and was first bred in this country in 1934 by a

Philadelphia hobbyist, Gustav Armbruster. He kept his breeding tank at 85 degrees and fed the fry on tiny aquatic organisms *(infusoria)*. He was able to raise only a few of the babies to maturity. Around the same time, Dwight Winter of Pittsburgh kept discus that spawned a few times in his 100-gallon tank, but he was unable to raise them to adulthood. He did, however, observe that the discus ate their infertile eggs, which indicated that the discus, like many other fish, insists on a near-sterile spawning site, free of debris that might infect the next batch of eggs. In 1949, Mrs. W. T. Dodd of Portland, Oregon, reported to the Oregon Aquatic Society that "the babies [discus] hung against the sides of the parents, receiving free rides, using the [parents] as landing fields." In 1955, another hobbyist, Gene Wolfsheimer of Sherman Oaks, California, reported on the discus's spawning ritual, which he had observed and photographed. After cleaning the spawning site, the female extended her ovipositor, rubbed it against the area, and deposited a stream of translucent eggs that stuck to the site; the male immediately sprayed milt (sperm) over the eggs. Both parents then provided a constant flow of fresh water over the eggs by fanning their fins, and they cleaned the eggs with their mouths. They took turns, one fanning and cleaning while the other stood guard. The eggs hatched after three days, but the fry remained attached to the site by organic threads through which they drew nourishment. After four more days, the yolks were fully absorbed, and the babies broke off and swam directly to the nearest parent. They dug their heads into the parents' skin and appeared to be nibbling, first the mother, then the father. They continued this activity for a week, after which they began to eat on their own.

Several months later, Mr. Templeton phoned me, too excited to explain what was going on in his tank, and I rushed to the leather factory. The male discus had assumed that red-eyed brilliance again, but instead of attacking, he was gently nudging his mate, and they took turns vacuuming a swordplant leaf with their mouths. I was extremely excited and hopeful. Were we going to witness the rarity of discus breeding in the aquarium?

I explained to Mr. Templeton that in their native waters, discus spawn on smooth submerged tree branches and roots. The young discus stay close among the woody tangles, which makes capture nearly impossible. That is why very few young discus are available. Mature specimens are not in abundant supply, either. The discus is too bony to be considered a delicacy, but natives of the Amazon regions consider it a staple and often eat it raw. To catch the fish, they chop up a poisonous plant root called *timbo*, throw it into streams and lagoons, and wait for their victims to rise to the surface. Those large specimens that are hunted for sale rather than for food are usually caught at night, one by one, by natives who must use flashlights to locate them—a time-consuming chore. It's small wonder that mature discus are so expensive ($10 to $20 each). All this made the prospect of breeding discus in the aquarium exciting. (Discus are bred at fish farms in Singapore, Hong Kong, and Miami, but the supply is still limited.)

Mr. Templeton and I provided the discus with all the comforts they could possibly desire. We gave them frequent small water changes, reduced the aeration, and turned off the power filter. We substituted a submergible heater for Mr. Templeton's tube heater so that the tank would have no unnecessary obstruction and raised the water temperature from 75 to 80 degrees. We gave the pair a varied diet, including live shrimp and bloodworms. The discus grew unnaturally bold, coming right to the front glass for their feedings. We considered placing a washed flowerpot, or a piece of one, in the tank because many breeders believe that the brown-orange color encourages discus to spawn. We even masked three sides of the aquarium with sheets of leather, hoping the light brown color would remind them of their muddy native waters. On the office door, we hung this sign:

ENTER WITH CAUTION
MOVE SLOWLY AND QUIETLY
AND DON'T GO NEAR MY
FISH TANK
—THE BOSS

And we waited.

Weeks passed, but the discus gave no further prenuptial indications. Then they chose another leaf or portion of the aquarium glass and began to clean again. Then nothing again. And so it went. We kept on waiting.

Four months passed. At 9:00 on a Monday morning, Mr. Templeton called nearly hysterical with joy over the fifty small ivory-colored eggs stuck in the crease of a Brazilian swordplant leaf. And the discus were laying more!

"Don't allow anyone in the room till I get there!"

When I got out of the subway, I ran all the way to his office. The scene that greeted me was unbelievable: All the secretaries and executives were pacing outside Mr. Templeton's office. It looked like a cartoon of a maternity ward. I thought that they were all awaiting news of the fish, but Marie, Mr. Templeton's secretary, muttered, "Everyone thinks the boss is nuts. He's brought business to a standstill because of those goddamn disc fish. He's locked everyone out of the office."

I knocked gently and announced my arrival. The door opened a little, and Mr. Templeton gleefully let me in, quickly closing the door behind me; it was as if he were defending a castle.

We approached the tank—slowly. The male discus, in brilliant blue breeding costume, rushed to view the intruders.

"They could gobble down all the eggs anytime they feel threatened," I whispered. "Keep the leather shades down around the tank, and let's mask the window with a paper flap."

We did it together, as quietly and gently as possible.

"Now you can get back to work. Don't keep lifting the flap. One look a day is all you're allowed. And don't feed them for the next week. Let the pair devote all their attention to hatching the brood. They have more than enough stored fat to sustain them for a while."

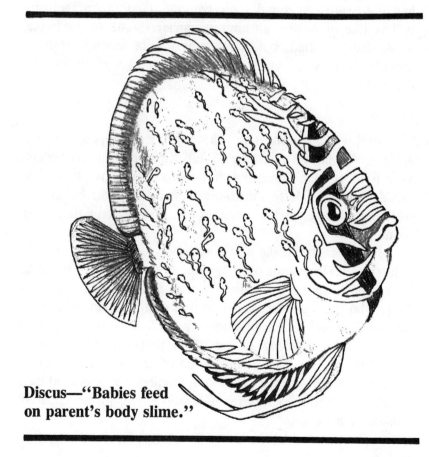

Discus—"Babies feed on parent's body slime."

The discus continued to fan and clean their eggs for two days, until the fry hatched and clung to the leaf like wriggling eyelashes. (For the first week, their tails look like short strands of hair.) Within a week, the parents began to move the babies, a mouthful at a time, from leaf to leaf. Almost every day, one discus would peck a leaf clean, and the other would spit babies onto it. We started frequent feedings of brine shrimp to relieve the parents' hunger so that they wouldn't be tempted to eat their fry. One parent ate while the other stood guard over the nursery, and then they traded places.

After two weeks, the babies were swimming free, and they began to cluster around their parents, landing on their flat bodies like planes on an aircraft carrier. Some of the babies weakened and died, but about twenty kept feeding from the parents' body slime until they were large enough to fend for themselves.

And what, you must be wondering, was happening in Mr. Jefferson's tank all this time? Well, those two discus became very fond of each other, but they never made any attempts to breed. Still, Mr. Jefferson found their affectionate behavior a welcome change, and he seemed to enjoy his aquarium a lot more.

I suspect that if the discus was not such a temperamental fish, it would lose some of its appeal. The challenge of breeding it or even raising it to maturity makes it attractive to the hobbyist who desires a rarity and who is willing to invest a great deal of time and patience pampering his fish. A discus is like a spoiled child, refusing to eat when unhappy. Often, these hunger strikes are the first indication of an oncoming ailment, but a discus is just as likely to stop feeding if it is bullied by a larger fish. And sometimes it will stop eating for no apparent reason whatsoever.

Discus are prone to more diseases than any other aquarium fish. This, in combination with their timid nature, makes it impossible to keep them successfully in a community tank. They are susceptible to ich, velvet flukes, and other afflictions that cause them to dash themselves against rocks and the sides of their tank in an effort to alleviate the pain and itching. They may also contract diseases not common in North American aquariums. Discus often carry fluke larvae in their stomachs; these flukes attack the birds and mammals that feed on the discus, but they do not kill the fish.

Few drugs are strong enough to eliminate the internal parasites that prey on the discus. If a toxic chemical is added to the aquarium water in an attempt to exterminate a parasite, the chemical is stored in the discus's fatty tissue. If the discus subsequently goes on a hunger strike, the toxin is released into its system because the discus then subsists on stored fat. The result is a slow death. Of all the medicines currently on the market, Maracyde and Protocure are about the most effective for curing a protozoan infestation. But these drugs must be used with caution because they are almost strong enough to finish off a weakened fish. I always use about 10 percent less than the recommended dosage.

Of course, the most effective medicine for keeping discus happy is preventive. Maintain a clean tank, be sure there is a little uniodized salt in the water (3 tablespoons for every 10 gallons), and replace one-third of the tank water with tap water once a week, always replacing the salt that gets removed in the process.

Certainly, there is a great deal of chance involved in sexing and pairing fish and attempting to breed them; furthermore, these problems are not unique to breeding discus. Nevertheless, an observant, attentive hobbyist comes to know his or her fish so intimately that it is not hard to recognize prenuptial behavior. The dedicated hobbyist is in an excellent position to provide breeding fish with everything needed to encourage them to raise a family. If you decide to take on the challenge of breeding discus, it is best to begin with six or eight tank-bred juveniles and condition them for breeding, allowing them to mature and pair off naturally. And, of course, you should choose the best breeding stock available. It might be best to begin with baby brown discus, which cost just a few dollars, and see if you can deal with the finicky discus nature. If you are successful in rearing them, and if you find them appealing, then it is time to move on to something very special in the way of discus varieties.

There are quite a few discus breeders in Miami who have refined breeding procedures and raised various hybrid strains whose unearthly beauty will take your breath away. They are well worth the special effort it takes to acquire them. These powder blue and turquoise discus have a brilliance that rivals any marine fish, and they have become the undisputed monarchs of aquarium fish. Breeders are generally importers as well as fish farmers. Because they deal in wholesale distribution on a wide scale, they are downright hostile when approached by a hobbyist, so begin by talking to the retailers in your area and find out if they do business with any of these men. Hybrid discus are expensive, and some retailers will be content to add a small percentage in return for procuring a half-dozen baby discus for you. Retailers are usually eager to try new fish suppliers; after all, their business is greatly affected by the quality and variety of fish that they offer for sale. You might ask to accompany your dealer on shopping trips to local wholesalers to see what is available. This way you can pick your own specimens from a wider selection.

You can also investigate the fish clubs in your area. Although fish farms disdain lone hobbyists, they will often do business with a group *if* the order is large enough. This goes for all types of tropical fish, not just discus. Six friends and I ordered a box of cardinal tetras (1,000 fish) for just a few pennies a fish. Importers generally deliver by air freight, and you or your group must arrange to get your fish from the airport to the aquarium.

Not long ago, I visited a few fish farms in Miami and got a good look at the big business of tropical fish. I met three different men who seemed to represent the types of people involved in handling aquarium fish before they reach the retail shops.

Mr. Crabbe is primarily a businessman. His greatest concern is moving his stock, and his business is run most efficiently. He deals in the greatest quantities possible, mass shipments from South America, Taiwan, and Singapore. He keeps many fish only long enough to repack them and ship them off to local wholesale distributors all over the country. He breeds only fish that reproduce prolifically and with little or no attention from him or his employees, which means that he sells undistinguished stock. He sells inferior stock at a cut rate. His place is frantic; workers run around the cluttered, factorylike tank rooms, snatching up and packaging fish. Visitors are not welcome unless a large sale is promised.

Mr. Oniz is more of a middleman than a breeder. He comes from South America, and he owns a rather shabby-looking open-air aquarium. His 200 tanks are surrounded by dogs, cats, pigeons, rabbits, and a host of other livestock. He came to America with an initial cash allowance and set up an effective fish boardinghouse primarily for discus, which are collected and shipped to him from the Amazon River basin by his family and friends. (He also handles cichlids and tetras.) Because the fish arrive in all kinds of conditions, Mr. Oniz makes a most conscientious effort to restore his stock to health. He is a dedicated and friendly man who keeps a giant red-tailed catfish as a mascot. He does not shield his procedures from hobbyists because he takes an active interest in the hobby as well as in the industry, and he is proud to belong to the coalition of Florida fish farmers.

Mr. Rekin's farm grows yearly. It is well organized, clean, efficient, and open to the hobbyist. It was once a city dump, and the concrete runoff vats converted into ideal breeding flats. Oversized hybrid live-bearers, bred in Singapore and shipped through Hong Kong, are housed in these outdoor pools for conditioning; they receive careful daily attention until they are completely healthy. What a fabulous sight: rows and rows alive with symmetrical schools of red and blue swordtails over 4 inches long; beautiful sailfin mollies (*Mollienisia latipinna*) in the peak of health, with tremendous sequined dorsal fins; hoards of tetras, catfish, and cichlids, all noticeably content.

Mr. Rekin retired from the carpet business and turned his hobby into a very profitable venture. He employs almost his entire family. He led me through aisles of prize specimens, dipping his net to display the crème de la crème. Next to the shipping room, there is an aluminum structure resembling a greenhouse. It houses tanks and pools where angelfish and discus breed with regularity and in privacy.

Mr. Rekin agrees that fish have personalities. He has had nearly a million finny friends over the last forty years, and he says that the bond between hobbyists is second only to the affection an aquarist has for his fish, especially when they start to pay for their own room and board.

I decided to choose a special fish to breed at home and then sell the offspring to recoup my initial investment and support my hobby. Once I had made up my mind, I immediately narrowed my choice to one of the African dwarf cichlids. All over the world, even in areas that have an abundant supply of beautiful native fish, hobbyists are more interested in exotic species;

novelty seems to be a major factor in a fish's popularity. So it is not surprising that although many species of dwarf cichlids are found in American waters, their African counterparts are more popular with aquarists. Because there are so many varieties of cichlids, well-cared-for specimens are always in demand. Furthermore, dwarf cichlids are easily bred in captivity, and they make few special demands on attention or space. Tank-bred specimens readily adapt to various "unnatural" environments and produce offspring with many color patterns. Professional breeders always reintroduce wild specimens in order to maintain true coloration.

Of course, I knew that as an independent cichlid breeder, I could never compete with the low prices charged by the large fish farms. But what I *could* do was develop fish of superior quality. I would have the advantage of being able to keep a close watch on all the progeny, and that way I could raise fish that far surpassed professionally mass-produced specimens.

I knew that I didn't have time to breed discus (an obvious first choice), but I also knew that I wanted to breed a fish I found especially personable and attractive. Then I remembered the first time I had seen a mature kribensis *(Pelvicachromis pulcher)*—radiant hues of rose, sapphire blue, aquamarine, and gold, all in one fish! At the time, I had told myself that if I ever had to be happy with only one fish, the krib would be my choice. I had my answer: I would breed kribensis. Quantities of kribs are limited, and because of their striking appearance, it would be easy to sell them for a good price.

The kribensis is the largest of the dwarf cichlids. Mature males reach a length of more than 3 inches; mature females, more than 2 inches. It is a relatively new fish to American hobbyists, but it has been enormously popular ever since it was first imported into this country in 1952. All kribensis available today are the descendants of that 1952 stock. Under aquarium conditions, so different from its African home, a new kind of

Kribensis *(Pelvicachromis pulcher)*

kribensis has been created: a man-made, domesticated fish well suited for survival. Today's krib is gentle enough to be a member in good standing in a community of other small fish. And if you give them a tank of their own, they will present you with families of 20 to 100 babies every two months throughout their reproductive period, which lasts about four years. Furthermore, each successive brood will increase in number because a breeding pair grows larger over its reproductive life.

I bought my first pair of kribs when they were quite small—less than 1 inch long. Their characteristic metallic blues and coppers were as yet only barely visible, giving scarcely a hint of the vibrant colors they would display as adults. I gave them their own 5-gallon tank and fed them very well indeed on tubifex worms. They were clearly content with their new home, and they grew steadily.

It is the female kribensis who assumes all family responsibilities, from seduction to care of the babies. She makes an excellent parent, not only protecting her fry but keeping a tidy house, which is why it is possible to breed kribs in a 5- or 10-gallon tank. Knowing this, I conditioned my female with plenty of protein, giving her both live and dry foods (tubifex worms, shrimp, chicken livers, and freeze-dried foods), and she grew plump and strong. Because she was to be the homemaker, I transferred the male to a community tank and allowed the female a week or two to inspect the breeding tank and set up her nest.

The kribensis does not require special tank conditions for breeding. Day-old tap water that has been allowed to aerate is fine. The tank water must circulate gently, and for this I used an air stone with a pump rather than an outside power filter, which could easily suck the babies out of the tank. I floated some water sprite to give the fish a greater feeling of security. As the water aged, little protozoans developed around the plants, providing a ready source of food for hungry infants. The kribensis needs to dig a depression in which to build its nest and will not feel secure unless its tank is provided with a coarse gravel substratum. Kribs will spawn on the slate bottom or glass side of their tank, but they prefer the smooth underside of a rock cave or a 2-inch clay flowerpot laid on its side. I chipped out the bottom of a clay pot with a lightweight hammer to give my kribs a back entrance, but my female had other ideas. She chose to spawn inside the plastic worm cup I had anchored in the gravel.

Once the female had chosen her breeding site and had developed a rosy copper glow, I reunited her with her husband. Their encounter stunned me. As soon as they saw each other, both fish changed color, exploding into a display of firecracker reds. She darted around with jerky movements and kissed her mate on the mouth and body, and he understandably grew more and more excited. She appeared to swell up. Then she arched her tail sideways, performing a kind of erotic dance. Again and again, she caressed and enticed the male into her nest, and they took turns excavating gravel and cleaning the breeding site. Their foreplay continued for the better part of a week.

The climax came one sunrise when the female turned upside down to lay her eggs, one at a time, on the underside of the cup. With very little coaxing, the male followed each time, releasing his sperm over each new egg. When she finished, she took full command of the situation, chased him away, and began her vigil. I did the henpecked husband a favor and returned him to the community tank, lest his spouse become overly protective and make herself a widow.

For two or three days, she continually fanned the oval yellow eggs to prevent fungus from destroying them before they had a chance to hatch. She cared for them tenderly with her mouth to ensure their safety.

At birth, the babies were the size of a peppercorn. Mama led them out of the nest a week and a half later, when they were able to swim on their own. By this time, too, they were ready to gobble down finely ground dry food and live or frozen baby brine shrimp. Like a mother hen, she herded her babies in a tight school to feed among the pebbles. And when she sensed danger, she signaled to them by making quick, jerky movements that sent them clustering to her side. After about two weeks of constant but conservative feeding, the babies developed their own identity and began to pay less attention to their mother, so I transferred her to the community tank, where her husband was happy to see her again. It was time to recondition her for future breeding.

I kept the babies' bellies full, and they seemed to grow right before my eyes. I would feed them as often as half a dozen times a day, adding a few tubifex worms now and then, so you can bet they got excited whenever I came near their tank. After one month, their diet consisted mostly of live worms and shrimp, and it wasn't much longer before they had outgrown the little breeding tank. I moved them to a new 20-gallon long tank, the ideal size for raising baby fish.

Before I knew it, a year had flown by, and I had made no

attempt to sell any of the babies. I couldn't even think of parting with any of the twenty-six beautiful kribs, who were now fully matured. They were larger and more vibrantly colored than their parents, and I was entranced by them. But they began to pair off, and the females started to wage war over territory. I was finally forced to give them away to friends or trade them for other fish. I was never able to bring myself to sell any of the kribs I bred—after all, I wanted to be sure that I knew who was going to care for them—so I never did turn breeding kribensis into a profitable endeavor.

The same 20-gallon tank now sits below the cichlid tank in my hall. Over the years, it has contained two more batches of kribensis, two paradise fish spawns, baby gouramis, swordtails, and angelfish. Most recently, it has become a dramatic battle-ground in which two enraged rams butt heads and joust for the attention of a very available female. Much like the kribensis in breeding habits, the ramirezi *(Apistogramma ramirezi)* is more difficult to spawn, but worth the effort. In a small, well-planted, and clean aquarium, rams vibrate with stunning pastel hues and males develop a graceful cockatoo headdress.

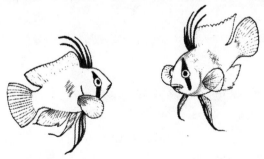

Ramirezi *(Apistogramma ramirezi)*

The thrill involved in having fish that breed and the pleasure of raising the offspring are rewards that we aquarists never tire of. There is always another fish, more exotic, more beautiful, more difficult to breed, or more expensive.

There is one fish with quite extraordinary breeding habits that I have not been able to find. It is the splash tetra *(Copeina arnoldi)*, a lovely red-hued rarity from the Amazon jungles. They are said to be peaceful and hardy and easily bred in a 10-gallon tank. In nature, their behavior is truly remarkable. They will pair off and search the river shoreline until they find a leaf hanging just inches above the water. Having found a suitable leaf, the male sizes up the situation, grabs the female, locking her fins forming a suction cup, and then leaps with her out of the water and straight at the leaf. Their fins serve as suction cups, keeping them secured to the leaf for about 10 seconds, enough time for them to lay and fertilize about a dozen eggs before plunging back into the water. This amazing action is repeated for an hour or so until about 100 eggs cover the underside of the leaf. They are laid in a perfect round mass the size of a silver dollar, and no two eggs overlap.

The male then finds a hiding place a short distance away.

Splash Tetra *(Copeina arnoldi)*

For the next three days, he dashes beneath the leaf every fifteen or twenty minutes, splashes water on the eggs with his tail to keep them from drying out, and runs away, using diversionary tactics to protect his family from predators. After three days, the embryos burst through their egg membranes and plop into the water, where they shoot to the bottom and find cover.

The feisty nature of the splash tetra reminds me of a heroic dwarf gourami I once knew. He raised a family of at least 200

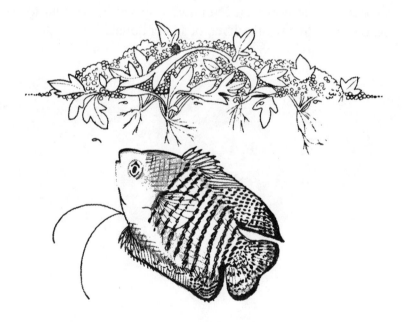

Dwarf Gourami—Tending its bubble nest

fry in a 5-gallon aquarium on my dresser, maintaining a protective bubble nest for two months. Whenever I approached the tank to feed him and the babies, he would leap out of the water with wild fury, bumping my finger to discourage me from coming any closer. Day after day, the same routine. I began to wonder whether he regarded me as a threat rather than a friend and provider and whether danger would instill in him a sense of parental obligation. To test him, I took a rubber toothy-mouthed shark, an awesome-looking fish to a dwarf gourami, and circled the tank with it, just as a real shark circles its victims. Then I submerged the shark in the tank. The gourami summoned his courage and ferociously attacked this decoy fish, which was twice his own size. I developed a great deal of respect for that noble little fellow, who was so willing to risk his own life to save the lives of his children.

AFTERWORD

I am always happy to arrive home in the evening. Then I can slowly shed the pressures of the day as I walk from one aquarium to another, greeting my friends, getting back in touch with the joy and peace they bring me. I believe that Pierre Van Paassen was right when he said that "a man who abandons nature has begun to abandon himself." I was a child of the suburbs, and I am a city man, but I have never lost touch with the natural world. My home is alive with plants, fish, and Sammy, my salamander, who sometimes sleeps with his head on a frog.

Although the world outside my windows is full of traffic, noise, and pollution, there is a certain peace in my house that comes only from the presence of nonhuman creatures. My interest in fish and my admiration for them will continue to grow. At the same time, I have acquired an insatiable need and an ever-deepening respect for nature.

Every one of my aquariums holds special memories. I pause to enjoy my tank of school fish as they create their wonderful patterns in their own world, and I remember Josh and the tank we set up to bring him nighttime quietude. I wander around my tank of goldfish and watch them sporting their tails like ancient Oriental fans, and I hope that Marian's fish are giving her pleasure, just as she does for others. I marvel at the colors and activity of my collection of African cichlids, and I wonder how Wallace is and wish he could see the many off-spring of the fish he left behind. I say good night to Clarias, whose popeyes seem to wink at me, and I know that Mrs. Newman is safely tucked in her chair, watching her oscars instead of *The Late Show*. I linger beside the tank that resembles a tiny portion of the Amazon, with its South American cichlids gliding past the swordplants, always on the lookout for a snack, and I pretend that I'm exploring the Amazon River in a canoe. I smile when I look at my tank full of nocturnal creatures. I am always amused by their odd ways, and I hope that Milly and Stanley and their gouramis will live happily ever after. I gaze in awe at my saltwater fish, as bright and colorful as a palette of fresh oil paints, and I think of Elmer bent over his books and his endlessly fascinating invertebrates.

Sometimes, when I'm all alone with my fish at night, or when a new batch of baby fish is born in my apartment, or even when the telephone rousts me out of bed on a house call, I am reminded of the many ways my aquariums have served and supported me as I have taken care of them.

Last, but certainly not least, I give a good-night snack to my tenth-generation guppies, which inhabit the first tank I ever owned. It always reminds me of Aunt Etta and the early days. I have tried, over the years, to remain true to the things she taught me. I have recommended aquariums for other people only after I have experimented with like ones for myself. I have encouraged people to master simple approaches to keeping fish rather than succumb to the seductions of gadgetry. I have done all I could to make happy matches between fish and aquarists.

I had just turned out the last light and snuggled comforta-bly into bed when the phone rang.

"Hello. Is this the fish doctor? You were recommended by a friend. My nine-year-old lionhead is suddenly listless. He stopped eating last Thursday. He won't swim around, and it looks like he's dying. What can I do?"

"Make a pot of coffee," I said.

"Goldfish drink coffee?"

"No. It's for me. I'll be over in twenty minutes." And I was out the door.

APPENDICES

APPENDIX A
SETTING UP AQUARIUMS

Set Up an Aquarium in Ten Easy Steps

Equipment

Tank
Canopy
Gravel
Pump and Filter
Light
Rocks
Plants
Heater
Thermometer
Tubing

1. Rinse the tank with warm salt water.
2. Place the tank on a sturdy base or stand. (Remember that 1 gallon of water weighs 8 pounds, and the stand must be able to support a full tank.)
3. Wash the gravel until the water runs clear. (This can be done easily, using a large bucket or a pail and a plastic colander.) Place the gravel in an even layer in the bottom of the tank.

4. Rinse the rocks and set them in the gravel to form a solid foundation (see diagram). Smooth the gravel around the rocks.

5. To prevent clouding when water is added, cover the flat surface of gravel with an ordinary dinner plate.

6. Fill the tank with tap water at 72 degrees. Add 1 teaspoon kosher salt per gallon. Remove dinner plate.

7. Attach the heater and plug it in. Never keep the heater plugged in when it is out of water. Set the thermostat to keep the water at 72 degrees.

8. Attach the canopy to limit evaporation. Attach the light and plug it in.

9. Add the plants when the tank water clears. Allow the plants to settle with the light on for 48 hours before adding fish.

10. When gas bubbles no longer collect on the aquarium walls, raise the temperature to 78 degrees by resetting the thermostat. Fish may now be added. Float plastic bags for 10 minutes before releasing the fish.

Setting Up a Budget Aquarium

You *can* create an elegant aquarium on a budget. The tank described here is ideal for raising fancy guppies, live-bearers, gouramis, or surface-swimming fish.

10-gallon, all-glass aquarium (20 inches
   long by 10 inches high), and canopy ....$10.00 *
fluorescent reflector 12.00
vibrator air pump 3.00
small bubble-up filter and filtering
   medium (charcoal and floss).................... 2.00
heater 4.00
6-inch-diameter glass bowl (3 to 3½ inches deep) .. .50
½ cup pebbles .... .25

½ cup no. 3 gravel .... .25
African violet soil .... .50
1 Amazon swordplant 1.00
1 thermometer 1.50
$35.00

*These prices are, of course, approximate.

1. Choose the location for your aquarium. An ideal spot is in front of a window that receives sunlight filtered through a light curtain. Take into account where you will sit to view the tank. For example, if you are going to sit on pillows on the floor, place the tank on the floor or on a 12-inch-high box.

If you have a radiator in front of a window and your houseplants are withering from the heat, don't despair. This is a perfect place to put a cast-iron stand to suspend the aquarium in midair, making full use of valuable sunlight.

2. Once the tank is in place, fill it with tap water. (Remember, do *not* move a tank once it is filled with water.) Now charge and connect the pump and filter, and set the heater's thermostat for 78 degrees. (Put a couple of marbles or pebbles into the filter to weight it down.) Allow the water to sit for 48 hours before you add fish.

3. Prepare the glass bowl as you would a flowerpot. Place a ¾-inch layer of pebbles in the bowl. Add a 2-inch layer of potting soil. (African violet soil is the best choice because it already contains humus and is porous.) Root the swordplant securely in the soil, and cover the soil completely with a 1-inch layer of no. 3 gravel (see page 218). Now carefully submerge the bowl in a pot full of tap water, and allow it to soak for 20 minutes.

4. Place the plant (still in the bowl) in the aquarium. Do this *slowly*. Inevitably, some loose soil will escape, but the filter will absorb it quickly. Allow the plants at least 48 hours to adjust to the tank water before adding fish.

I have had great success with this dish-garden method of

cultivating rooted plants. The only trick is to remember to keep the crown of the plant slightly above the gravel level. Within a few months, Amazon swordplants may grow to a height of over 12 inches, producing dozens of broad green leaves and sending out streamers with baby plantlets that can be transferred to new bowls and new aquariums.

5. Add the fluorescent reflector and a plate-glass canopy or tank cover.

6. Now for a dramatic touch: This aquarium lends itself to showing off your favorite crystal or glass objets d'art or quartz crystal cluster. I designed just such an aquarium as a display case for a client's trio of gorgeous Baccarat fish as a home for her baby swordtails. She was so delighted with the results that she presented me with one of the glass fish. I ran right home and added it to the same kind of tank, which sits near my bedroom window and which I use to breed veiltail guppies.

7. Because there is no gravel on the tank bottom to absorb mulm and house helpful bacteria, you must stick to a routine of weekly water changes. Use a narrow siphon tube to vacuum deposits from the bottom, and replace a third of the tank water with tap water of equal temperature. (When you are replacing no more than 50 percent of the water with tap water, it is not necessary to let the tap water stand first.)

Curing Coral and Driftwood

Aquarium books generally advise against placing coral and driftwood in a fish tank, but I have had great success with both. I have kept angelfish with driftwood, cichlids with coral. Both can add a dynamic touch to any aquarium.

The secret is to be sure one item balances with another to maintain the proper pH. Shells and coral are limestone and will gradually turn aquarium water alkaline. Driftwood and peat moss release organic compounds quickly and will turn aquarium water acid. However, if coral (and shells) and driftwood (and peat moss) are properly cured and the tank water is changed frequently, pH levels will not reach toxic extremes.

Curing coral and shells

1. Clean thoroughly under a strong jet of water to remove all organic material. Allow to dry in the sun (if possible).
2. Soak in a solution of chlorine bleach and water (1 quart chlorine to each gallon of water) for at least 24 hours.
3. Soak in salt and water (either marine or rock salt, 1 pound to 5 gallons water) for 24 hours.
4. Rinse, and soak in fresh water for 4 hours.
5. If possible, dry the coral in sunlight for 2 days.

The coral is ready for either a saltwater or freshwater aquarium when it is free of any organic odor and any smell of chlorine. Be careful that the coral does not collect waste materials. Take it out and rinse it about once a month.

Curing driftwood

Use only true driftwood: wood that has spent a long time underwater and been allowed to dry in the sun.

1. Sand the wood with sandpaper or nylon tulle to remove surface dirt.
2. There are three ways of accomplishing this step: (a) Boil driftwood for 4 hours (longer if the water becomes red or cloudy), changing the water at least 3 times. (b) *Or* soak the driftwood in laundry bleach and water (1 part bleach to 5 parts water) for 48 hours. Rinse, and soak in fresh water for 24 hours. (c) *Or* soak the driftwood in salt water (½ pound kosher or rock salt to 5 gallons water) for 1 week; then soak it in fresh water for 24 hours.
3. Rinse the driftwood, and allow it to dry in the sun. *Or* soak the driftwood in fresh water for 24 hours, and dry it in the sun to keep it light-colored.

APPENDIX B
COMMUNITY TANKS

Community Fish

When you create a community aquarium, your major concern *must* be the selection of compatible tankmates. About 70 percent of the tropical fish varieties available in retail pet shops are considered good community fish. Small angelfish, gouramis, tetras, various live-bearers, barbs, catfish, and many small cichlids can happily share the same aquarium. However, as fish mature, they develop individual personalities. For example, one male betta will be as gentle as a lamb; another of equal size might bully every other fish in the tank. Overcrowded fish or territorial fish such as cichlids may wreak havoc among their tankmates, especially when they are ready to spawn.

The logical answer to stocking a community aquarium is:

1. Know the temperament of any fish before you buy it—by reading a tropical fish encyclopedia, talking to a reliable fish dealer, and/or using the chart at the end of this section. The more you know, the better your choices and chance for success.

2. Keep a spare tank on hand for fish that suddenly become aggressive, and be very aware of tank protocol. If some

fish in your tank are continually cowering in corners, have torn fins, or are wounded or dead, look carefully for the culprit.

3. When adding new fish to an existing community, re-arrange the rocks or coral, and feed the old fish immediately before you add the new ones. This will keep your old fish busy enough to allow the new fish an opportunity to examine their new home and make themselves comfortable.

The following tables suggest a few sample communities of fish according to various tank capacities. They are arranged in four groups; for each tank size, each family member is inter-changeable with others in the same group. (Following these tables is a list of members in each fish family, with the representative life expectancy of that family indicated in parentheses.) Where a "pair" of a given fish is suggested, a male and female are required.

Group I: *Primary fish* are the dominant fish in a community tank. The tank is based on the needs of its primary inhabitants; the others will adapt to the conditions of the community.

Group II: *Secondary fish* are less aggressive and adapt more easily to a variety of tank conditions.

Group III: *School fish* are desirable members of a community tank because of their organized activity. They are best kept in groups of six or more.

Group IV: *Scavengers* are a vital addition to any aquarium. Algae eaters and plecostomus catfish keep algae under control. Other catfish, loaches, and even goldfish function as housekeepers. Most scavengers are quite peaceful and are protected against aggressive tankmates by armored plates and sharp spines.

To ensure the success of a community aquarium, avoid overcrowding the tank, avoid overfeeding, and change a third of the water every 2 weeks.

Fish Communities for the 10-Gallon Aquarium[1]

Fish		Environment
I	(2) Angelfish	Rooted plants; tall rocks
	(2) pair Swordtails	
II	(4) Silver tip tetras	
	(2) Kissing gouramis	
III	(4) Neon tetras	
IV	(2) *Corydoras* catfish	

Fish		Environment
I	(2) Fancy goldfish	Rooted and floating plants;
	(1) pair Fancy guppies	rock caves; driftwood
II	(1) pair Dwarf gouramis	
	(2) Black tetras	
III	(4) White clouds	
IV	(1) Algae eater	
	(1) *Corydoras* catfish	

[1]Groups of interchangeable species for the 10-gallon community tank:

I	II	III	IV
Angelfish	Gouramis	Danios	Loaches
Dwarf cichlids	Tetras	Rasboras	Small catfish
Goldfish			
Live-bearers			
Oddities			
Sharks			

Fish Communities for the 20-Gallon Aquarium[2]

Fish	Environment
I (5) Swordtails (4) Platies	Tall rooted plants; flat rocks and caves
II (2) Kissing gouramis (2) Silver dollars	
III (6) Tiger barbs	
IV (2) Algae eaters (2) *Corydoras* catfish (1) Angelica catfish	

Fish	Environment
I (1) pair Kribensas (1) pair Ramirezi	Rooted and floating plants; rock caves or flowerpot
II (1) pair Opaline gouramis (1) pair Bleeding hearts	
III (4) Pearl danios (4) Hatchets	
IV (2) Clown loaches (1) Angelica catfish (2) Kuhli loaches	

[2]Groups of interchangeable species for the 20-gallon community tank:

I	II	III	IV
Angelfish	Gouramis	Small barbs	Loaches
Dwarf cichlids	Large tetras	Small tetras	Catfish
Oddities	Goldfish	Danios	
Live-bearers		Rasboras	
Sharks			

Fish Communities for the 30-Gallon Aquarium[3]

Fish	Environment
I (6) Angelfish (1) pair Festivum **II** (4) Black ruby barbs (1) pair pearl gouramis (1) Elephant-nose **III** (4) Serpae tetras (4) Black tetras (6) Rasboras **IV** (1) Black shark (1) *Plecostomas* catfish (2) *Corydoras* catfish	Tall rooted plants; flat rocks and caves
I (1) pair Blue acaras (1) pair Severum **II** (3) Clown barbs (1) pair Paradise fish **III** (6) Zebra danios (6) Rummy noses **IV** (1) Raphael catfish (1) Red-fin shark (2) *Corydoras* catfish (2) Kuhli loaches	Rooted and floating plants; rock caves; driftwood

[3]Groups of interchangeable species for the 30-gallon community tank:

I	II	III	IV
South American cichlids Oddities Angelfish	Large barbs Gouramis Live-bearers Dwarf cichlids	Tetras Small barbs Rasboras Danios	Sharks Loaches Catfish Goldfish

Fish Communities for the 55-Gallon Aquarium[4]

Fish		Environment
I	(1) pair Jack Dempseys	Rock caves
	(1) pair Convicts	
	(1) pair Firemouths	
	(1) Black ghost knife fish	
II	(1) pair Kissing gouramis	
	(1) pair Paradise fish	
III	(2) Tinfoil barbs	
	(4) Silver dollars	
	(6) Tiger barbs	
IV	(2) Raphael catfish	
	(2) *Plecostomus* catfish	
	(4) *Corydoras* catfish	
	(1) Black shark	
I	(2) Butterfly fish	Tall rooted plants;
	(2) Discus	flat rocks and caves
II	(1) pair Honey gouramis	
	(5) pair Fancy guppies	
III	(20) Cardinal tetras	
	(12) Black neons	
	(6) Silver tip tetras	
	(4) Brass tetras	
IV	(4) *Corydoras* catfish	
	(4) Bumblebee catfish	
	(4) Fancy goldfish	

[4]Groups of interchangeable fish for the 55-gallon community:

I	II	III	IV
South American cichlids	Angelfish	Barbs	Catfish
	Gouramis	Tetras	Loaches
Oddities	Dwarf cichlids	Danios	Sharks
	Live-bearers	Rasboras	Goldfish

Rooted plants; tall rocks

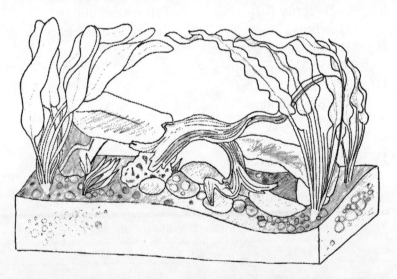

Rooted and floating plants; rock caves; driftwood

Tall rooted plants; flat rocks and caves

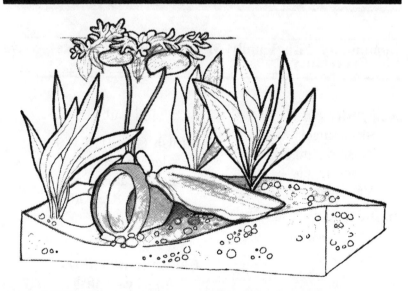

Rooted and floating plants; rock caves or flowerpot

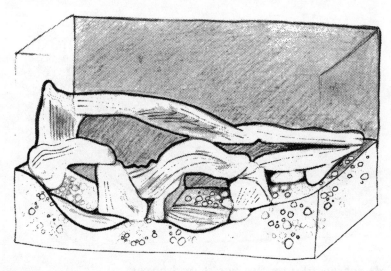

Rock caves

Community Fish Family Members and Their Respective Life Expectancy

Angelfish *(6 to 10 yrs)*
   Black angels
   Blushing angels
   Silver angels
   Veil angels

Barbs (small) *(5 yrs)*
   Cherry barb
   Rosy barb
   Tiger barb

Barbs (large) *(7 yrs)*
   Black Ruby barb
   Clown barb

Tinfoil barb

Catfish (small) *(5 yrs)*
   Algae Eater
   Banjo catfish
   Bumble Bee catfish
   Corydoras
   Glass catfish

Catfish (large) *(8 yrs)*
   Angelica catfish
   Plecostomas catfish
   Raphael catfish
   Synodontis catfish

Danios *(3 to 5 yrs)*
  Giant danio
  Leopard danio
  Pearl danio
  Zebra danio

Dwarf Cichlids *(5 yrs)*
  Kribensas
  Orange Chromide
  Ramirezi

Goldfish *(10 to 90 yrs)*
  Black Moor
  Bubble Eye
  Celestial
  Comet
  Fantails
  Koi
  Orandas

Gouramis *(4 yrs)*
  Blue gourami
  Chocolate gourami
  Dwarf gourami
  Honey gourami
  Kissing gourami
  Opaline gourami
  Pearl gourami
  Silver gourami
  Betta
  Paradise Fish

Live-Bearers *(2 to 3 yrs)*
  Guppies
  Platies
  Mollies
  Swordtails

Oddities *(3 to 15 yrs)*
  Arowana
  Butterfly Fish
  Elephant-Nose
  Archer Fish
  Fire Eel
  Head Stander
  Knife Fish
  Leaf Fish
  Mono
  Datinoid
  Puffer
  Rope Fish
  Scat
  Snakehead
  Stingray

Rasboras and School Fish
  (3 to 6 yrs)
  Blind Cave Fish
  Bloodfin
  Glass Fish
  Hatchets
  Rasboras
  Rummy Nose
  White Cloud

Tetras (small) *(3 to 4 yrs)*
  Black Neon
  Black Phantom
  Brass tetra
  Cardinal tetra
  Glowline tetra
  Neon tetra
  Pristella
  Serpae tetra

Silver Tip tetra
Von Rio tetra

Tetras (large) *(4 yrs)*
Black tetra
Bleeding Heart tetra
Silver Dollar

Loaches *(4 to 15 yrs)*
Clown loach
Kuhli loach
Botia
Weather loach

Sharks *(4 to 10 yrs)*
Bala shark
Black shark

Black Red-Tail shark
Rainbow shark

South American Cichlids
(5 to 12 yrs)
Acara
Convict
Discus
Festivum
Firemouth
Geophagus
Jack Dempsey
Jewel Fish
Oscar
Severum

APPENDIX C
AQUARIUM PLANTS

The best way to bring an aquarium to life is with an underwater garden. Plants are not an absolute necessity in the aquarium, but they provide numerous advantages. They help to filter the water and participate in the gas exchange cycle. They provide food, shelter, and spawning sites, and give a general sense of well-being to your fish. Plants absorb organic waste materials and help to keep tank water crystal-clear.

It stands to reason that there is a "formula" for keeping plants alive: a combination of water conditions and light much like that in the plant's natural habitat. Many plants respond surprisingly well to 2 or 3 hours per day of filtered sunlight, supplemented by 12 to 16 hours of fluorescent light from plant bulbs placed above the tank. If no sunlight is available, substitute a few hours of incandescent light (25 to 40 watts). And remember that it is always important to select plants for their freshness and vigor.

Plant your aquarium as soon as the water is conditioned and ready. Any delay in introducing plants will give algae a chance to develop. Because algae and plants compete for the same elements, the first to settle into a new tank usually thrives.

Another important factor is the gravel bed or planting medium. Crushed quartz gravel no. 3 is adequate, but plants need a finer ground mixture to support their roots. Colored silica, gravel coarser than sand and finer than no. 3 gravel, especially in dark colors, works very well. The use of peat moss and loamy potting soil (as described in the Leiden garden project) either mixed with gravel, or, more practically, in pots, bowls, or trays, is highly recommended (see illustration).

Well-tended plants will not only enhance the aquarium but will grow and propagate, furnishing plants for other tanks. Don't be discouraged if your first attempt at aquatic gardening is unsuccessful. It really is easy to grow beautiful water plants

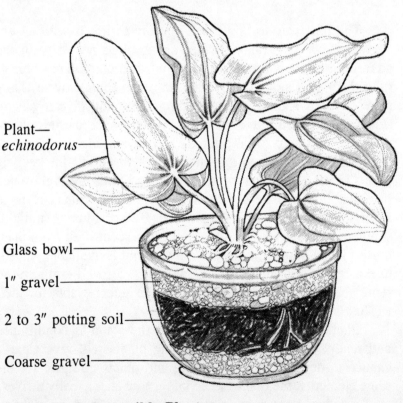

Plant— *echinodorus*

Glass bowl

1″ gravel

2 to 3″ potting soil

Coarse gravel

Making a Submergible Planter

once you get the hang of it. I recommend feeding plants; tablets or liquid aquarium plant foods given at monthly intervals seem equally effective. Remember to do partial water changes. When in doubt, supply more light rather than less, but give plants at least 8 hours of darkness, and you'll find yourself pruning dense thickets of luxurious plant growth.

Here are several groups of aquatic plants. They *will grow* under the proper conditions.

Best Bets

All of these plants are hardy, fast-growing, and readily available throughout the year. They will grow profusely with 2 or 3 hours of full or indirect sunlight each day.

Hair Grass. A very fine cluster of dark green hairlike needles that branch into tufts. Very hardy. Excellent plant for maternity tank or with breeding egg-scatterers. Propagates by runners.

Hygrophila. This excellent plant has long, thin stems of slender, closely paired oval leaves. Their color is pale yellow-green. Choose plants that appear symmetrical, and plant immediately. Untie bunches and strip off leaves to expose 1 or 2 inches at the bottom of the stems. Anchor the stems in the gravel, singly or in pairs. Plant is adaptable to a variety of temperature and light conditions, but it grows best with 10 to 14 hours of bright light. Will twist and turn to reach the light. To propagate, pinch back bushy top growth; insert cuttings in gravel.

Temple Plant *(Nomaphila).* Strong, firm stems support a burst of large, broad-veined, pointy yellow-green leaves. This makes a lovely contrast to finer-leaved plants. Look for plants with at least 5 healthy leaves. The fleshy roots grow rapidly and profusely. Give it plenty of light, including sunlight, so that the leaves develop fully. A happy *Nomaphila* will continue to grow for years. Propagate by cuttings; pinch back and reroot leafy tops often; any portion of stem will grow. Does not like to be moved.

Wisteria. A lovely fernlike leaf, light-green and bushy on a brittle stem. Trim soft or scraggly segments off stems, and anchor in gravel in small clumps. Stems should be thick and well rooted. Propagate by taking cuttings. Floating leaves will root and grow. A striking and hardy plant, excellent for hiding baby fish. Grows best under the same conditions as livebearers. Grows quickly; likes some sunlight. Terrestrial form has small serrated edges that will branch out into angular leaves when submerged.

Background Clusters

These plants have feathery tufts of delicate leaves. They cover a lot of space, grow tall, and should be used in corners or along the back of the tank. They require strong light; be sure light is able to penetrate to the stem bottoms. Good water circulation is essential. Strip away bottom leaves to make room for root growth.

Ambulia. Leaves are a lighter spring green and puffier than those of Cabomba (below) but are similarly feathery. Will decay unless it gets excellent circulation. Propagate by cuttings. Stems must be firm; choose carefully. Be sure light reaches entire plant.

Anacharis *(Elodea).* Deep green fleshy stems and crisp translucent leaves will grow amazingly fast in cool nonacid water. Stems should be crisp. Strip leaves from the bottom of the stem and plant in bunches of two and three. Should be pruned—propagate with these cuttings. Excellent food plant for herbivorous fish, especially goldfish. Good oxygenator and water purifier.

Cabomba. This all-time favorite is also known as fanwort. Fine, dark green leaves that resemble supple pine needles fan out from a slender main stem. Strip leaves from the lowest 2 inches of the stem. Plant in groups of from 2 to 4. Requires cool temperatures. Give sunlight if possible, otherwise strong artificial light. Frequently drops its leaves, which should be removed from the tank promptly. Propagate by cuttings. Often blooms—small white bell-like flowers—in the aquarium.

Foxtail. Lovely, rust-to-green feathery tufts truly resembling a fox's tail. This native of northeastern America is easily collected and easily grown; look for it in freshwater ponds. It makes a nice contrast to other plants. Look for specimens with full puffs of leaves and a few stringy silver roots. Rinse specimens carefully before planting them. They require moderate light and acid water. Propagate by cuttings.

Centerpiece Plants

These are relatively low-growing plants with leaves growing in a cluster from a crown, or central growing point. If you are careful not to cover the crowns with gravel, they will thrive.

Cryptocoryne. Here is a rarity in aquatic plants; it requires little light for hearty growth. Indeed, it adapts well to a variety of conditions and is very hardy. Cryptocorynes make a striking accent in the tank foreground. Slender individual leaves may have red and green streaks. There are many varieties with interesting differences in the markings. Although they are expensive and hard to find, they are worth the effort. Propagates prolifically by short runners; will often cover an entire patch of aquarium floor. Don't worry if initial leaves die; be patient.

Echinodorus. From five to fifty leaves of various shapes and sizes radiate from the crown of this Brazilian native. It is also known as Amazon swordplant. Makes a luxurious centerpiece. Many adhesive-egg layers prefer this as a spawning site. For best results, plant in a soil mixture in a planter, then set planter into gravel in the tank. Appreciates filtered sunlight. Propagates by runners or division, but don't separate baby plant from parent until it is quite large. Once it is planted, try not to disturb it. Buy only fleshy plants with lots of roots.

Sagittaria. Brittle, dark green, slender leaves with sharp tips curving out from the crown. Named for the heavenly archer. Propagates by runners, and often blooms in the aquarium. Grows fast; prefers some loam, and good light. Look for thick roots and crisp leaves.

Vallisneria *(Eelgrass).* The long, slender, tapelike leaves of this plant may be only a half-inch wide but they can grow until they are several feet long. Corkscrew-like, val twists gracefully to the surface in delicate ribbons. Buy only fresh, crisp plants with lots of white roots. Crowns must be planted with root tops peeking out of gravel. Propagates by runners and when happy; multiplies quickly to create a thicket. An all-time favorite; likes plenty of room and sunlight, good circulation, and a cool temperature.

Bulbs

Many aquatic plants grow from a fleshy root or bulb, which indicates that they usually go through a period of dormancy. These are very hardy plants, since their bulbs provide for the storage of nutrients.

Aponogeton. Ruffled, light, translucent leaves up to 10 inches long unfurl quickly from the bulb. Often flowers above surface. An easy plant to grow, and perhaps the most splendid showcase aquarium plant. All but the top quarter-inch of the bulb should be submerged under gravel. A soil planter will encourage luxuriant growth. Soft, slightly acid, clean water encourages growth. Under proper conditions will bloom above water surface in 6 weeks. Save seed to germinate in soil flats covered by only a few inches of water. Bulbs may be left in the aquarium during the dormant stage. Purchase only firm, rounded bulbs. At this time, keep at 60 to 65 degrees. Requires little attention.

Banana Lily. An available and hardy little plant with fleshy banana-shaped roots which may sit above or be buried below gravel surface. Round, lily-type, dark green leaves are often patterned with reddish mosaic patches. Leaves unfurl atop cordlike stems which often reach the surface. Very long-lived but difficult to propagate. Reliable grower when either floated or rooted.

Madagascar Lace Leaf. Very tough dark green leaves with interesting open lattice structure. Grows slowly. Still relatively expensive and rare. Member of the Aponogeton family. Needs at least a 6-inch circle of its own territory to thrive. Likes 10 hours of moderate light daily, and cool, soft acid water. Propagates by division. Difficult to grow, but does best in plenty of loam and peat at cool temperatures (68 degrees optimum). Good luck!

Spatterdock *(Cow Lily)*. Delicate filmy leaves grow quickly from the fleshy bare rhizome. Excellent for alkaline aquariums. Needs moderate to high light, but not sunlight. Does very well for 2 or 3 months. Beautiful centerpiece or accent plant. Available at most pet shops. Before selecting a bulb or root, squeeze the bottom to be sure it is not mushy; smell it to be sure it is not foul-smelling. It should be firm and light-colored.

Cold Water Plants

All of these come from nontropical areas. They are brittle and fleshy. If kept in a warm aquarium, they tend to disintegrate quickly and foul the water.

Bacopa. A swamp plant native to the southern United States. Brittle stems with lustrous dark green leaves. Grows in pairs and often has lovely blue blossoms. A close relative of watercress. Easily grown if water temperature is not allowed to exceed 68 degrees. Propagate by cuttings. Requires some sunlight. Strip leaves 2 inches from the bottom of the stems. Stems should be crisp and sweet-smelling.

Cardamine. Delicate, stringy version of moneywort (see below) with spring-green lobed leaves. Light color and leaf shape makes this a good contrast plant. Can grow in very long tangles. Grows fast and is easily propagated by cuttings. Prefers cool water but is tolerant up to 80 degrees. Provide moderate to high light levels. Very hardy.

Ludwigia. Spade-shaped green or red-and-green variegated leaves. Bushy dense growth on supple stems. Often drops leaves. Clean up after shedding leaves. Choose small compact plants, not leggy ones. Needs good circulation as well as light to the base of the stem. Strip leaves 2 inches from stem bottoms and plant in two's and three's. Likes plenty of light and temperatures between 60 and 70 degrees.

Moneywort. Light-green rounded leaves grow quickly on straight, thin stems. Tolerant of a range of temperatures, but does best in a cold-water tank kept at 70 degrees. Propagates quickly by cuttings. A fine accent plant for foreground niches. Grows well for a few months, then dies and must be propagated by cuttings or replaced.

Bog Plants

In nature there are aquatic plants and terrestrial plants, and then there are a few plants which are adaptable to a semi-aquatic life. Their roots are submerged but their leaves poke above the surface. These are called bog plants, and are used with limited success in the aquarium.

Brazilian Swordplant. Dark green slender leaves on a wiry stem. Very popular. May be grown in a soil medium underwater, or as a house plant. Excellent for breeding cichlids. Slow grower; initial leaves are large, but subsequent leaves remain small in the aquarium. Doesn't like to be moved. Look for well-rooted specimens.

Sandriana. Strong, woody stem supports a burst of stiff green-and-white-striped leaves. Easily rooted, this popular house plant will last for months in the aquarium, and sometimes grows. Striking leaf blades and nice contrast to aquatic plants. Grow in soil planter. Rooted plants will do well if fed.

Spider Plant *(Aluminum Plant)*. Small offshoots from this hanging plant do quite well for months in the aquarium.

Violet. Often found clinging to riverbeds. Try some roadside varieties. A challenge for the water gardener. Will grow for quite a while when submerged.

Floating Plants

Limited but useful form of aquatic plant which may or may not be rooted. They provide the perfect shelter for newborn fish that like to congregate at the surface, and act as a light filter for plants below.

Hornwort. Rootless long billows of weak stems grow to as long as 8 feet, with Christmas tree–like needles. An excellent spawning grass. Likes hard alkaline water with a minimum of light. Usually acquired while in a dense dormant stage. Within weeks in a warm aquarium will grow into a beautiful spray, continually branching out. However, has a limited life span. Requires a cool aquarium when in the dormant or semidormant state. Look for compact bushy plants which do not shed.

Water Sprite *(Indian Fern)*. Very prolific. Unfurls irregular fernlike leaves not unlike those of the chrysanthemum. Brittle stems should not be discarded if a leaf snaps off. Baby plantlets spring up between plant separations and send out new leaves and roots until a plant detaches itself from the old leaf. May be used floating or rooted. Well-established plants may be planted, leaving at least a half-inch of root above the gravel surface. An excellent plant, hardy. Adapts famously to artificial light. Requires the same conditions as guppies; consequently, if you can grow sprite, you can raise guppies. And vice versa.

Here is a quick reference table of plants usually found in local pet stores. It gives their requirements for water temperature, light, and pH, as well as their maximum size.

Aquarium Plants and Their Conditions for Growth

Key
D–Dim
M–Medium
H–High
S–Grows to water surface
V–Variable
N–Normal
A–Acid
ALK–Alkaline

	TEMPERATURE (IN DEGREES)	LIGHT CONDITIONS	WATER CONDITION	HEIGHT (IN INCHES)
Ambulia	60 to 75	H	N	S
Anacharis				
(Elodea)	50 to 70	H	ALK	S
Aponogeton	65 to 80	M to H	N to A	S
Bacopa	60 to 70	H	N	10
Banana Lily	60 to 85	D to M to H	V	S
Brazilian				
Swordplant	50 to 90	M to H	A	4 to 20
Cabomba	60 to 80	H	A	S
Cardamine	50 to 65	H	N	S
Cryptocoryne	65 to 80	D to M	A	2 to 8
Echinodorus	65 to 85	D to M to H	A	2 to 12
Foxtail	60 to 75	M to H	A	S
Hair Grass	60 to 90	D to M to H	N	12
Hornwort	75 to 90	M to H	N to ALK	S
Hygrophila	60 to 85	M to H	V	S
Ludwigia	60 to 80	H	N	S
Madagascar				
Lace Leaf	65 to 78	H	A	10
Moneywort	50 to 80	H	N	S
Sagittaria	55 to 80	H	N to A	5 to 18
Sandriana	60 to 80	D to M to H	V	8 to 20
Spatterdock				
(Cow Lily)	60 to 75	M to H	N to ALK	6
Spider Plant				
(Aluminum Plant)	50 to 80	M to H	V	12
Water Sprite				
(Indian Fern)	60 to 90	H	V	S
Temple Plant				
(Nomaphila)	50 to 85	H	V	S
Vallisneria				
(Eelgrass)	50 to 80	M to H	A	7
Violet	50 to 70	M	A	8
Wisteria	60 to 80	M to H	N to A	10

Leiden Garden

While Americans are only now becoming concerned about creating a natural-appearing environment, Europeans have long been devoted to the natural look. This type of gar-

Leiden Garden

den, in which a planter contains earth, peat moss, and vitamins to encourage growth, was popularized by the Dutch. It results in a splendid underwater garden. It is so luxuriant that it can be enjoyed without any fish, or it can be maintained solely to propagate aquatic plants for other tanks. Any plant that will root will do well in a Leiden garden. The trick is in the layering of the planting mediums.

Choose a well-lit 20- to 55-gallon aquarium. For best results use a tank that is as wide as it is high.

Prepare the planting strata in these four layers, starting from the bottom:

1. 1"—1 part each unwashed builder's sand, 1 part coarse gravel or dolomite
2. 2"—1 part African violet soil, 1 part terrarium soil, and 1 part unwashed builder's sand, mixed together thoroughly
3. ¾"—unwashed builder's sand
4. ½"—washed clean gravel

Place tank near filtered sunlight, if possible.

Add rainwater to compensate for evaporation, again if possible.

Allow plants 2 weeks to adjust, root, and begin to grow before adding fish.

Use a power filter for thorough water circulation to all parts of the tank.

APPENDIX D
FISH NUTRITION

Water

No single factor is more important for a healthy aquarium than the water quality. Because an understanding of how a fish uses its environment is so crucial, this information deserves to be emphasized. Water is composed of oxygen and hydrogen, but because the chemical bond linking these two elements is not easily broken, fish cannot draw breath from the oxygen in water. Water can absorb other substances—gases and solids—in quantities that vary, depending upon temperature and pressure. The oxygen that fish do breathe is constantly being absorbed from the atmosphere into the water. It passes through the gills of the fish, from which it enters the bloodstream. The blood carries CO_2 waste back to the gills for discharge into the water. This is a fish's most immediate life-support system.

When a fish becomes sick, it is often because its water has too high a toxic content. If aquarium water is saturated with CO_2, fish are unable to exhale. This CO_2 waste prevents absorption of fresh oxygen, and sends fish gasping to the surface. When fish have difficulty breathing, you should aerate the water; this will supply new oxygen and allow the accumulated CO_2 to escape into the air.

Tap water is generally acceptable for aquarium use. Its mild concentration of chlorine helps control bacteria. But you should never plunge a fish into 100 percent tap water. A mixture of equal parts of aged water (water that has been left standing) and tap water is advisable.

Under pressure in pipes, water can absorb a variety of gases which dissipate and collect as bubbles in a freshly filled fish tank. This water should filter for 24 hours with a strong circulation before adding fish. It is a good idea to acquaint yourself with the water quality in your district. Your local fish dealer might be able to give you specific information. If you live where the air is not polluted, you can catch rainwater, which is soft enough to replace evaporated or distilled water.

Water hardness is measured by the amount of salts (sodium chloride, potassium sulfate, magnesium sulfate) dissolved in the water. Hard water is usually alkaline; soft water is usually neutral or slightly acid.

Test kits to monitor water hardness are available, but there is really no effective way, other than changing aquarium water, to alter hardness. Evaporation leaves salts behind, and replacing evaporated water with tap water without removing additional aquarium water will leave a heavier concentration of salts in the tank water, which will become increasingly hard.

The easiest way to determine water hardness is to wash your hands with some tank water. Soap lathers quickly in soft water; hard water dissolves soap with difficulty, and doesn't encourage lathering. Of course, do not ever allow soaps or detergents to come in contact with your fish or the water they live in.

Fish which require hard water should be provided with the following per 10 gallons of aquarium water:

1 tbsp. rock salt
1 tsp. epsom salt (magnesium sulfate)
1 tsp. potassium sulfate

(Epsom salt produces the medicinal effect of water from sulfuric hot springs.)

I believe an overemphasis has been placed upon the pH factor. The pH will be kept within the appropriate limits by the contents added to the aquarium. Dolomite and coral are added if an alkaline condition is desired. Fish which thrive in acid water should be housed with plants, driftwood, and perhaps a peat planting medium. In either case, prevent the buildup of excessive alkaline or acidic material by making frequent partial water changes.

An overcrowded aquarium should be avoided for many reasons. Too many fish will produce too much waste material. With inadequate aeration, a tank crowded with fish is capable of using up all the available oxygen in a short time, resulting in suffocation. At warmer temperatures water holds less gas and therefore warm-water tanks require more aeration. Oxygen is absorbed by water when air comes in contact with it. That is why a tank with a large surface area is always recommended over a tall, narrow tank. Circulation by the power filter alone is often inadequate for sufficient aeration, especially in a tall tank. A moderate stream of bubbles emanating from the bottom is recommended. One or two columns of air supplied by an under-gravel filter is ideal, which is why it is a good idea to install an under-gravel filter when the tank is initially set up.

There are many subsand or under-gravel filters available. The most effective model consists of a plastic platform with molded and perforated ridges which covers the entire tank floor beneath the gravel. A wide plastic tube is attached to the filter platform and an air stream forces water up through these tubes, creating suction under the platform and through the gravel. The gravel actually becomes the filter itself, a biological filter which houses cultures of denitrifying bacteria and provides nourishment for plants while, in turn, plants supply the fish with food.

Live Foods to Buy

Brine Shrimp. Brine shrimp can be purchased at most pet shops. (To raise your own, see page 235.) When adding store-bought brine shrimp to an aquarium, be careful not to add any of the brine solution that they come in to the water in the aquarium. The brine solution contains unknown quantities of salt, as well as bacteria. Always wash the shrimp in a net held under cold running tap water for at least 10 seconds. Because the brine water is likely to contain hundreds of baby brine shrimp, collect it in a wide-mouthed jar. Add 1 cup of tap water and 1 teaspoon of rock salt to this, and place the jar next to a strong light. Collect them with an eye-dropper. Sift this water through a handkerchief to drain off the baby shrimp.

Tubifex Worms. Tubifex worms are the best source of live protein for fish. However, because they are often collected in sewage areas, they are likely to carry parasites such as leeches and flukes. To clean the worms, rinse them in a fine-mesh net under cold running water for at least 3 minutes before feeding them to fish. Take particular care to keep them from falling onto the aquarium gravel because they can burrow deep, proliferate, and clog the under-gravel filter. My favorite worm feed consists of two perforated plastic cups that lock into place on a suction cup, allowing them to be placed where I can enjoy watching my fish while they are enjoying their special treat. Floating cone-shaped or square worm feeders are fine, too. Even a little cup nestled in the gravel and filled with worms is better than simply putting worms into the tank. Live worms can be easily stored in the refrigerator. There are little plastic worm baskets which hook inside the toilet tank for efficient worm storage; they will be rinsed whenever the toilet is flushed and the tank refills. I usually put unused tubifex in a dessert dish in the refrigerator and cover them with ⅓inch of water, and I rinse them at least twice a day. They can be kept alive for over a week in this way.

Recipes

Here are recipes that will delight your fish and keep them healthy:

Recipe #1:

1 pound dry dog food
1 pound fish meal
1 egg
2 cups water
1 teaspoon salt

1. Preheat oven to 250 degrees.
2. Grind dog food. Sift over fish meal and mix.
3. Beat the egg into the water.
4. Add egg mixture to dog food mixture and stir to combine. Add salt. Add more water if necessary, stirring until mixture becomes thick, pasty, and even-textured.
5. Spread mixture evenly in aluminum pie plates.
6. Bake in preheated oven for 2 hours or until it is dry and brittle. It can also be baked in the sun in summer or on a radiator in the winter. The heat exposure should be long enough to be sure no moisture is left in the mixture.
7. Slice and leave at room temperature a few hours longer or until you are absolutely sure it is completely dried out.
8. Crumble into flakes and store in an airtight container in a cool, dry location.

Recipe #2:

1 pound beef liver
1 pound (regular, not quick-cooking or instant) oatmeal
1 pound shrimp meal (optional)
½ pound fresh spinach, washed and with coarse stems
    removed, coarsely chopped
    OR

1 package frozen chopped spinach
water

1. Preheat oven to 250 degrees.
2. Cut liver into strips about 1 inch by 1 inch by 4 inches long.
3. In a large saucepan bring 1 quart water to the simmering point. Add liver and cook gently 8 to 10 minutes or until liver is firm. Remove liver with a slotted spoon, reserving water.
4. To water remaining in saucepan add another quart of water and bring to a boil.
5. Add oatmeal, shrimp meal, and spinach to saucepan, stirring, and cook gently for 8 to 10 minutes, or until oatmeal is cooked. Stir occasionally.
6. Meanwhile grind liver. Add ground liver to mixture in saucepan and cook over low heat, stirring until mixture is very thick and smooth.
7. Spread mixture evenly on a cookie sheet and bake in a preheated oven at 250 degrees for 30 minutes to 1 hour, or until it is completely dry and brittle.
8. Cut into 3-inch squares and leave at room temperature a few hours or until you are absolutely sure it is completely dried out.
9. Crumble into flakes and store in an airtight container in a cool, dry place.

Recipe #3:

1 pound beef heart
1 pound dry baby cereal
1 pound fresh fillets of any white fish
water

1. Preheat oven to 250 degrees.
2. Cut beef heart into strips about 1 inch by 1 inch by 4 inches long.

3. In a large saucepan bring 1 quart water to the simmering point. Add beef heart strips and cook gently for 20 minutes or until meat is firm and cooked throughout. Remove meat with slotted spoon, reserving water.

4. To water remaining in saucepan add another quart of water and bring to a boil.

5. Add baby cereal gradually, stirring to avoid lumps. If mixture gets too thick, it may be necessary to add more water. Add fish, stir to mix. Continue cooking, stirring occasionally, until fish is done and mixture is smooth.

6. Meanwhile, grind the beef heart. Add ground beef heart to fish mixture in saucepan and cook over low heat, stirring, until mixture is very thick and smooth.

7. Spread mixture evenly on a cookie sheet and bake in preheated oven at 250 degrees for 30 minutes to 1 hour, or until it is completely dry and brittle.

8. Cut into 3-inch squares and leave at room temperature a few hours or until you are absolutely sure it is completely dried out.

9. Crumble into flakes and store in an airtight container in a cool, dry place.

And remember, your fish will be delighted if you treat them to any raw meat—chicken, beef, lamb, clams, or fish—cut into ⅛- to 1-inch dice. Rinse meat thoroughly before serving, so that aquarium water will not cloud up when raw food is added.

Raising Brine Shrimp

When you are raising baby fish, it is necessary to have a supply of live food on hand. Baby brine shrimp (also called artemia or sea monkeys) are the ideal food for fish, not only because of their high degree of protein, but also because their entire life cycle takes only a few weeks. Artemia breed at six weeks of age. Eggs are encased in a tough shell, and in nature accumulate at the shoreline where they dry out in the sun. When rains fill the salt flats again, baby shrimp burst from their eggs within 24 hours.

Raising brine shrimp is easy. Here are the tricks:

1. The larger the volume of water, the more shrimp you will be able to grow. A 5-gallon tank is excellent, but you can also use a 1-gallon mayonnaise jar, as long as you provide constant aeration. Fill the tank with water.

2. Allow water to age 1 day with aeration before adding brine mixture.

After 1 day, add 6 tablespoons rock salt and 1 tablespoon epsom salt for every gallon of water.

3. Add brine shrimp eggs. Make sure they are fresh and have been kept very dry. Eggs are available in a dry state and vacuum-packed. They can be used even after several years if they have been kept dry and at an even temperature.

Use no more than ¼ teaspoon of eggs per gallon of water. If you use too many eggs at a time, they will all hatch at once and die of overcrowding.

Eggs float until they hatch, at which point they sink to the bottom of the tank. They hatch in 24 hours at 75 degrees, but take a week or more at temperatures lower than 70 degrees.

4. Baby shrimp will collect at a strong light source when aeration is stopped. They may then be siphoned out for feeding to fish.

To avoid adding brine water to the fry tank along with the brine shrimp, drain them through a napkin or paper towel.

5. Keep tank in front of a sunny window. Shrimp grow quickly, feeding on algae or a quarter-teaspoon bakers' yeast.

6. When shrimp are 1 week old, give them a stronger salt solution. For each gallon of aged tap water, add:

10 oz. rock salt
2 tablespoons epsom salt
1 tablespoon baking soda

APPENDIX E

BREEDING

How to Create a Breeding Room

For you die-hard do-it-yourselfers, I include this plan to turn a basement or garage corner into an efficient breeding room with very little investment in equipment:

You will need:

10 to 16 styrofoam shipping boxes (available on request from most aquarium shops at about $2 apiece)

1 large, heavy dark sheet of plastic tarpaulin (available from building suppliers)

A level corner of the floor in a warm basement or garage (not on a wooden floor)

Procedure:

1. Clean plastic and boxes carefully with salt water.

2. Using the two corner walls as two sides of the rearing vat, place the boxes at right angles to the walls, forming the other two sides of the rearing vats.

3. Fill the boxes with water to keep them secured.

4. Line the rearing vat with heavy plastic and secure with adhesive-backed cloth tape.

5. Fill the vat with about 10 inches of water.

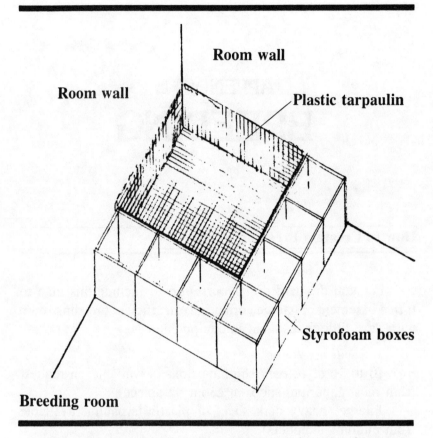

Breeding room

The vat will be shallow, but will have a large surface area, enabling you to raise hundreds of baby fish. The boxes may be set up as breeding tanks, hospital tanks, male segregation tanks, etc.

The vat is not suitable for larger cichlids because of their sharp spines.

Similarly, you can make a fry tank out of a cardboard box or wooden crate. You will need:

2 sheets of heavy plastic sheeting
1 square, sturdy styrofoam box

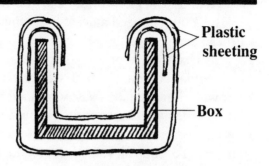

Fry tank

1. Line the inside of a box with one plastic sheet, letting edges overhang the top of the box.

2. Set the box down in the center of the second plastic sheet and wrap the plastic over the sides of the box so it hangs over the top edges to the inside. Tape all around, or around corners only, with adhesive-backed cloth tape for added support if desired. Fish are most comfortable in a dark environment.

In a well-lit room, use dark plastic for both projects. If the room is dimly lit, use plastic of a light tan color.

How to Breed Fancy Guppies

No fish offers as great a challenge for improving the breeding stock as do fancy guppies. Hybrids may be purchased for from $3 a pair and up in pet stores, but the true aristocrats among guppies may be purchased through the mail from specialized guppy breeders at a cost of more than $10 per fish.

It is advisable to begin with store-bought specimens while establishing your own techniques of breeding and raising guppies. But when guppies become an obsession, as they are apt to do, and you want to produce bigger and more beautiful fish, the initial expense for breeding stock can be considered an investment.

Here's how the professionals do it:

1. You will need at least four aquarium tanks, one in each of these sizes: 5-gallon, 10-gallon, 20-gallon, and 30-gallon.

2. Use the 10- or 20-gallon tank for breeding. Set it up as for a regular community tank with these additions: a) use a box or power filter, which is easily cleaned and changed; b) floating plants, especially water sprite, should be used; c) except for a *Coryadoras* or *plecostomus* catfish, the tank should house only guppies. To control selective breeding, one male should be housed with three females.

3. Use the 5-gallon tank as a maternity tank. Make it ready for newborn fry by suspending a plastic open-bottom or net breeding trap at the water surface. If the trap is to be covered, allow at least ½ inch above the water surface to prevent female from suffocating. Maternity tanks should be equipped with a special foam sponge filter.

A 5-gallon tank will hold from 30 to 40 young. In a tank this size they will become accustomed to "frenzied feeding" and get a good growth start. Fry will not feed ravenously in a large tank.

Each brood should have its own 5-gallon tank, since baby guppies born a few days apart are already at different growth stages, and smaller fish will not feed properly if they are competing with larger ones.

4. After fry reach 1 month of age, move them to a 20- or 30-gallon tank.

At this time it is important to cull, or remove and dispose of young which are underdeveloped. The trick here is to have no more than one fish per gallon of water, and to maintain temperature at 80 degrees.

5. As the young continue to grow, male guppies will enter puberty. The young male's bottom fin grows into a gonopodium, or sex organ.

If males are allowed to breed before they reach full maturity, their growth will be stunted. To prevent this, young males must be segregated from the females before they reach puberty.

6. Perhaps the most important trick in raising guppies is frequent water change.

When adolescent specimens reach the 20- or 30-gallon rearing tanks, 25 percent of the water must be changed once or twice a week.

No gravel or plants should be used because guppies tend to rest on the tank bottom at night. Here their long flowing tails would be susceptible to bacteria which collect in gravel. The absence of gravel and rocks also leaves more room in the tank for growth. And a bare tank is the easiest tank to keep clean.

7. Babies are best kept at 80 degrees to increase their metabolism and induce fast growth.

Breeders should be kept at 75 degrees to keep their metabolism relatively high and their breeding rate active.

Mature specimens should be kept at 70 to 72 degrees to retard their metabolism. The average guppy life span is only 2 years. By slowing down their metabolism, you can increase their life expectancy.

8. Here is a feeding schedule for raising splendid guppies. It may be followed also for raising most of the varieties of baby fish to maturity:

	Babies	Adults
7 AM	live baby brine shrimp	dry food
10 AM	fine-ground dry food	
1 PM	frozen beef heart or chicken hearts	
4 PM	fine-ground dry food	
7 PM	live baby brine shrimp	brine shrimp
10 PM	fine-ground dry food	

With heavy feedings, daily water changes are recommended.

When babies are 3 months old or 1½ inches long (whichever occurs first), transfer them to adult diet.

As your guppy breeding operation grows, it is important to keep a record of crosses to remember how a certain hybrid was produced. Here is a typical ID card:

> **Date of birth**
> **ID #**
> **Type of strain or cross**
> **Parents' ID ♂ # ♀ #**

How to Hatch Angelfish Eggs

Often a pair of angelfish will spawn in the community aquarium. The eggs will surely be eaten unless they are removed to be hatched away from their parents. Here are some tips for hatching and rearing the fry with the same attention their parents would give them.

You will need:
5- or 10-gallon tank
5-inch net with large mesh
sponge filter and pump
heater
thermometer
methylene blue
large tweezer
plastic pipette or straw
liquid fry food

1. When the fish have finished spawning and begun to fan their eggs, it is safe to remove the eggs. But first the nursery tank must be prepared. Clean the tank carefully with warm salt water. Half-fill the tank with water from the breeding tank. Add

2 to 3 gallons of tap water and set the heater's thermostat at 80 degrees. No gravel is used for this tank.

2. Insert the sponge filter and pump, allowing it to bubble for 8 hours.

3. Add 4 drops of methylene blue to the new tank. This will protect the eggs from fungus.

4. Bend the handle of the net so that it fits securely over the top edge of the aquarium. Move the filter so that it is adjacent to the net. When the net and filter are positioned correctly, a stream of bubbles should rise *next to,* but not *into*, the net.

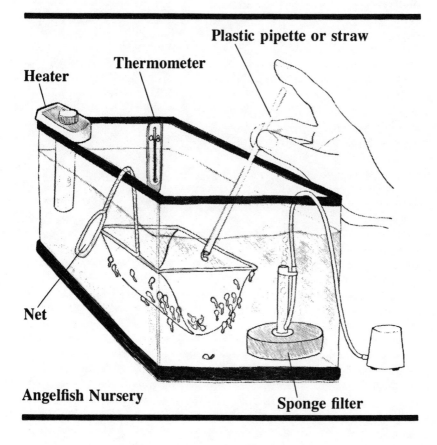

Plastic pipette or straw

Thermometer

Heater

Net

Angelfish Nursery

Sponge filter

5. Gently transfer the leaf with eggs from the community aquarium to the net in the nursery tank. During the next 48 hours remove any eggs that turn white, using a large tweezer.

6. Eggs will hatch in 2 days and fry will cling to the net. Babies that fall to the tank bottom should be drawn up, using a pipette or straw, and returned to the net.

7. Place 2 to 3 drops of liquid food into the center of the net twice daily.

8. When fry are free-swimming, in about 7 to 10 days, the net may be removed. Feed babies live baby brine shrimp 2 or 3 times daily. Give dry food when babies are 1 month old and hardy.

APPENDIX F
DISEASES AND TREATMENTS

The body of a fish is symmetrical and perfectly arranged. Each scale and every ray are exactly spaced, smooth, and lustrous. Consequently it is easy to see when a fish is in distress because its symmetry is jarred, its perfection marred. Most symptoms of disease are visible; diagnosing and treating them is intuitive. Sometimes I wish I could take a fish's blood pressure, or look down its throat with a tiny tongue depressor, but obviously that isn't possible. There are only two methods of maintaining your fish's health. First is preventive medicine: providing clean and proper conditions for a healthy tankful of fish. Second is chemical treatment for fish displaying unhealthy symptoms.

An extra clean tank is very handy for treating sick fish. It is a good idea to get a 10-gallon aquarium to begin with. Then, when you graduate to a larger tank, you can use this smaller one as an infirmary. I always keep one tank ready for emergencies. Being prepared can be essential for curing an ailing fish. Immediate action is often necessary to arrest and prevent the spread of disease. A parasite-infested fish must be isolated in a tank that houses no future hosts.

Treat skin infections in a salt bath in a hospital tank. Prepare tank by filling it with equal parts of water from the fish's regular aquarium and fresh tap water at the same temperature.

Place fish in prepared tank. One-half hour later begin gradually to add salt, in the proportion of a) 3 tablespoons kosher salt per 1 gallon of water, or b) 2 tablespoons epsom salt plus 2 tablespoons kosher salt per 1 gallon of water. Add total salt requirement gradually for 4 hours. Let fish stand in salt bath for one-half hour longer. Then remove half of salt bath water and replace with fresh tap water at the same temperature. Leave fish in hospital tank for an additional one-half hour, then return to the original tank.

If the fish is in extremely delicate condition, use a weaker salt solution and reduce the amount of time the fish is in the salt bath. If the fish seems strong, it can remain in the salt bath for the full time.

When a fish shows the slightest sign of disease, I like to quarantine it for close observation and treatment. I keep a 5-gallon tank for the infirmary, as well as a few 1-gallon mayonnaise jars for hatching brine shrimp, transporting fish, and even breeding fish and raising fry. I examine my fish daily for the visual symptoms of fish disease and consult my chart of symptoms and treatments.

Symptoms	Treatments
1. white spots on fins	treat for ich
2. frayed or deteriorating fins; red streaks in veiltails	treat for fin rot
3. white cottony patches	treat for fungus
4. white glaze over eyes	treat for fungus or bacteria
5. injuries	isolate and add salt

6. brownish velvety patches	treat for velvet
7. swollen eyes	treat for pop eye
8. tiny pin holes in body mainly cichlids)	treat for hole in head
9. shimmies	raise temperature; add salt
10. constipation	vary diet; epsom salt bath; raise temperature
11. inflamed gills	isolate and treat for flukes; more aeration
12. pale color	check pH; provide more plants and hiding places
13. gasping for air	change water; more aeration
14. loss of appetite or lying on tank bottom	change water; vary diet; add salt

These are usually the first signs of disease. When any of these symptoms appear, immediately transfer sick fish to their own clean, well-aerated tank, with at least 1 teaspoon salt per gallon of water. Treated properly and promptly, most aquarium diseases are easily cured. Any aquarist with an infirmary tank and a first-aid kit will be able to save the lives of his fish.

Fortunately, the most common diseases are easily recognizable. Parasites (including protozoans, bacteria, and fungus) which attack and find nourishment in the skin and external organs of fish appear as whitish splotches, spots, bumps, or fuzz. Internal diseases are less common, difficult to diagnose

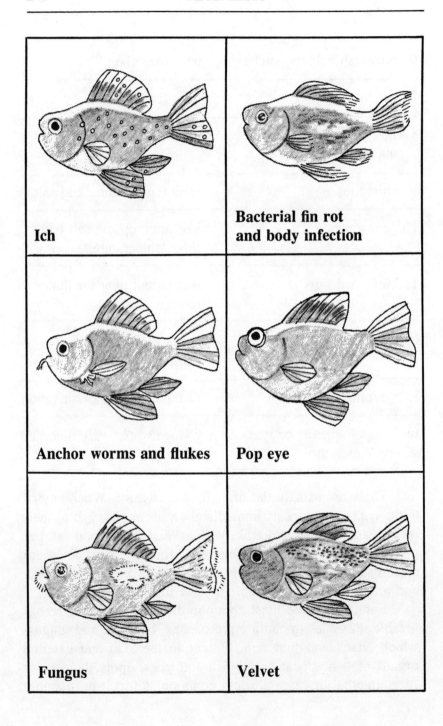

Ich

Bacterial fin rot
and body infection

Anchor worms and flukes

Pop eye

Fungus

Velvet

positively, and tricky to treat. If proper care is taken in selecting healthy initial stock, and subsequent additions are kept isolated for about a week, there is very little chance that your fish will become infected. It is important to inspect your fish frequently—without overdoing it, of course.

I don't like to recommend antibiotics or pesticides for the aquarium. A fish weakened by disease can often be killed by the cure. Remember that the addition of foreign chemicals to the water may change its quality. The aquarium's ecosystem can become unbalanced if helpful nitrogen-fixing bacteria are destroyed along with the pathogenic or harmful bacteria. Unless fish show specific symptoms, or tank water is cloudy and foul-smelling, chances are that bacteria are not a problem.

Alas, it is sometimes necessary to dispose of a fish in order to prevent it from contaminating its tankmates. According to one noted author, the most humane manner of "getting rid" of an undesirable fish is to bash its little body against a wall. I can't do that. I always opt for the gentler flushing method.

Here is a list of fish diseases:

External Parasites

Skin Ich (Ichthyophthirius)

Spores of this protozoan pest are always present in aquarium water, but they rarely infect healthy fish. However, when a fish's resistance is lowered, as a result, for example, of a sudden drop in temperature, the condition of its body slime allows ich parasites to take hold. Within 4 days the ich parasite matures and completes its life cycle, dropping from its host to the gravel, where it develops into a cyst, producing thousands of free-swimming spores. These spores search out a new host, and can only thrive in the presence of light at moderate (60 to 80 degrees) temperatures. Left untreated, ich can reach epidemic proportions, and wipe out an entire tankful of fish in a short time. Ich spores look like white sugar grains clinging to fins and scales. Magnification reveals their spherical shape. They cause itching and noticeable discomfort, and, inevitably, affect a fish's disposition. Since this parasite has such specific requirements for survival, there are various options for a successful cure.

Symptoms: Small white spots cling to the victim's fins, tail, and body. They appear gradually, only a few at first, but then more and more, until the fish seems to be covered with tiny raised grains of sugar.

Treatment: Keep the tank quite dark and raise the temperature to 90 degrees, at the rate of 1 degree every 2 hours. Maintain these conditions for 1 week. Because ich is unable to reproduce at high temperatures, it will die off when its 4-day life cycle is completed. Use Formalin or methylene blue, or 1 ml. of a 1%-per-gallon commercial ich medicine (most are effective) and maintain a tank temperature of 85 degrees without light.

For cold-water fish, start by adding 3 grains of quinine sulfate per gallon; add a bit more each day until all white spots are gone. Once exterminated, ich rarely recurs, unless it is introduced by new fish or plants. While it attacks most fish, it seldom causes irreparable damage because it is easily arrested in time.

Another method of exterminating ich is to move the infected fish to a fresh isolation tank every day for 1 week and discard the water. When parasites leave the fish's body, they will die without a new host to attach to. Impractical, perhaps, but effective all the same.

Velvet (Oodinium)

Symptoms: This is a flagellate parasite which penetrates and coats the skin, appearing as milky off-white, yellow, or brown velvet patches. Not nearly as common as ich, velvet must be caught and treated quickly, as it is often fatal in young fish. Magnification reveals that the oodinium organisms move and look like powdery particles similar in appearance to ich, although the particles are much smaller.

Treatment: Treat with acriflavine and kosher salt and raise the water temperature to 85 degrees for 3 days. Repeat treatment after 1 week if necessary, after a partial water change. If the symptoms persist, or if the fish suffers a relapse, give it a 30-minute bath in copper sulfate (in isolation, of course) once a day until all symptoms have disappeared.

Anchor Worm

Symptoms: This is a multicellular transparent worm which attaches itself to various places on a fish's anatomy, notably around the jaws, mouth, and gills. Hard to spot at first, these little pests are able to expand and contract, and cling fast to their host.

Treatment: The most effective treatment involves dealing directly with the worm. Dampen a washcloth and fold it into a pad. Place the fish on the cloth and wrap it carefully, leaving only the parasite exposed. It's surprising to see how trusting and obliging your patient will be, as if it knows you want to help. A fish out of water has a good 3 to 4 minutes without discomfort, if kept moist. Soak a cotton swab with Formalin or methylene blue and carefully dab the worm, avoiding contact with the fish. Return the fish to the hospital tank. The worm should drop off within 24 hours. If the first treatment is unsuccessful, swab the worm with a slightly stronger solution. You should be able to remove the softened worm with a tweezer.

Bacterial Fin and Tail Rot

Symptoms: Tail rot usually occurs in unsanitary aquariums. It takes the form of an infection along torn fins or tail and gradually consumes the tissue as the fins seem to shrink. Because it progresses gradually, it can readily be diagnosed and treated.

Veiltail goldfish are susceptible to another form of tail rot which appears as red streaks running along veins in their elongated tails. Treatment is the same for both bacterial infections.

Treatment: Mobility of the affected fish is, of course, hampered, and to ensure proper feeding, essential in curing them, patients should be placed in a clean hospital tank. Use an antibiotic, penicillin or tetracycline, 50 mg. per gallon. Repeat the treatment after 4 days if necessary. In extreme cases trim excessively ragged areas with a surgical scissor while cradling fish in a wet washcloth (as described in treatment for anchor worm). Then watch in amazement as tails and fins regenerate, becoming bigger and more beautiful than ever.

Fungus (Saprolegnia)

Symptoms: This appears as a cottony fuzz covering patches on the body and fins, or as a cloudy film over the eye. Fungus usually takes hold of previously injured tissue. The best preventive is not to expose fish to sharp objects or "bullies" which might cause such injuries.

Treatment: Fungus is destroyed easily by adding salt in progressively increasing amounts as described on page 258. The protective body slime prevents fungus from feeding and gives the injury a chance to heal. Advanced or persistent cases should be treated with salt plus a commercial fungicide, such as malachite green.

Mouth Fungus (Cotton Mouth)

Symptoms: White cottony tufts attached to the fish's jaw are not a true fungus, but a bacterial infection. Untreated, this disease will completely consume the jaw and face.

Treatment: Place the patient in isolation and treat with an antibiotic. For immediate results, hold the fish in a wet washcloth (as described in treatment for anchor worm), and apply tincture of merthiolate by means of a cotton-tipped swab to the infected area.

Internal Parasites

Dropsy (Pseudomonas)

Symptoms: This is perhaps the most pathetic-looking disease of all. Bacteria invade the fish's entire body, causing general swelling and severe protrusion of scales.

Treatment: Dropsy is difficult to treat; victims should be isolated, even though dropsy attacks individual fish and rarely causes an epidemic. But to minimize aggravation, I advise destroying any infected fish. Even if the bacteria are exterminated, fish rarely recover completely. For larger fish or favorite specimens try an antibiotic treatment in a hospital tank with frequent salt baths. Do not raise water temperature. Keep isolated.

Pop Eye (Exophthalmus)

Symptoms: This is a strange condition caused by gas-forming bacteria around one or both eyes. Affected fish develop bulging eyes, often accompanied by loss of appetite and weight loss. Often pop eye will disappear on its own or after medication and will either leave the victim unaffected or recur.

Treatment: To relieve gas accumulation: hold fish in a wet washcloth (as described in treatment for anchor worm). Brush the eyes with a 1:1 solution of argyrol and glycerine, using a very soft watercolor paint brush. Fish may remain out of water for up to 3 minutes to ensure penetration. Repeat as necessary.

To eliminate bacteria: treat fish in a separate tank with 1

teaspoon salt per gallon and 50 mg. penicillin or tetracycline per gallon.

Hole in the Head (Ichthyophonas)

Symptoms: This versatile parasite is capable of infecting most areas of a fish's anatomy: eyes, fins, gills, reproductive organs, liver, kidney, and even the brain. About half of all deaths in the aquarium may be blamed on this fungus-like organism. Generally, it enters the digestive system on infected food, and is then able to penetrate the bloodstream and reproduce throughout the body. It manifests itself on the skin in the form of pin-sized holes or blemishes, lumps, and lesions, often on the forehead. Ragged fins, popeyes, emaciation, and gasping for air are all symptoms.

Treatment: Treatment is difficult because this organism reproduces rapidly through skin lesions and gills, and is transmitted through feces. Therefore, isolation is essential. Add antibiotics, chlorphenicol or penicillin diluted at 250 mg. per 4 gallons of water. Soak food—chopped chicken or beef heart—in a 1% solution of chlorphenoxethol, or Flagyl®.

Gill Worms and Flukes

Symptoms: Tiny, filamentous milky-white worms attached to fleshy tissue within the gills cause fish to dash themselves wildly against rocks and tank sides. Flukes and worms induce redness and swelling of the gills, making it difficult for their host to breathe and may cause death in a matter of weeks.

Treatment: Treat in a separate bare-bottom tank. Add $^1/_{16}$ grain potassium permaganate per gallon or 20 drops Formalin per gallon. Treatment should last from 10 to 30 minutes, or until fish seems tired. Then siphon out half of the water to get rid of dead flukes and replace with conditioned water. Repeat the treatment every 2 or 3 days if necessary.

Nutritional Maladies

Prevention of disease depends upon fish that are resilient and strong. Proper environment conditions are essential for keeping fish in tiptop condition. Extremes of temperature, pH, and water hardness may lead to diseases of the skin and gills. Even more important is proper nutrition. Fish food manufacturers go to great lengths to provide dry foods that are fortified with essential vitamins and nutrients. But no single food is adequate. Fish require a varied diet of meat protein, roughage, fish meal, and cereal. Live foods should be fed weekly if possible. Within a month, you will be able to judge the quantities of food your fish require. Overfeeding and underfeeding both may cause nutritional damage.

Constipation

Most often encountered in fish with compressed bodies (angelfish, discus, scats, etc.), constipation causes a lack of appetite coupled with body swelling and a continued string of feces trailing behind an uncomfortable fish. Constipation results from feeding too much starchy dry prepared food. Fish given live food and red meat frequently will not become constipated. Treated with a varied diet at the first sign of constipation, a fish will usually perk up. In advanced cases fish may gulp for air at the surface, and look very swollen. Treat in a salt bath using epsom salts—3 tablespoons per 5 gallons of aquarium water for 10 minutes. Repeat daily until fish recovers.

Obesity

This goes beyond the swollen appearance of constipation and is a state of being unhealthily overweight. Too much food coupled with lack of activity in a small tank may produce lethargic and fat fish. Because feeding your fish is the greatest exchange between you and your pet, overfeeding them over a period of months or years is very common. Fattening of the liver and ovaries follows, leading to death or rampant invasion by parasites. *Overfeeding must be avoided.* Feed fish daily, and time their food intake with a clock. Determine how much food they will consume *completely* within *5 minutes,* and feed no more.

Egg Binding

This is also a very common condition of pampered aquarium fish. A female produces eggs, but is unable to spawn under given conditions. The eggs harden as she produces more until her internal organs are ruptured and squashed together. This can be seen as an exaggerated balloon-like swelling in a female which has reached breeding condition. The eggs must be dissolved and their protein reabsorbed within the female's body. Epsom salt baths are effective. To prevent egg binding, simply permit ripe fish to breed under proper conditions.

Stunting

Crowding and insufficient feeding may cause fish to remain dwarves all their lives. Feed juvenile fish frequently during the day (many small feedings are better than one great meal). Follow the size rule: 1 inch of fish per 1 gallon of water.

Recommended Drugs and Stock Solutions

The chart below lists drugs available from local pet dealers. (Kosher salt is available in supermarkets or grocery stores.)

Dosages vary according to manufacturers. The chart gives references for standard dosages and stock solutions (percentage of chemicals to be dissolved in water before putting into tank).

A stock solution is either the strength of the medication as purchased, or the strength to which you will have to mix it before adding to your fish tank.

Bear in mind that rocks and gravel displace water, and so a

10-gallon tank will contain perhaps 8 gallons of water. Adjust dosage to the actual water content of an aquarium, not to the maximum capacity of the tank.

In general, I recommend underdosing. Too great a proportion of any medication can harm a fish whose condition is already weakened. As the fish gains in strength, the treatment can be repeated with a more concentrated dosage.

Drug	Stock Solution	Dose/Aquarium Water
ACRIFLAVIN③ (*use with kosher salt*)	1 tablet/ 10 oz. water	2 tsp./1 gal.
COPPER SULFATE②	1%	1½ tsp./1 gal.
CHLORAMPHENICOL④	250 mg. tablet	1 tablet/ 10 gal.
ERYTHROMYCIN①	200 mg. tablet	1 tablet/ 5 gal.
FORMALIN	1%	1 tbsp. /1 gal.
QUININE HYDRO-CHLORIDE③	10 gr./oz. water	3 tsp./1 gal.
MALACHITE GREEN②	5%	5 drops/ 1 gal.
METHYLENE BLUE④	5%	5 drops/ 1 gal.
POTASSIUM PERMANGA-NATE④	1%	2 drops/ 1 gal.
TETRACYCLINE④	250 mg.	1 tablet/ 10 gal.

KOSHER SALT *for* *treatment*⑤	uniodized	1 tbsp./1 gal.
KOSHER SALT *for* *tonic*⑤	uniodized	1 tsp./1 gal.

Key:
① Repeat dose daily. Change half the water after third dose.
② Repeat after 2 days.
③ Treat for 3 days; repeat once before changing half of aquarium water.
④ One dose, change half of aquarium water before repeating.
⑤ Use salt only once. When removing water, be sure to dissolve appropriate amount of salt in new water before adding to the aquarium.

Standard Drug Measurements[1] and Their Metric Equivalents

	FLUIDS		DRY WEIGHT	
	oz. fluid	*metric*	*wt. grains*	*wt. grams– metric*
1 drop	1/160 oz.	1/20 cc.	1 gr.	
1 teaspoon	⅛ oz.	4 cc.	75 gr.	5 g
1 tablespoon	⅔ oz.	20 cc.	300 gr.	20 g
1 cup (teacup)	6 oz.	180 cc.	3300 gr.	220 g

[1]*Note that in some cases drug measurements are different from standard or culinary measurements. Use your standard kitchen measuring spoons for teaspoon and tablespoon measurement, but note that a 1 cup is a 6 fluid ounces, not a standard 8-ounce cup.*

COMMONLY KEPT FRESH-WATER FISH CHART

LEGEND

pH

−N	slightly acid
N	neutral
N+	slightly alkaline
NC	not critical

Foods

A	live shrimp
B	live tubifex
C	dry food
D	vegetables
E	red meat
F	goldfish
G	earthworms, insects
H	frozen shrimp
I	algae
J	trout chow

Sex Differences

♂	male
♂	male breeding tube

♀	female
♀	female breeding tube

Breeding Tank Environment

1	no. 3 gravel
2	dolomite
3	bare bottom
4	pebbles
5	peat moss
6	flowerpot
7	vertical slate
8	horizontal slate
9	broad-leafed plants
10	floating plants
11	rooted plants
12	rock caves
13	net breeder
14	community tank
15	box filter
16	power filter
17	under-gravel filter
18	sponge filter
19	aeration only

Fish	Habitat	Size	Coloration	Hardi-ness	Temper-ament Range	Function	pH	DH/Salt
Algae eater (*Gyrinocheilus aymonieri*)	Thailand Cambodia	6″	Tan fish with variable dark markings.	sturdy	gentle active	scavenger	−N	soft
Angelica catfish (*Pimelodus pictus*)	South Africa	6″	Sleek silver body with black polka dots, long graceful barbels.	fairly hardy	playful territorial active	scavenger nocturnal	N+	hard
Angel fish (*Pterophyllum scalare*)	Amazon basin, Guyana	6″	Compressed body, silver or silver-and-black variations.	sturdy	intelligent hostile alert	primary fish	N	soft
Aphyosemion killy (*Aphiosemion australe, Aphiosemion calliurum, Aphiosemion arnoldi*)	Tropical Africa	2″	Long, brilliantly colored species with lyretails and jewellike red and blue iridescent flecks.	fairly hardy	intelligent playful alert territorial	loner	acid	soft
Archer fish (*Toxotes jaculator*)	India Burma Malaya Philippines East Indies Thailand	6″	Silver-yellow body, six thick dark bands. Metallic, sturdy-looking.	fairly hardy	jumper intelligent hostile territorial	loner	N+	salt
Arowana (*Osteoglossum bicirrhosum*)	Amazon	18″	Long, sleek silver body, large metallic scales.	fairly hardy	gentle intelligent playful alert jumper	loner	N	NC

Foods	Temperature Range[a]	Breeding Habits	Optimal Tank Environment[b]	Age or Size at Maturity	Sex Distinctions	Fry Care and Comments
C D I	70° **78°** 85°	substratum breeder	1, 8, 11, 18	5″	♀ fuller	Not often bred. Algae eaters like a tank with some filtered sunlight to promote algae growth.
A B C D G H	70° **76°** 80°	substratum breeder	1, 2, 11, 12, 17	*Not bred in captivity*		One of the loveliest scavengers for a community tank.
A B C D H	72° **78°** 85°	plant-adherer	1, 7, 9, 11, 18 or 3, 7, 19	9 months	♂ fuller fins ♀ plumper ♂ pointed	Good parents. Both parents will tend eggs and transport them to a new clean site every day. From 500–1,000 eggs hatch in 3 days Feed live foods in separate tank when free-swimming.
A B C	70° **76°** 80°	plant-adherer	5 gal. 1, 10, 19	5 months	♂ larger ♀ plain	If well fed and in good condition, fish will spawn daily. Remove eggs on floating plants and hatch separately. Feed live food.
E G	74° **78°** 85°		*Not bred in captivity*			This interesting fish actually spits down flying prey with a jet stream of water.
A B C E F G	76° **78°** 85°	mouth-breeder	55 gal.	12″		Not often bred. Female protects 12–24 young until they have absorbed large egg sac. Good pet fish—do not move once settled into a tank.

[a]*Temperatures in degrees Fahrenheit. Figure in boldface is optimal temperature within the range tolerated by the fish.*

[b]*Optimal tank environment provides conditions which are ideal for the encouragement of breeding.*

Fish	Habitat	Size	Coloration	Hardi-ness	Temper-ament Range	Function	pH	DH/Salt
Australian rainbow (*Melanotaenia nigrans*)	Australia	4″	Gray body with pink, yellow, or greenish lines.	sturdy	gentle playful jumper active	school fish	+N	salt
Bala shark (*Tri-color shark*) (*Balantiocheilos melanopterus*)	Thailand Sumatra Borneo	14″	Large silver scales, striking sharp fins edged in black.	sturdy	intelligent playful alert jumper active	secondary fish	N+	NC
Banjo catfish (*Bunocephalus coracoldeus*)	Brazil	6″	Dark brown markings.	sturdy	shy territorial	scavenger nocturnal	NC	NC
Betta (*Betta splendens*)	Thailand Malaya	2½″	Brilliant hues of red, blue, crimson, turquoise, etc.	sturdy	shy hostile playful	loner	NC	NC
Black ghost knife (*Sternarchus albifrons* or *Apteronotus albifrons*)	Amazon Surinam	8″	Chocolate brown body with white ring around tapering tail. No dorsal fin.	fairly hardy	shy playful territorial alert jumper	loner nocturnal	NC	NC
Black molly (*Mollinesia sphenops*)	Mexico Central America	4″	Jet black or marbled, new strains with orange flecks.	fairly hardy	playful dumb jumper active	primary fish	N+	salt

Foods	Temperature Rangeᵃ	Breeding Habits	Optimal Tank Environmentsᵇ	Age or Size at Maturity	Sex Distinctions	Fry Care and Comments
A B C	70° **76°** 80°	plant-adherer	15 gal. 1, 11, 17	3″	♂ more colorful	Allow well-fed pair to spawn in fine-leaved plants (cabomba). Remove parents (even though they seldom eat eggs). Hatch in 1 week; fry are hardy.
A B C G	72° **76°** 82°		55 gal.	*Not bred in captivity* 8″		Handsome fish—very skilled jumpers. Feed live food.
A B C	60° **78°** 90°	substratum breeder	10 gal. 1, 6, 11, 12, 17	2″	♀ fuller	Not often bred. Very shy. Apparently good parental care.
A B C	65° **78°** 85°	bubble-nest builder	10 gal. 1, 10, 19 or 3, 10, 18	6 months	♂ long fins, colorful ♀ plain	Easy to breed. Fill tank with 8″ of aged water, feed parents well. Remove female after spawn, and male in 2 weeks when fry are free-swimming. Keep them warm and feed live food. Fry are quite delicate.
A B C E G	70° **80°** 85°		*Not bred in captivity*			A bizarre and funny fish. Shy until you gain their confidence. May be tamed to handfeed.
A B C D I	70° **80°** 90°	live-bearer	10–30 gal. 1, 2, 10, 11, 14, 17	2″	♀ larger ♂ larger dorsal fin ♂ pointed gonopodium	Parents will not bother babies if all are well fed. Keep in 2 tsp. kosher salt per gallon.

Fish	Habitat	Size	Coloration	Hardi-ness	Temper-ament Range	Function	pH	DH/Salt
Black neon tetra (*Hyphessobrycon herbertaxelrodi*)	Brazil	1½"	Brilliant black and opaline stripes, red eye.	sturdy	gentle playful dumb alert active	school fish	−N	soft
Black phantom tetra (*Megalamphodus megalopterus*)	Brazil	1½"	Smoky to jet black fins.	fairly hardy	gentle alert shy active	school fish	−N	soft
Black red-tail shark (*Labeo erythrurus*)	Thailand	6"	Light gray to velvet black body, red tail.	fairly hardy	playful alert territorial active	primary fish scavenger	N+	hard
Black ruby barb (*Puntius nigrofasciatus*)	Ceylon	3"	Males are a deep crimson color with black trim on fins.	sturdy	playful alert mated pairs advised jumper active	school fish	N	soft
Black tetra (*Gymnocorymbus ternetzi*)	South America	3"	Round silver-and-black-striped body. Bold black tuxedo-like markings.	sturdy	gentle dumb mated pairs advised active	school fish	NC	NC
Bleeding heart tetra (*Hyphessobrycon rubrostigma*)	Colombia	3"	Rosy-hued translucent body. White and black trim on fins. Red spot on gill plate.	sturdy	shy gentle playful mated pairs advised jumper active	secondary fish school fish	−N	soft

Foods	Temper- ature Range[a]	Breeding Habits	Optimal Tank Environ- ment[b]	Age or Size at Maturity	Sex Distinc- tions	Fry Care and Comments
A B C	72° **78°** 82°	egg- scatterer	10–15 gal. 1, 11, 18 2♀ : 1♂	9 months	♀ fuller	100 eggs hatch in 24 hours. Feed live food. Remove parents after spawn.
A B C	72° **78°** 82°	egg- scatterer	10–15 gal. 1, 11, 18 2♀ : 1♂	9 months	♂ elongated dorsal fin ♀ some red in fins	100–300 eggs hatch in 24 hours. Keep tank clean—susceptible to fungus. Feed live foods. Interesting community fish.
A B C	70° **78°** 85°	substratum breeder	15–20 gal. 1, 2, 11, 12, 17	1 year 3 years	♀ plumper	Condition fish in separate tanks to avoid bullying. 30–60 eggs are tended by male for 3 days until they hatch; then remove him. Fry are free-swimming in 3 days.
A B C	65° **80°** 85°	egg- scatterer	15–20 gal. 1, 11, 13, 18	12 months	♀ deep red	Fry hatch in 48 hours. Feed infusoria. Remove parents after spawn.
A B C	65° **78°** 85°	egg- scatterer	15–20 gal. 1, 11, 13, 18	2″ 10 months	♂ smaller	Remove parents after spawn. Feed infusoria or liquid food.
A B C	65° **80°** 90°	egg- scatterer	15–30 gal. 1, 11, 13, 18	12 months	♂ extended dorsal fin ♀ larger, more robust	Well-conditioned pair will spawn regularly. Remove parents, feed fry infusoria.

Fish	Habitat	Size	Coloration	Hardiness	Temperament Range	Function	pH	DH/Salt
Blind cave (*Anoptichthys jordani*)	Mexico	3″	Albino pink.	fairly hardy	shy gentle jumper active	school fish	N+	hard
Bloodfin (*Aphyocharax anisitsi*)	Argentina	2″	Sleek silver body, red tail.	sturdy	active jumper	school fish	−N	NC
Blue acara (*Aequidens pulcher*)	Venezuela Colombia Panama	6″	Bluish body, fine turquoise lines on face, dark bands and bright blue and red flecks.	sturdy	intelligent hostile alert territorial mated pairs advised	primary fish	N	NC
Blue gourami (*Trichogaster trichopterus*) (*Three-spot gourami*)	Sumatra	6″	Sky blue body, round spot in center and at tail base.	sturdy	hostile mated pairs advised	primary fish	−N	NC
Botia (*Botia modesta*)	Thailand Vietnam Malaysia	10″	Slate gray, dolphin-like body, orange fins.	sturdy	shy intelligent playful territorial jumper	scavenger nocturnal	−N	soft
Bumblebee goby (*Brachygobius xanthozona*)	Sumatra Borneo Java	2″	Black and yellow bumblebee stripes.	requires special attention	shy gentle playful territorial	primary fish	N+	salt 1 tsp. per gal.
Bumblebee catfish (*Microglanis poecilus*)	Brazil	8″	Bronze and black marbled stripes.	sturdy	shy playful territorial	scavenger nocturnal	+N	NC

Foods	Temperature Range[a]	Breeding Habits	Optimal Tank Environment[b]	Age or Size at Maturity	Sex Distinctions	Fry Care and Comments
A C	68° **78°** 90°	egg-scatterer	10–15 gal. 1, 11, 13, 18	2½″	♀ fuller	Remove parents after spawn. Eggs hatch in three days.
A B C	70° **78°** 80°	egg-scatterer	20 gal. 1, 11, 13, 18	3″	♀ fuller ♂ more colorful, hooks on anal fin	Nonadhesive eggs hatch in 30 hours. Pair often jump out of water during spawning. Remove parents, feed fry liquid food or fine dry food.
A B C E G H	65° **80°** 85°	substratum breeder	10–20 gal. 1, 6, 11, 12, 17	4″	♂ pointed anal fin ♀ bronzer	Easy and fascinating to breed. Condition pair on live food. Pair will lock jaws and raise the young. Just feed well and watch.
A B C	60° **78°** 90°	bubble-nest builder	10 gal. 1, 10, 18	10 months	♂ long dorsal fin ♀ plumper	200–800 eggs hatch in 2 days. Remove female after spawn, male after 1 week. Feed fry anything finely ground. Very strong fish—often outgrow community.
A B C	65° **78°** 85°	substratum breeder		4″ *Not bred in captivity*	♀ fuller	Interesting scavenger with retractable spines behind gills.
A B C	75° **82°** 85°	substratum breeder	5 gal. 2, 12, 17	1½″	♀ fuller	120 eggs hatch in 4–8 days. Fish breed much as dwarf cichlids. Feed adults and fry live foods.
A B C	65° **78°** 80°	substratum breeder	10 gal. 1, 11, 12, 16	4″ *Not often bred*	♀ fuller	Small specimens usually available. Will grow and gobble up baby fish at night.

Fish	Habitat	Size	Coloration	Hardiness	Temperament Range	Function	pH	DH/Salt
Butterfly (*Pantodon buchholzi*)	West Africa	4"	Tan with dark markings.	requires special attention	shy playful alert jumper	primary fish loner	−N	soft
Cardinal tetra (*Cheirodon axelrodi*)	Amazon Rio Negro	2"	Brilliant red and blue luminescent stripes.	fairly hardy	gentle active playful	school fish	−N	soft
Cherry barb *Capoeta titteya*)	Ceylon	2"	Light brown to brilliant red hue.	sturdy	gentle playful mated pairs advised active	secondary fish	−N	soft
Chocolate gourami (*Sphaerichthys osphromenoides*)	Sumatra Malaya	2"	Chocolate brown body with four ivory rings.	requires special attention	shy gentle intelligent mated pairs advised jumper	primary fish loner	−N	very soft
Clown barb (*Barbodes everetti*)	Borneo Malaya	10"	Gold body, red fins, 3 black bands.	sturdy	gentle dumb playful active	school fish	N	soft
Clown loach (*Botia macracantha*)	Sumatra Borneo	12"	Gold and black bands, red fins; "goofy" face.	fairly hardy	shy jumper gentle playful intelligent territorial	scavenger secondary fish nocturnal	N	soft

Foods	Temper-ature Range[a]	Breeding Habits	Optimal Tank Environ-ment[b]	Age or Size at Maturity	Sex Distinc-tions	Fry Care and Comments
A B C G	68° **80°** 85°	egg-scatterer	20–30 gal. 1, 10, 11, 17 Float a piece of cork, keep water level low.	3½"	♀ straight anal fin ♂ anal fin edge incised, central rays form a tube	Hatch fry separately. Feed live food.
A B C	70° **78°** 82°	egg-scatterer	10–20 gal. 1, 5, 11, 18	9 months	♀ fuller	Remove parents after spawn. Feed babies infusoria.
A B C	72° **78°** 85°	egg-scatterer	10 gal. 1, 4, 11 18	1½"	♀ fuller ♂ redder	Raise fry separately. Hatch in 36 hours and soon take live baby brine shrimp.
A B C	78° **80°** 82°	mouth-breeder	15 gal. 3, 10, 18	2½"	♀ heavier before spawning; hard to determine sex	A delicate and rare fish, even in native waters. 40–50 eggs are incubated by male for 14 days.
A B C	70° **78°** 85°	egg-scatterer	10–20 gal. 3, 10, 18	3"	♀ fuller	Fin nippers; should not be kept with smaller fish. Plant eaters.
A B C	65° **76°** 80°	substratum breeder	20–30 gal. 1, 6, 11, 12, 14	4"	♀ fuller ♂ brighter reds	Reports of clown loaches spawning very privately in a well-planted tank, but no observation of spawning or parental care.

Fish	Habitat	Size	Coloration	Hardi-ness	Temper-ament Range	Function	pH	DH/Salt
Convict cichlid *(Cichlasoma nigrofasciatum)*	Guatemala Panama Costa Rica El Salvador	6"	Cadet-blue sides, black vertical stripes like convict suit. Golden albino form has black eyes, female has brilliant copper-orange glow.	sturdy	intelligent hostile alert territorial mated pairs advised	primary fish	NC	NC
Corydoras catfish	South America	3"	Variable markings.	sturdy	shy gentle playful	scavenger	NC	NC
Datinioid *(Datinioides microlepis)*	Thailand Sumatra Borneo	15"	Bold yellow and black tiger stripes.	fairly hardy	intelligent alert keep with larger fish	primary fish	−N	N
Discus *(Symphysodon aequifasciata)*	Brazil	8"	Brown compressed round body; blue lines glow in face and fins.	requires special attention	shy intelligent alert mated pairs advised jumper	primary fish loner	−N	soft
Dwarf gourami *(Colisa lalia)*	India	2½"	Males have beautiful blue and red iridescent diagonal stripes; females, silver.	sturdy	shy gentle mated pairs advised active	secondary fish	−N	NC
Elephant-nose *(Gnathonemus petersi)*	Congo River Central Africa	12"	Black with white art deco-markings.	requires special attention	shy intelligent playful alert territorial jumper	primary fish scavenger	−N	soft, some salt

Foods	Temper-ature Range[a]	Breeding Habits	Optimal Tank Environ-ment[b]	Age or Size at Maturity	Sex Distinc-tions	Fry Care and Comments
A B C E F G	65° **78°** 85°	substratum breeder	10–20 gal. 1, 6, 11, 12, 17	3″	♂ longer, pointed dorsal fin ♀ rosy blush on sides	100 fry hatch in 3 days. Good parental care by both parents. Hardy fish, easy to breed.
A B C	70° **75°** 80°	plant-adherer	10–20 gal. 1, 11, 15	2 years	♀ fuller	100–150 eggs hatch in 3 days. Remove parents; feed fry infusoria.
A B C E F G	72° **76°** 80°	*Not bred in captivity*				Feed live food and red meat. This fish is most intelligent and feisty.
A B C G H	70° **80°** 85°	substratum breeder plant-adherer	10–30 gal. 1, 7, 9, 11, 18	5″	♂ more colorful, longer, pointed dorsal, bump on forehead	Pair will tend eggs and feed fry until free-swimming. Bullying in small fish a problem. Discus require daily attention.
A B C	65° **78°** 85°	bubble-nest builder	10 gal. 1, 10, 11, 19	9 months	♂ more colorful ♀ fuller	Easy to breed, this beautiful little fish is always a favorite. Keep a lid on breeding tank to avoid drafts. Male takes care of fry. Remove female after spawn.
A B C	72° **76°** 80°	*Not bred in captivity*				These curious fish should be provided with their own rock cave. Shy at first, the elephant-nose may be trained to recognize its friends.

Fish	Habitat	Size	Coloration	Hardiness	Temperament Range	Function	pH	DH/Salt
Festivum cichlid *(Flag cichlid)* *(Cichlasoma festivum)*	Amazon	6"	Green-gold shimmery body, unique body shape; black line runs from eye thru top fin.	sturdy	shy hostile alert territorial mated pairs advised keep with larger fish	primary fish	−N	soft
Fire eel *(Mastacembelus)*	Java Borneo Sumatra	18"	Chestnut brown body, bright red spots.	sturdy	shy gentle intelligent playful territorial jumper	primary fish nocturnal scavenger	N	NC
Firemouth cichlid *(Cichlasoma meeki)*	Northern Yucatán	5"	Brilliant red on throat.	sturdy	alert territorial mated pairs advised keep with larger fish	primary fish loner	NC	NC
Gambusia *(Gambusia affinis)*	Southern U.S.	2"	Tan with bluish shimmer.	sturdy	hostile alert territorial jumper active	loner	−N	NC
Geophagus *(Geophagus jurupari)*	South America	9"	Blue spots shimmer on long snout and flat body.	sturdy	gentle intelligent playful territorial keep with larger fish	primary fish	−N	soft
Glass catfish *(Kryptopterus bicirrhis)*	India	4"	Transparent.	delicate	shy gentle	primary fish scavenger	N+	N

Foods	Temper-ature Range[a]	Breeding Habits	Optimal Tank Environ-ment[b]	Age or Size at Maturity	Sex Distinc-tions	Fry Care and Comments
A B C	65° **78°** 85°	substratum breeder	10–20 gal. 1, 7, 9, 17	2½"	♂ more colorful, longer fins ♀ thicker	Difficult to breed. Same procedure as for angelfish. Condition on live food.
A B C	70° **78°** 80°	egg-scatterer	*Not bred in captivity*			A very personable pet fish. Likes to burrow in gravel. Keep tank tightly covered.
A B C	65° **78°** 85°	substratum breeder	20 gal. 1, 6, 8, 9, 12, 16	3"	♀ duller ♂ pointed fins	100–200 eggs hatch in 3 days. Parents sometimes eat young. Feed young live foods. A hardy fish.
A B C	60° **75°** 85°	live-bearer	5–10 gal. 1, 10, 11, 15	9 months	♀ larger ♂ gonopo-dium	Breed prolifically. Hungry, greedy eaters.
A B C E F G	70° **78°** 82°	substratum breeder mouth-breeder	20 gal. 1, 8, 9, 12, 17	2 years	♂ longer fins, brighter color	Both parents incubate and care for young—mouthbreeding begins after fry hatch.
A B C	72° **80°** 82°	bubble-nest builder	5 gal. ½ full 1, 10, 11	1"	♀ fuller	100 eggs hatch in 2 days. Remove male. Cover and aerate tank. Feed fry infusoria.

Fish	Habitat	Size	Coloration	Hardiness	Temperament Range	Function	pH	DH/Salt
Glass fish (*Chanda ranga*)	India Burma	2″	Transparent.	sturdy	shy gentle jumper active	secondary fish scavenger	N+	N
Goldfish (*Carassius auratus auratus*)	China	12″	Variable orange, white, bronze.	sturdy	gentle dumb playful	primary fish scavenger	N	NC
Guppy (*Lebistes reticulatus*)	Brazil Trinidad Venezuela	2″	Variable man-made strains with multicolored veiltails. Males sport every color found in the rainbow.	sturdy	intelligent playful alert mated pairs advised jumper active	primary fish	N+	1 tsp. salt per gal.
Hatchet (*Carhegiella marthae*)	Venezuela Peru Brazil	1½″	Silver body with thin black lateral line. Some species have brown marbled design.	fairly hardy	shy gentle playful dumb jumper active	secondary fish scavenger	−N	soft
Headstander (*Abramites microcephalus*)	Amazon Guianas	5″	Body light brown with yellow hue, six or seven wide bars.	sturdy	shy gentle playful territorial	secondary fish scavenger	−N	soft
Honey dwarf gourami (*Colisa chuna*)	India	2″	Female, silver; male, bright orange with yellow dorsal fin and bright blue anal fin when in spawning dress.	requires special attention	shy gentle mated pairs advised	primary fish loner	−N	soft

Foods	Temperature Range[a]	Breeding Habits	Optimal Tank Environment[b]	Age or Size at Maturity	Sex Distinctions	Fry Care and Comments
A B C	78° **90°** 95°	egg-scatterer	15 gal. 1, 11, 13, 18	1″	♂ fins edged in black and white	Hatch 200 eggs separately; feed infusoria.
A C D	50° **65°** 70°	egg-scatterer	20–50 gal. 1, 10, 18	2½″	♂ tiny bumps on operculum when spawning	Thousands of eggs hatch in 4 days. Fry are delicate. Feed baby brine shrimp after 2 weeks.
A B C D	60° **78°** 90°	live-bearer	10–20 gal. 3, 10, 18 or 1, 10, 11, 13, 14, 17	9 months	♂ smaller, more color ♂ gonopodium	Well-fed guppies in top condition may bear 50–150 fry once a month for over a year. Frequent water changes and feedings of live food ensure success. Young males must be isolated from females or they will be stunted.
A B C	75° **82°** 85°	egg-scatterer	5–20 gal. 1, 10, 11, 18	1¾″	♀ plumper when viewed from above	Separate parents after spawn. Much leaping and splashing about during mating. Rarely spawned. Excellent jumpers.
A B C D I	65° **76°** 85°	egg-scatterer	1, 9, 11, 17	3″	♀ fuller, plainer	Breed much as black tetras. Remove parents after spawn. Protect eggs from fungus by keeping tank clean and adding methylene blue.
A B C	72° **80°** 85°	bubble-nest builder	5–10 gal. 1, 10, 11, 18 Water about 8″ deep	1½″	♀ plain ♂ red, yellow, and blue	A delicate and rare fish—worth the trouble. Breeds like other gouramis. Good parental care if tank remains unbothered. Condition on live shrimp. Keep tank covered.

Fish	Habitat	Size	Coloration	Hardiness	Temperament Range	Function	pH	DH/Salt
Jack Dempsey cichlid (*Cichlasoma biocellatum*)	Amazon	8″	Dark body with beautiful blue, green, and red shiny mosaic flecks.	sturdy	intelligent hostile alert territorial mated pairs advised keep with larger fish	primary fish loner	NC	NC
Jewel cichlid (*Hemichromis bimaculatus*)	Tropical Africa	6″	Both have pink hue, turn brilliant red with blue flecks in breeding dress.	sturdy	intelligent hostile alert territorial mated pairs advised keep with larger fish	primary fish loner	NC	NC
Julidochromis mbuna (*Julidochromis marlieri, J. ornatus*)	Lake Tanganyika Africa	3″	Yellow and dark brown tiger stripes in various geometric patterns.	fairly hardy	shy gentle playful alert territorial mated pairs advised	primary fish	Alk	salt
Kissing gourami (*Helostoma rudolfi*)	Sumatra Borneo Java Malaya Thailand	8″	Pink.	sturdy	gentle playful mated pairs advised	primary fish	NC	NC
Knife fish (*Xenomystus nigri*)	Africa	8″	Brown.	sturdy	shy intelligent alert territorial jumper	primary fish nocturnal	−N	soft
Koi (*Carassius hybrid*)	Europe	18″	Variations of black, yellow, white, red, and orange splotches.	sturdy	gentle playful dumb keep with larger fish	primary fish loner	N+	NC

Foods	Temper-ature Range[a]	Breeding Habits	Optimal Tank Environ-ment[b]	Age or Size at Maturity	Sex Distinc-tions	Fry Care and Comments
A B C E F G J	65° **78°** 85°	subtratum breeder	10–30 gal. 1, 6, 8, 10, 12, 16	3″	♂ longer; dorsal fin with red edge	Easy to breed and raise. Love to dig. Build a nest and spawn in typical cichlid fashion. Parents may be removed after 300 eggs hatch in 3 days. Good parental care.
A B C E	70° **80°** 85°	substratum breeder	10–30 gal. 1, 6, 8, 9, 12, 16	3″	♀ stouter	Interesting courtship. Easy to breed—but what do you do with 300 pugnacious jewel fish? Good parental care.
A B C	76° **80°** 82°	substratum breeder	20 gal. 1, 2, 6, 12, 17	3″	♀ lighter markings on nose	Good parents. Provide pair with a large conch shell. They do the rest.
A B C	72° **80°** 85°	egg-scatterer	30 gal. 1, 10, 11, 18	4″	none visible	100–1,000 floating eggs hatch in 48 hours. No parental care.
A B C E G	75° **80°** 82°	*Not bred in captivity*				Interesting fish. Able to swim backwards and forwards using long deep anal fin.
A B C	50° **70°** 80°	egg-scatterer	Bred in large ponds using artificial spawn grass	8″		Personable.

Fish	Habitat	Size	Coloration	Hardi-ness	Temper-ament Range	Function	pH	DH/Salt
Kribensas *(Pelmato-chromis kribensas)*	West Africa	6"	Beautiful copper-rose and blue iridescent hues.	delicate	shy intelligent playful alert territorial mated pairs advised	primary fish loner	−N	soft
Kuhli loach *(Acanthoph-thalmus species)*	Malaya Burma Java Sumatra Borneo Singapore	4"	Yellow gold body with variable brown stripe patterns.	fairly hardy	shy gentle playful jumper	scavenger	NC	soft
Labeotropheus mbuna *(Labeotropheus fuelleborni, L. trewavasae)*	Lake Malawi, Africa	7"	Blue bands; some red in body and fins.	fairly hardy	intelligent playful alert territorial mated pairs advised	primary fish loner	alk	hard
Lamprologus mbuna *(Lamprologus savori birchardi)*	Lake Tangan-yika	5"	Chic gray body, white trim on lyretail; turquoise trim on face.	fairly hardy	intelligent playful territorial mated pairs advised alert	primary fish loner	alk	hard
Leaf fish *(Monocirrhus polyacanthus)*	South America	4"	Mottled brown markings. Well camouflaged.	fairly hardy	shy jumper	primary fish	−N	soft
Mono *(Monodacty-lus argenteus)*	Malaya African coast	8"	Silver, yellow tint, black trim and stripes.	requires special attention	playful active jumper	primary fish	alk	hard salt
Mudskipper *(Perioph-thalmus barbarus)*	Indo-Pacific region	8"	Mud gray body. Blue iridescence on jagged dorsal fin.	requires special attention	gentle intelligent playful jumper	primary fish loner	alk	soft

Foods	Temperature Rangeᵃ	Breeding Habits	Optimal Tank Environmentᵇ	Age or Size at Maturity	Sex Distinctions	Fry Care and Comments
A B C	78° **80°** 82°	substratum breeder	5–20 gal. 1, 6, 11, 12, 18	1″	♂ pointed dorsal fin, pale ♀ stocky, rosy glow on side	Excellent fish to breed. Interesting courtship, good parental care by female. Remove male after spawn. 20–100 eggs hatch in 3 days. Feed them live tubifex at 3 days.
B C	75° **70°** 80°	egg-scatterer	20 gal. 1, 6, 11, 12, 18	*Breeding not observed*	♀ heavier	Provide the kuhli loach with plenty of hiding places.
A B C D E I	72° **80°** 82°	substratum breeder mouth-breeder	20–30 gal. 2, 8, 12, 14, 17	4″	♂ more colorful, egg spots	Good parental care; typical mbuna breeder.
A B C D	72° **80°** 82°	substratum breeder	10–20 gal. 2, 6, 10, 11, 12, 17 (large conch shell)	3″	♂ bump on head	Breed like dwarf cichlids; good parents. 50 or so babies are quite small at birth; feed powdered food. Like privacy.
A B C E	70° **78°** 85°	plant-adherer	10–20 gal. 1, 7, 9, 17	2″	Not visible	Eggs hatch in 4 days, are cared for by female. Feed live food.
A B C	76° **80°** 82°	egg-scatterer, rarely bred	55 gal.	3″ 2 years	♀ fuller	Parents often eat eggs. Fry hatch in 24 hours. Quite delicate; must be carefully raised away from parents.
A B G	65° **70°** 78°		10 gal. aquaterrarium	*Not bred in captivity*		Delightful pet; tamable. Needs aquaterrarium.

Fish	Habitat	Size	Coloration	Hardi-ness	Temper-ament Range	Function	pH	DH/Salt
Neon tetra *(Paracheiro-don innesi)*	Amazon	1½"	Blue neon stripe across body.	delicate	shy dumb active	secondary fish school fish	−N	soft
Nothobran-chius killy	East Africa	2"	Varied, brilliant red and blue patterns.	requires special attention	territorial playful	primary fish loner	acid	soft
Orange chromide *(Etroplus maculatus)*	India Ceylon	3"	Speckled yellow or orange. Bottom fins black to gray.	delicate	intelligent alert territorial mated pairs advised keep with larger fish	primary fish	N	salt
Ornate tetra *(Hyphessobry-con ornatus)*	Guianas	2"	Translucent pinkish-green body. Elongated dorsal and anal fins marked in black and white.	sturdy	shy gentle playful mated pairs advised active	secondary fish scavenger	−N	soft
Oscar *(Astronotus ocellatus)*	Amazon basin Southern U.S.	18"	Variable suede-like red and black stripes, solids, or mottled.	sturdy	intelligent playful alert keep with larger fish mated pairs advised	primary fish	NC	NC

Foods	Temper-ature Range[a]	Breeding Habits	Optimal Tank Environ-ment[b]	Age or Size at Maturity	Sex Distinc-tions	Fry Care and Comments
A B C	65° **76°** 80°	egg-scatterer	10 gal. 1, 5, 11, 18 or 3, 13, 18	10 months	♀ fuller	150 eggs hatch in 24 hours. Remove parents after spawn. Feed fry protozoa. Frequent water changes.
A B C	75° **78°** 82°	egg-scatterer	5½ gal. 5, 19 1♂ : 2♀	10 months	♂ colorful ♀ drab	Remove parents after spawn. Drain tank but allow peat moss and eggs to stay slightly moist for 1 month. Eggs hatch almost immediately after tank is refilled. Feed live food.
A B C	72° **78°** 82°	substratum breeder plant-adherer	10 gal. 1, 6, 8, 15	2″	♀ fuller, smaller ♂ redder eyes	Breed much like convict cichlid. Usually good parents. Feed fry and breeders live shrimp.
A B C	72° **76°** 80°	egg-scatterer	10–15 gal. 4, 13, 18	1 year	♂ extended dorsal	Breed like black tetra. A handsome fish for most communities.
A B C E F G H J	70° **80°** 85°	substratum breeder	55 gal. 1, 6, 8, 9, 16	6″	♀ stockier ♂ longer fins, more color ♀ blunt	Give breeders lots of room and red meat. Wonderfully affection-ate courtship. Good parental care. Feed fry liberally.

Fish	Habitat	Size	Coloration	Hardi-ness	Temper-ament Range	Function	pH	DH/Salt
Panchax killy *(Pachypanchax playfairi)*	East Africa	4″	Tan body with metallic green sheen, red spots.	sturdy	intelligent hostile alert territorial mated pairs advised jumper	primary fish loner	N+	salt
Paradise fish *(Macropodus opercularis)*	China Formosa	3″	Red and blue sparkling patterns; albino form pretty, too.	sturdy	intelligent playful alert mated pairs advised	primary fish secondary fish	NC	NC
Peacock cichlid mbuna *(Aulonocara nyassae)*	Lake Tangan-yika	10″	Pale to deep azure or Prussian blue when mature.	delicate	shy gentle territorial mated pairs advised	primary fish loner	alk	salt
Pearl danio *(Brachydanio albolineatus)*	Borneo Sumatra Thailand India	2½″	Mother-of-pearl body, red pin-stripe at tail.	sturdy	playful dumb jumper active	school fish	NC	NC
Pearl gourami *(Trichogaster leeri)*	Thailand Malaya Sumatra Borneo	4″	Exciting multicolor mosaic blue-green pearl speckles. Males have ruby-red throat.	sturdy	shy gentle mated pairs advised	primary fish secondary fish	−N	soft
Pencil fish *(Nannostomus)*	British Guiana Amazon	2½″	Lateral stripes of yellow and black with red accents.	sturdy	territorial jumper	secondary fish	−N	soft
Piranha *(Serrasalmo mattereri)*	Amazon	12″	Silver-flecked gray body, red belly; big teeth.	sturdy	hostile territorial	primary fish loner	−N	soft

Foods	Temperature Rangeᵃ	Breeding Habits	Optimal Tank Environmentᵇ	Age or Size at Maturity	Sex Distinctions	Fry Care and Comments
A B C	75° **80°** 85°	egg-scatterer	10 gal. 1, 10, 11, 19	3″	♀ smaller	Remove 100–150 eggs from spawning tank, attached to floating plants. Hatch in clean bare tank to combat fungus. Hatch in about 2 weeks.
A B C	60° **70°** 90°	bubble-nest builder	5–10 gal. 1, 10, 19	2″	♂ longer fins and tail ♀ plump	Half-fill a 10-gallon tank with tap water, add floating plants; aerate. Add paradise fish; feed and breed. Very hardy. Good outdoor fish.
A B C	72° **78°** 82°	mouth-breeder	20 gal. 2, 8, 12, 17	4″	♂ egg spots, more brilliant azure blues	Breeds like other mbunas. Fry are quite hardy at ¼ inch. One of the more peaceful African cichlids.
A B C	68° **76°** 82°	egg-scatterer	10–20 gal. 4 with spawn grass or 3, 13, 18 2♀ : 1♂	1½″	♀ fuller	Protect eggs from parents and fungus. Feed fry infusoria or liquid food.
A B C	70° **78°** 85°	bubble-nest builder	10 gal. 1, 10, 19	3″	♂ longer dorsal fin	Easy to breed and raise. A truly splendid fish for most communities. Male is good parent for first 2 weeks; then remove him. Feed fry liquid food.
A B C	72° **78°** 80°	egg-scatterer	10 gal. 1, 10, 11, 18 2♂ : 1♀	1¾″	♀ pale colorless fins	Remove parents after spawning; protect 100 eggs from strong light.
E F	70° **76°** 80°	egg-scatterer		*Not often bred in captivity*		

Fish	Habitat	Size	Coloration	Hardiness	Temperament Range	Function	pH	DH/Salt
Platy (*Xiphophorus maculatus*)	Mexico-Guatemala	2½"	Various red, gold, blue, black varieties—high fin, black tail, red tail, etc.	sturdy	gentle playful mated pairs advised jumper active	primary fish secondary fish	N+	hard salt
Plecostomus catfish	Amazon	12"	Variable brown & dark markings.	delicate	shy gentle intelligent playful alert jumper keep with larger fish	scavenger	−N	salt
Pristella tetra (*Pristella riddlei*)	South America	2"	Delicate pink hue, white on fins.	sturdy	shy gentle active	scavenger	−N	soft
Pseudotropheus mbuna (*Pseudotropheus zebra, P. auratus, P. tropheops, P. microstoma, P. lucerna, P. johanni, P. elongatus*)	Lake Malawi, Africa	4–8"	Various color varieties even within a species: blues, reds, oranges, yellow.	sturdy	intelligent playful alert territorial keep with larger fish mated pairs advised	primary fish	alk	hard salt
Puffer (*Tetradon schoutdeni*)	Malaya India	6"	Iridescent green with black polka dots and white belly.	requires special attention	hostile	primary fish	alk	hard salt
Ramirezi (*Apistogramma ramirezi*)	Venezuela	2"	Gold body, ruby sides with blue flecks; lovely.	requires special attention	shy playful alert territorial mated pairs advised	primary fish	−N	soft

Foods	Temperature Rangeᵃ	Breeding Habits	Optimal Tank Environmentᵇ	Age or Size at Maturity	Sex Distinctions	Fry Care and Comments
A B C	70° **78°** 85°	live-bearer	10–20 gal. 1, 10, 11, 14, 17	10 months	♀ larger ♂ gonopodium	Well-fed parents won't bother babies, which grow quickly. Hardy fish
A B C D I	72° **78°** 80°	egg scatterer	20–30 gal. 1, 11, 12, 17	7″	♂ black on anal fin does not cross fin.	100–120 eggs hatch in 60 hours.
A B C	70° **78°** 82°	egg-scatterer	10 gal. 1, 5, 10, 11, 18	1 year	♂ longer dorsal	Breed same as most tetras.
A B C E G	70° **78°** 82°	mouth-breeder	55 gal. 1, 2, 6, 8, 12, 14, 17	1 year	♂ more colorful, bright egg spots.	These fish like lots of room, so it's easier to let them pair off and mate in community. Remove female when her buccal sac is distended. Fry, released in 3 weeks, are self-reliant.
B C	72° **76°** 80°	substratum breeder	10–20 gal. 2, 12, 17		♀ larger, lighter color	Best kept in brackish water tank with larger fish. Needs frequent water changes. Feed mussels.
A B C	72° **78°** 82°	substratum breeder	10 gal. 1, 6, 11, 12, 17	12 months	♀ has solid blue on spot ♂ extended front dorsal rays	Good parental care, usually by both parents. Difficult to spawn.

Fish	Habitat	Size	Coloration	Hardiness	Temperament Range	Function	pH	DH/Salt
Raphael catfish *(Platydoras costatus)*	Amazon	12″	Chocolate brown body with ivory stripes.	sturdy	shy playful territorial	scavenger nocturnal	+N	hard
Rasbora *(Rasbora heteromorpha)*	Malaya Sumatra Java Thailand	1½″	Copper metallic body with geometric black "T" down lateral line.	sturdy	gentle playful dumb active	scavenger	acid	soft
Red-fin shark *(Rainbow shark) (Labeo erythrurus)*	Thailand	5″	Gray body, reddish fins and tail.	fairly hardy	intelligent playful territorial keep with larger fish	scavenger	N	soft
Rope fish *(Calamoichythys calabaricus)*	Cameroon	15″	Brown with orange underside and fins.	sturdy	intelligent playful territorial jumper keep with larger fish	primary fish loner	NC	NC
Rosy barb *Puntius conchonius)*	India	6″	Silver males have a rosy hue when mature.	fairly hardy	playful dumb alert jumper active	school fish	NC	NC
Rummy nose *(Hemigrammus rhodostomas)*	Amazon	3″	Silver body, black and white tail stripes; red nose.	delicate	shy gentle playful jumper active	scavenger	−N	soft

Foods	Temperature Range[a]	Breeding Habits	Optimal Tank Environment[b]	Age or Size at Maturity	Sex Distinctions	Fry Care and Comments
A B C	70° **78°** 85°		*Not bred in capitivity*	4″	not apparent	Good scavenger for a cichlid tank.
A B C	72° **80°** 82°	plant-adherer	10 gal. 1, 5, 11, 14, 18	9 months	♂ better defined "T"	300 eggs hatch in 24 hours. Difficult to spawn.
A B C I	70° **78°** 85°	substratum breeder	55 gal. 1, 11, 12, 16	4″	♀ fuller lighter	Nice scavenger for larger fish (i.e., goldfish and cichlids, but not discus). Breeds secretly.
A B C	72° **78°** 82°		*Not often bred*		♂ anal fin pointed	Adhesive eggs.
A B C	70° **78°** 85°	egg-scatterer	10–20 gal. 1, 4, 11, 17 or 3, 13, 18	9 months	♂ red	Breed like most egg-scatterers. Keep fry tank clean.
A B C	70° **78°** 82°	egg-scatterer	10–20 gal. 1, 11, 18 or 3, 13, 18	1″	♀ fuller	Rummy nose, like most tetras, are happy in a well-planted aged aquarium and breed in same manner. Difficult to spawn.

Fish	Habitat	Size	Coloration	Hardiness	Temperament Range	Function	pH	DH/Salt
Rusty cichlid mbuna (*Iodotropheus sprengerae*)	Lake Malawi	6″	Velvety lavender-brown body, yellow egg spot.	sturdy	intelligent playful alert territorial mated pairs advised	primary fish	N+	hard
Sailfin molly (*Mollinesia latipinna, M. velifera*)	Yucatán	4″	*latipinna:* Velvet black. *velifera:* Silver, amber, green iridescence.	requires special attention	playful hostile alert territorial mated pairs advised jumper	primary fish loner	N+	N
Scat (*Scatophagus argus*)	Indo-Pacific region	12″	Variable silver to green body, dark spots; red subspecies.	delicate	gentle playful intelligent alert active	primary fish scavenger	alk	salt
Serpae tetra (*Hyphessobrycon serpae*)	Amazon	1½″	Crimson body, fins trimmed in black and white.	sturdy	gentle playful active	scavenger secondary fish	−N	soft
Severum (*Cichlasoma severum*)	Northern South America to Amazon River	8″	Gray to green body; often turquoise lines decorating face and sides resembling discus coloring. Red eyes. Gold form lovely, too!	sturdy	intelligent alert territorial	primary fish	NC	NC
Silver dollar (*Mylossoma aureum*)	Amazon	9″	Silver with dark spots, red anal fin.	sturdy	gentle playful jumper active	primary fish secondary fish	−N	soft

Foods	Temper-ature Range[a]	Breeding Habits	Optimal Tank Environ-ment[b]	Age or Size at Maturity	Sex Distinc-tions	Fry Care and Comments
A B C I	70° **78°** 82°	mouth-breeder	20–50 gal. 1, 2, 6, 12, 14, 17	1½″	♂ has one yellow egg spot	Mouthbreeding females should be moved to the safety of a nursery tank.
A B C D I	76° **80°** 85°	live-bearer	10–20 gal. 1, 2, 10, 14, 16	9 months	♂ larger dorsal fin ♂ gonopo-dium	Mollies either thrive or die, depending on individual care. Water changes, live food, algae, and salt are all necessary.
A B C E	74° **78°** 80°	*Not bred in captivity*				Comical and perky addition to a tank of cichlids. If a scat lasts for a month, it will probably live for many years.
A B C	65° **78°** 85°	egg-scatterer	10–15 gal. 1, 10, 11, 13, 18	9 months	♂ has hooks on anal fin, slimmer, brighter	Hatch fry separately and feed liquid food. Breeds like most tetras.
A B C E G H I	65° **78°** 85°	substratum breeding	30 gal. 1, 8, 9, 11, 17	6″	♀ fuller ♂ longer fins, brighter colors	Breeds as most cichlids. Fry are hardy and should be fed live baby brine shrimp at 1 week old.
A B C	70° **76°** 85°	egg-scatterer	10–20 gal. 1, 10, 11, 18	3″	♀ fuller	Spawn when in good condition in same fashion as black tetra.

Fish	Habitat	Size	Coloration	Hardi-ness	Temper-ament Range	Function	pH	DH/Salt
Silver gourami *(Moonlight gourami)* *(Trichogaster microlepis)*	Thailand	6″	Silver body with bluish sheen.	sturdy	gentle alert jumper keep with larger fish	primary fish	−N	soft
Silver tip tetra *(Hemigrammus hanus)*	Brazil	1¾″	Bronze body with frosted white fins and split tail.	fairly hardy	gentle active	scavenger	−N	N
Snakehead *(Chana micropeltes)*	India	up to 3′	Red with black racing pin-stripes.	sturdy	hostile alert territorial jumper	primary fish loner	NC	NC
Stingray *(Potamotrygon laticeps)*	Amazon	up to 4′	Changeable brown-gray with spots.	requires special attention	playful keep with larger fish	primary fish loner	N+	NC
Sunfish *(Enneacanthus)*	U.S.	6″	Orange and blue iridescent flecks.	sturdy	intelligent hostile alert jumper keep with larger fish	primary fish	N	NC
Swordtail *(Xiphophorus helleri)*	Southern Mexico	4″	Variegated, bold reds or greens, or blacks with emerald sheen.	fairly hardy	gentle hostile mated pairs advised jumper active	primary fish	N+	N

Foods	Temperature Rangeª	Breeding Habits	Optimal Tank Environmentᵇ	Age or Size at Maturity	Sex Distinctions	Fry Care and Comments
A B C	75° **78°** 85°	bubble-nest builder	10–15 gal. 1, 10, 19	4″	♂ orange ventral fins	Pretty fish; breeds much as pearl gourami does. Occasional fish become bullies.
A B C	72° **78°** 82°	egg-scatterer	10–15 gal. 1, 5, 10, 11, 18	9 months	♀ fuller	Remove parents after spawn. Raise fry on liquid food and infusoria.
A B C D E F G H J	70° **80°** 85°	egg-scatterer bubble-nest builder	55 gal.	*Bred in pools*		200–1000 eggs are left floating unattended.
A B E H	70° **78°** 85°		55 gal.	*Not bred in captivity*		Interesting addition to a large tank with flat gravel bottom.
A B C	60° **70°** 80°	substratum breeder	29 gal.	*Not bred in captivity*		
A B C	70° **76°** 84°	live-bearer	10–20 gal. 1, 2, 10, 11, 15	9 months	♂ smaller, extended lower tail ♂ gonopodium	Keep fish well fed. Provide plenty of room for babies to hide. 1–2 tsp. salt per gallon. Feed live food and change water every 2 weeks.

Fish	Habitat	Size	Coloration	Hardi-ness	Temper-ament Range	Function	pH	DH/Salt
Synodontis catfish *(Synodontis decorus)*	West Africa Congo	8″	Brown with yellow spots, or silver with dark spots.	sturdy	gentle playful territorial	scavenger nocturnal	N	N
Texas cichlid *(Herichthys cyanoguttatus)*	Texas Northern Mexico	12″	Beautiful turquoise metallic mosaic.	sturdy	intelligent hostile mated pairs advised keep with larger fish	primary fish loner	NC	NC
Thick-lip gourami *(Colisa labiosa)*	India Burma	4″	Maroon and Prussian blue in body, and dorsal and anal fins.	sturdy	gentle playful mated pairs advised	secondary fish	NC	NC
Tiger barb *(Capoeta tetrazona)*	Borneo Sumatra	3″	Yellow-gold sides, 4 wide black bands; red and black fin tips.	sturdy	playful active keep with larger fish	school fish	NC	NC
Tinfoil barb *(Barbodes schwanenfeldi)*	Sumatra Borneo Thailand	to 14″	Sleek metallic silver body.	sturdy	playful jumper active keep with larger fish	secondary fish school fish	NC	NC
Tropheus moori mbuna	Lake Tangan-yika	5″	Black with red patches on side and dorsal fin.	requires special attention	gentle playful territorial keep with larger fish	primary fish loner	alk	hard salt

Foods	Temper-ature Range[a]	Breeding Habits	Optimal Tank Environ-ment[b]	Age or Size at Maturity	Sex Distinc-tions	Fry Care and Comments
A B C G	65° **76°** 80°			*Not bred in captivity*		A rare fish, even in native waters.
A B C E G H J	65° **75°** 80°	substratum breeder mouth-breeder	55 gal. 1, 6, 8, 12, 17	5″	♀ fuller ♂ bump on head	500–1000 eggs hatch in 5–7 days. Parents should be condi-tioned in separate tanks prior to spawn. Raise fry on baby brine shrimp.
A B C	70° **76°** 80°	bubble-nest builder	10–15 gal. 1, 10, 19	12 months	♂ more colorful	Easy to breed. Male is good parent. Keep tank clean and covered. Remove female after spawn.
A B C	65° **78°** 85°	egg-scatterer	20 gal. long 1, 13, 18	9 months	♂ rosy nose	Colorful and easy to breed, the tiger barb is very popular. Breed in water softer than normal tank. Separate and raise young on live foods.
A B C D	70° **76°** 80°	egg-scatterer	55 gal. 1, 10, 11, 13, 17	5″	♂ more colorful	Not often bred. Breeds like most barbs.
A B C	70° **76°** 82°	mouth-breeder	20–30 gal. 2, 6, 8, 12, 17 or a conch shell	2½″	not visible	2–6 babies are incubated by female for 3–4 weeks. A deli-cate, finicky fish.

Fish	Habitat	Size	Coloration	Hardi-ness	Temper-ament Range	Function	pH	DH/Salt
Von Rio tetra *(Hyphesso-brycon flammeus)*	Rio de Janeiro	1½"	Red hue in body, darker in anal fin. Black and white fins.	delicate	shy gentle playful mated pairs advised active	school fish	−N	soft
Weather loach *(Spined loach)* *(Cobitis taenia)*	Europe Asia	6"	Brown body with dark markings.	sturdy	territorial jumper active keep with larger fish	scavenger nocturnal	NC	NC
White cloud *(Tanichthys albonubes)*	White Cloud Mt., Canton, China	1½"	Tarnished silver, tan stripe, red in tail.	sturdy	shy gentle playful dumb jumper keep with larger fish	school fish	NC	NC
Zebra danio *(Brachydanio rerio)*	India	2"	Silver body with steel-blue lateral stripes.	sturdy	playful dumb jumper active	school fish	NC	NC

Foods	Temperature Range[a]	Breeding Habits	Optimal Tank Environment[b]	Age or Size at Maturity	Sex Distinctions	Fry Care and Comments
A B C	70° **78°** 82°	egg-scatterer	10–20 gal. 1, 11, 18	6 months	♂ smaller brighter	100–200 fry hatch in 48 hours. Remove parents after spawn. Keep fry tank clean and feed infusoria and live food.
B C	65° **72°** 80°	egg-scatterer	10–20 gal. 1, 6, 11, 17	4″	♀ fuller	Up to 1,500 eggs settle to sediment and feed from bottom debris.
A B C	60° **78°** 85°	egg-scatterer	10–20 gal. 1, 10, 11, 14, 17	6 months	♀ fuller ♂ brighter	100 eggs are scattered and usually not eaten by parents. Very easy to breed and raise.
A B C	65° **72°** 80°	egg-scatterer	10–20 gal. 3, 13, 18 2♂ : 1♀	1½″	♀ heavier	Easy to breed. 200 eggs hatch separately from parents in 2 days. Feed liquid food or strained egg yolk.

APPENDIX H
NATIONAL SPECIALTY ORGANIZATIONS

American Catfish and Loach Association (ACALA)
J. Gayle Hoskin, Jr., Membership Chairman
6511 Johnson Street
Hollywood, FL 33024

American Cichlid Association (ACA)
Jonathan and Lee Pierce, Membership Chairpersons
15019 North 21 Place
Phoenix, AR 85022

American Killifish Association (AKA)
Jerry and Bev Sellers, Membership Chairpersons
P.O. Box 4231
Sarasota, FL 33578

Federation of American Aquarium Societies (FAAS)
Rich and Val Olcott, Membership Chairpersons
1853 Snowden
Memphis, TN 38107

Goldfish Society of America (GSA)
Susan Law, Membership Chairperson
1510 William Way
Concord, CA 94520

International Betta Congress (IBC)
Aurelia Ogles, Membership Chairperson
4540 Gifford Road, Apt. 24-B
Bloomington, IN 47620

International Fancy Guppy Association (IFGA)
Midge Hill, Membership Chairperson
9903 Candia Drive
Whittier, CA 90603

American Livebearer Association (ALA)
John Buhr, Membership Chairman
512 South 12 Street
Clear Lake, IA 50428

North American Native Fishes Association (NANFA)
Robert T. Rosen, Membership Chairman
Princeton Arms South—Apt. 70
Cranbury, NJ 08512

INDEX